Improving the
Extended Value Stream

Improving the Extended Value Stream

Lean for the Entire Supply Chain

Darren Dolcemascolo

New York

Most Productivity Press books are available at quantity discounts when purchased in bulk For more information, contact our Customer Service Department (888-319-5852). Address all other inquiries to:

Productivity Press
444 Park Avenue South, 7th floor
New York, NY 10016
United States of America
Telephone 212-686-5900
Fax: 212-686-5411
E-mail: info@productivitypress.com
ProductivityPress.com

Library of Congress Cataloging-in-Publication Data

    Dolcemascolo, Darren.
    Improving the extended value stream : lean for the entire supply chain /
Darren Dolcemascolo.
      p. cm.
    Includes index.
    ISBN-13: 978-1-56327-333-9 (alk. paper)
    ISBN-10: 1-56327-333-0
    1. Business logistics. 2. Manufacturing processes. 3. Industrial management.
4. Industrial efficiency. I. Title.
HD38.5.D65 2006
658.7—dc22

                                  2006004344

10 09 08 07 06 5 4 3 2 1

Dedication

*To Cari and to my parents—without all your love,
support, and encouragement throughout the
years this book would not have been possible.
I thank God for each of you every day.*

Table of Contents

Acknowledgments

I would like to thank Mike Sinocchi of Productivity Press for approaching me with the idea of writing this book. I would also like to thank the rest of the team at Productivity Press and Ruth Mills.

Introduction

Many organizations have reaped the benefits of implementing lean manufacturing internally. When most people think about a lean value stream, they tend to focus on *internal processes*. However, the total value stream for a typical product crosses many different organizations. Thus, much of the total cost of a product depends on *supplier processes*, which are not addressed in a typical lean manufacturing implementation. For many lean manufacturers, this has resulted in major frustration.

Today, the most popular approach to reducing supply chain costs is to switch from local to offshore suppliers. Although this reduces the "per-unit" product cost, offshoring often does not result in bottom-line improvement because it simultaneously creates excess inventory and other wastes. Therefore, the lean solution to reducing overall supply chain cost is to apply the principles of lean in a systematic way to the entire supply chain. I felt there was a need in the marketplace for a comprehensive implementation guide to creating a complete lean supply chain. For this reason I decided to write *Improving the Extended Value Stream*.

Improving the Extended Value Stream is a system for extending lean manufacturing across the entire supply chain. In it, I will make the case for improving the extended value stream by demonstrating the benefits:

- Increased profitability,
- Reduced lead times and inventory, and
- Better quality.

I will then include a step-by-step plan for extending lean to the entire supply chain, from planning through implementation. Finally, I will teach you proven methods for sustaining success and continuously improving. Techniques addressed in the book include:

- Extended value-stream mapping,
- Internal value-stream mapping,
- Process *kaizen*,
- Outsourcing strategy,
- Supplier evaluation, and
- Supplier integration activities as they relate to a lean supply chain.

How This Book Is Organized

Improving the Extended Value Stream will teach you how to extend lean manufacturing to the entire supply chain, magnifying the benefits of lean manufacturing to your bottom line. Each technique addressed in the book includes a case example from a fictitious manufacturing organization, EVS Corporation.

The book is divided into three parts:

1. Planning and analysis of the lean extended value stream,

2. Implementation of a lean supply chain (which is the heart of the book, comprising six chapters), and

3. Sustaining and continuously improving the lean extended value chain.

Chapter 1 briefly reviews the tools, benefits, and implementation timeline of lean manufacturing. It then builds the case for extending the benefits of lean to the entire value stream and gives you an overview of the implementation steps.

Chapters 2 and 3 cover the techniques of extended value-stream mapping. Chapter 2 will teach you how to map and analyze a current-state value stream across an extended value stream. Introducing the techniques of value-stream identification and selection, the chapter begins by discussing the steps necessary to get started. Then, it offers a detailed step-by-step method for current-state mapping. Finally, the chapter discusses each of the metrics used for analysis of the current state.

Chapter 3 will teach you how to create a lean extended value stream. It discusses each of the elements in detail: lead and cycle times, inventory levels, information flow, and transportation. It then describes the steps to creating a lean extended value stream using extended future-state value-stream mapping. Finally, it teaches the reader how to create a plan for implementing the lean extended value stream.

Chapter 4 begins Part II, the implementation section of the book. Again using the EVS case study for illustration, Chapter 4 describes when it makes sense to outsource and how to develop and execute an overall outsourcing strategy for the extended value stream.

Chapter 5 provides step-by-step instructions for evaluating current and potential suppliers. It includes financial and nonfinancial metrics and auditing techniques essential to successful supplier selection.

Chapter 6 will teach you how to set up effective operating relationships with suppliers. It describes the roles and responsibilities of the buyer and supplier and techniques for setting up effective contracts.

Chapter 7 describes each of the key process-level kaizen tools to be used in developing a lean extended value stream. It begins by explaining the use of door-to-door value-stream maps at supplier locations to plan process-level improvements.

Chapter 8 describes various process-level tools including 5S, quick changeover techniques, process improvement and statistical analysis, detailed level process mapping, and total productive maintenance.

Finally in Part II, Chapter 9 uses another detailed EVS case study for illustration, and the chapter describes a step-by-step methodology for implementation, using kaizen events and other techniques.

Part III, which comprises Chapters 10 and 11, covers methods for sustaining and improving the lean extended value stream. Chapter 10 describes the methods for sustaining a lean extended value stream. Each of the key elements of an effective supplier association is described. Then, the chapter gives the reader a step-by-step plan for putting each element in place.

Chapter 11 describes the next steps that can be taken to continuously improve the extended value stream. This chapter outlines a method for involving suppliers in the design process to enhance the cost benefits of a lean extended value stream even more. It then discusses reducing transportation waste through the use of supplier parks and alternatives such as co-locating supplier processes.

This workbook serves as an action guide for the planning, implementation, and continuous improvement steps necessary to create a lean supply chain. So, turn the page and let's take the first steps on this journey together.

Part I

Planning and Analysis of the Lean Extended Value Stream

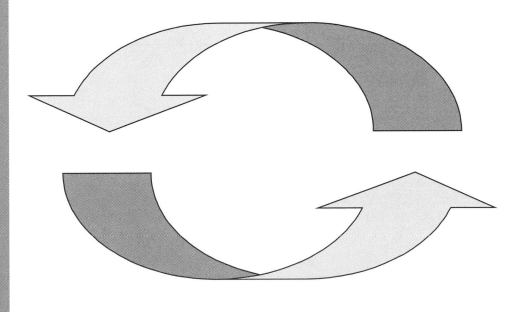

Chapter 1

Lean and the Extended Value Stream

Lean Manufacturing Overview

The power of lean manufacturing or "The Toyota Production System" is undeniable. Toyota has repeatedly proven its effectiveness. According to Jeffrey Liker's book *The Toyota Way*,[1] Toyota's $8.13 billion annual profit in 2003 was 8.3 times higher than the industry average and larger than the combined earnings of "the big 3." Toyota's automobiles are consistently at the top of the quality rankings; the company has the fastest product development process in the world; and it is benchmarked as best-in-class for high quality, high productivity, manufacturing speed, and flexibility.

If implemented properly, lean manufacturing will dramatically increase cash flow and operating profits of an organization by achieving the following benefits:

- Reducing inventory and lead time,
- Improving productivity and quality,
- Increasing overall customer satisfaction, and
- Improving employee involvement, morale, and company culture.

Five Principles of Lean

Lean organizations achieve such benefits by using a set of tools and principles to eliminate waste or non-value-creating activities. They create a culture of continuous improvement, and within that culture, they employ the tools of lean to eliminate waste and sources of waste. In the book *Lean Thinking*,[2] James Womack and Daniel Jones define five principles of lean, described in the following list.

---

1. *The Toyota Way*. Jeffrey K. Liker. McGraw Hill, 2004, pp. 4–5.
2. *Lean Thinking*. James P. Womack and Daniel T. Jones. Simon & Schuster, 1996, p. 10.

1. *Specify value.* The process, then, begins with the customer (not the plant manager or industrial engineer). The customer is the definer of value. If customers are willing to pay for something, then it is of value. If they are not, it is waste.

2. *Identify the value stream.* After value is clearly defined, then value streams are clearly identified. A value stream is the set of all actions necessary to bring a product from raw materials into the hands of the customer; this includes both material and information flow.

3. *Make value flow.* Within the value-stream-mapping model, single-piece flow is applied where possible.

4. *Let customers pull.* Pull systems are applied where single-piece flow is impossible (e.g., to control batch processes or between facilities).

5. *Pursue perfection.* After using value-stream-mapping techniques to create a plan to achieve this, process kaizen is used to eliminate waste and continuously improve.

The 7 Wastes of Manufacturing (Plus 1)

Taiichi Ohno, the former Chief Engineer at Toyota who popularized the Toyota Production System, is responsible for identifying the seven wastes of manufacturing:

1. Overproduction
2. Transportation
3. Unnecessary Inventory
4. Inappropriate Processing
5. Waiting
6. Excess Motion
7. Defects

The so-called eighth waste is usually considered to be the waste of underutilized employees (with respect to their ideas/minds). This eighth waste is addressed by creating a culture of continuous improvement, in which employees at all levels of an organization are participants in the lean transformation. Although top management commitment is an essential element for full lean implementation, lean is not solely a management activity. It is important to involve employees at all levels.

Process kaizen tools are used to eliminate these wastes at the shopfloor level. Such tools are often employed in events called kaizen events or kaizen blitzes, in which teams focus on improving a particular area in a 3- to 5-day period of time. Following is a brief review of some of the key tools.

The "5S" System of Improvement

The intent of 5S is to have only what you need available in the workplace, a designated place for everything, a standard way of doing things, and the discipline to maintain it. Created in Japan, the five Ss are: *seiri, seiton, seiso, seiketsu,* and *shitsuke.* Translated into English, we have:

1. *Sort.* Remove all items from the workplace that are not needed for current production.
2. *Set in order.* Arrange needed items so they are easy to find and put away. Items used often are placed closer to employees.
3. *Shine.* Make sure everything is clean, functioning, and ready to go.
4. *Standardize.* Develop and follow a method to maintain the first 3Ss.
5. *Sustain.* Create a habit and culture of properly maintaining correct procedures.

The 5S system is a powerful method for involving factory floor employees in lean early on, in the transformation to lean. The discipline required to implement and sustain 5S is the same type of discipline necessary to implement and sustain lean; consequently, 5S is often thought of as a foundational tool of lean; the five Ss are often called the "Five Pillars."

The SMED/Quick Changeover System

To achieve one-piece flow, manufacturers must reduce the time to switch between products in their processes. The Single Minute Exchange of Die (SMED) system, created by Dr. Shigeo Shingo, takes a three-step approach to reducing changeover time:

1. *Separate internal and external setup.* This involves breaking down each step in the process and categorizing. External setup includes steps that are done outside of the machine (e.g., retrieving tools). Internal setup includes steps that are done inside the machine.
2. *Convert internal setup to external setup* wherever possible.
3. *Streamline all aspects of the setup process.* This involves analyzing the internal setup steps in detail and applying improvement principles to them.

Although it began in the automobile industry on large metal-stamping equipment, this three-step method has been proven to work in any industry, using any piece of equipment.

One-Piece (aka Continuous-Flow) Manufacturing Cells

To facilitate one-piece flow (sometimes called continuous flow), manufacturing cells are often created. Creating one-piece-flow manufacturing cells includes analyzing and engineering the manufacturing steps, customer demand, equipment, labor, and physical layout. The goal is to create a continuous-flow environment, that is, a cell in which material moves from one value-creating step to the next, with no work-in-process (WIP) in between. One-piece flow does not always mean literally one unit at a time. In many cases, it makes sense to move small batches of product one unit at a time.

This is often much more difficult than it may first appear. Most manufacturing cells that have been set up do not have continuous flow; most changes to cells have been layout changes only. That is, machines were moved in a cellular arrangement and nothing more was changed. A change in layout alone does not create continuous flow; therefore, it is important to combine training in one-piece flow with analysis and implementation. Implementation must include a system for scheduling the manufacturing cell and auditing to ensure that standard work is done consistently.

Pull Systems

Pull systems (sometimes called *kanban* systems) are used to control inventory in a warehouse and to control production runs of upstream batch processes. Using a traditional material requirement planning (MRP) system for scheduling a factory, every production area is scheduled independently. There is no link between customer orders and actual production on the factory floor, and there is no link between production in one manufacturing area and the need of the next downstream process. In lean manufacturing, pull systems are used to remedy this problem; items are scheduled based on actual consumption rather than forecast.

Kanban is a Japanese word meaning "signboard" or "sign." A kanban signal, usually a card, is used to provide instructions to withdraw parts from a supermarket (warehouse) or to produce parts. Because parts are made or are moved only when a signal is given, pull systems prevent overproduction and excess inventory. As part of implementation, an auditing system should be instituted; audits will ensure that the proper number of kanban are in the system and that standard work is performed.

Total Productive Maintenance

Total Productive Maintenance (TPM) is used to increase machine uptime. By ensuring that equipment is properly maintained at all times, organizations can eliminate inventory and maintain consistency. TPM involves operators, engineers, and maintenance personnel working together in a team environment to ensure consistent maintenance and to eliminate the so-called "six big losses":

1. Breakdown losses
2. Setup and adjustment losses
3. Idling and minor stoppage losses
4. Speed losses
5. Quality defects and rework
6. Startup/yield losses (i.e., reduced yield between machine startup and stable production)

The key metric of TPM is Overall Equipment Effectiveness (OEE). By implementing TPM, OEE is dramatically increased, resulting in significantly more capacity out of the same set of equipment.

Flow Kaizen

Value-stream improvement, sometimes called flow-level kaizen, is the tool for identifying and planning opportunities for process kaizen. People often mistake value-stream mapping for process mapping. Process mapping simply involves mapping any given process. Value-stream mapping involves mapping information and product flow for a given value stream. The mapping is done in such a way that it allows one to visualize the current state and to plan and implement a future state with measurable goals. The key goal of value-stream mapping is reduction of lead time.

Before value-stream mapping was popular in the United States, organizations utilized process kaizen tools while largely ignoring their effect on the entire value stream. This led to successes in individual areas without the ability to demonstrate significant improvement to the value stream as a whole. Value-stream mapping allows organizations to target the right areas for process kaizen and to track, measure, and demonstrate the effects that process kaizen improvements will have.

The Case for Extended Value-Stream Improvement

Value-stream mapping has been used successfully by many organizations to plan and identify internal improvements. However, most companies that have embraced lean have not yet considered their extended value streams for improvement. The extended value stream is the value stream of material and information flow from raw materials to the end user; it crosses suppliers, customers, and facilities.

Why would an organization want to analyze and improve its extended value stream? Most organizations have outsourced a significant percentage of their manufacturing. According to outsourcing expert Michael F. Corbett, 62 percent of companies are outsourcing component manufacturing, and an additional 14 percent are considering it.[3] This implies that a large benefit is to be gained by improving the extended value stream: if most of the value stream for a given product consists of supplying organizations, then improving the entire value stream including the supplying organizations will have a much greater effect on the overall cost of the value stream than improving the door-to-door value stream alone.

For example, if your organization outsources its entire component manufacturing and does only assembly operations in house, a much greater benefit will accrue by improving the *extended* value stream than by only improving the *door-to-door* value stream. More specifically, if we assume that 70 percent of the cost of the product is material cost (i.e., purchased components) for a given value stream, then extended value-stream improvement would allow an organization to tap into the 70 percent that would otherwise remain untouched.

Without improving the extended value stream, an organization's suppliers will be building in "mass-production" style, which implies that the pull systems such organizations have set up with their suppliers are not true pull systems. Instead, suppliers are still building in large batches and holding huge amounts of inventory, and this cost is passed on to their customers. The approach most companies take is to "squeeze" their suppliers by demanding lower prices; however, it is important to keep in mind that someone must pay for the drop in price. This generally leads to lower quality and poor on-time delivery; sometimes it leads to suppliers going out of business. This is certainly not in the best interest of the customer. Instead, by improving the extended value stream, suppliers will be strengthened, and each participant in the value stream will benefit.

When to Begin Extending Lean

On the lean implementation timeline, extending lean to suppliers and customers depends on the organization's business model and its size. In general, lean should be extended after

---

3. *The Outsourcing Revolution*. Michael F. Corbett. Dearborn Trade Publishing, 2004, p. 92.

the company has worked through its door-to-door value streams and completed an initial lean implementation.

If the organization's business model is such that it outsources a significant percentage of manufacturing (i.e., material cost is a large percentage of a product cost), then extending lean should be done early—as soon as the initial lean implementation has been completed. This can be one to two years after the organization has begun lean implementation, depending on the size of the organization.

If the organization is more vertically integrated, then extending lean would likely be done two to four years after the organization has begun lean implementation. This is because it will take longer for the organization to implement lean internally, and the benefits to be gained through extending lean will be fewer. It may benefit a vertically integrated company to focus on continuing to improve its door-to-door value streams rather than extending improvement too early.

Implementation Overview

Because it involves people outside of the organization, extending lean is a more complex undertaking than implementing lean internally. In the chapters that follow, we will show you how to extend lean effectively. Successful implementation of lean throughout the extended value stream will result in short lead times and lower overall cost. There are eight major implementation steps, described in the following sections. Steps 1–3 can be considered the planning steps, whereas Steps 4–8 involve implementing and sustaining success. Figures 1-1 and 1-2 depict these steps, the rest of this chapter describes them briefly, and the rest of the book describes each step in detail.

Figure 1-1. Extending Lean: Steps 1–3, Planning

Figure 1-2. Extending Lean: Steps 4–8, Implementation

Step 1: Map Your Value Streams

Begin by identifying value streams and selecting a single value stream to begin improving. Next, create a *current-state* extended-value-stream map: this will show the material and information flow for the extended value stream. Then, develop a *future-state* map that shows an attainable material and information flow that will be achievable in approximately 12 months.

Develop an implementation plan for each future state. The plan should include the following information:

- Projects that need to be accomplished in order to achieve the future state,
- Due dates for each project, and
- Personnel responsible for each project.

Optionally, the team can develop an additional future-state map for 24 months.

Step 2: Define Your Core Competencies

Part of the process of developing the future-state maps and the plan to achieve them is to analyze core competencies. Visualizing the current-state extended-value stream will help you determine which processes should be done internally versus externally. In Chapters 4 to 6, we will show you the best way to determine this.

Step 3: Develop a Plan

The next step is to develop an outsourcing plan to achieve the future state based on your future-state value-stream maps and implementation plan and on the results of your core-competency analysis. Here's how:

- First, select key suppliers with which you plan to continue doing business and plan to forge a long-term relationship.
- Next, decide which suppliers you can no longer afford to keep. These key decisions should be based on your current relationship and ranking of your suppliers. It should also be based on their willingness to embrace lean.
- Then, develop an outsourcing plan. Decide which suppliers will handle which business activities. List the voids you have and put together a plan to find new suppliers to fill the voids. Ideally, new suppliers should already be on a lean journey.

Step 4: Identify New Suppliers and Contract with New and Existing Suppliers

Next, you need to search for new suppliers based on your outsourcing plan. Based on your goals of the future state, the types of supplier relationships you will need to build, and business requirements, you should develop a set of criteria and apply the criteria to potential future suppliers. After you've selected your suppliers, develop appropriate agreements (i.e., contracts) with new and existing suppliers within the value stream.

Step 5: Work with Suppliers/Customers to Map Their Door-to-Door Value Streams

This is where the actual lean implementation begins. Improvements at the shopfloor and information flow levels need to be made to achieve the future-state maps from Step 1. Value-stream maps for each key supplier and customer should be created.

Step 6: Work with Suppliers/Customers to Implement Their Future-State Plans Using Process Kaizen

After developing door-to-door value streams, suppliers and customers will work using the implementation plan. This will involve using process kaizen tools such as cell manufacturing, 5S, quick changeover, and TPM.

Step 7: Develop a Supplier Association to Sustain, Improve, and Expand Lean

Develop a supplier association that, unlike most supplier associations, encourages lean thinking and continuous improvement. The supplier association will be used for expanding the system as well as to include additional value streams and suppliers.

Step 8: Find Creative Ways for Additional Improvement from Suppliers

This step creates additional improvement for the supply chain in two ways: first, by bringing all of the supply chain processes closer together to combine the benefits of outsourcing with the benefits of vertical integration, and second, by involving suppliers in product design to improve the manufacturability of your product designs.

Now let's look at how one (fictitious) company, EVS Corporation, extended lean to its suppliers.

Case Study:
Introducing EVS Corporation and Its Suppliers

EVS Corporation manufactures electronic testing equipment in San Diego, California. When it was founded in the mid-1980s, it was vertically integrated. It manufactured most components for the equipment, assembled subassemblies that were used in the equipment, and assembled and tested the final product.

As the final product became more complex in the 1990s, management decided to outsource the manufacture of components and later, subassemblies, with the expectation that costs would be lower. Despite their efforts, costs did not go down, and, in 2001, the company was forced to downsize severely due to a recession, particularly in the electronics industry. It was then that EVS decided to embrace lean manufacturing.

In 2002, the company began to implement lean manufacturing internally. It was able to grow over the next two years while hardly increasing head count; and costs were dropping—but not fast enough.

In late 2003, the organization's VP of Manufacturing attended a conference in which he learned about extending lean to suppliers and customers. Because 80 percent of the cost of a typical EVS product was material cost (i.e., purchased parts), the VP realized that EVS would greatly benefit from a lean extended value stream.

Currently, EVS has more than 100 suppliers; the key suppliers (those that currently supply 80 percent of the total in dollar terms) are listed and described in Table 1-1.

Table 1-1. EVS Corporation Suppliers

Supplier Name	Parts Supplied to EVS
Electro-Mechanical Assembly, Inc., San Diego, CA	Major electromechanical subassemblies for each product line. 40 percent of all assemblies supplied to EVS come from Electro-Mechanical Assembly, Inc.
San Simeon Assembly House, Los Angeles, CA	Major electromechanical subassemblies for each product line. 45 percent of subassemblies supplied to EVS come from San Simeon Assembly House.
Trotsky Metals, Newark, NJ	Machined components going into each product line. 50 percent of all machined components in EVS products come from Trotsky. Most are shipped to Electro-Mechanical Assemblies, Inc., for use in subassemblies.
GTX Machining, Inc., Carlsbad, CA	Machined components going into each product line. 20 percent of all machined components supplied to EVS come from GTX. Most are shipped to Electro-Mechanical Assemblies, Inc., for use in subassemblies.
Al's Machine Shop, Phoenix, AZ	Single machined component (vacuum ring) going into each product line; the supplier is a single source for this product. The operations group is convinced that this component can only be made by this organization. This is used by EVS directly in its assembly cells.
Joe's Machine Shop, Portland, OR	Machined components going into each product line. 10 percent of machined components supplied to EVS come from Joe's. These are used by EVS directly in its assembly cells.
Electronics, Inc., Los Angeles, CA	Electronic subassemblies for each product line. 50 percent of all electronics components supplied to EVS come from Electronics, Inc. Most of these are shipped to Electro-Mechanical Assemblies, Inc., or San Simeon Assembly for use in subassemblies.

Throughout this book, we will use EVS Corporation as a case example for each of the implementation steps. Although every situation is unique and EVS Corporation may be dissimilar to your own organization, the principles and techniques that are used throughout this book can be applied to any industry. Examples of how to handle unique situations will be included throughout the book to help you tailor the techniques to your company's unique circumstances. Chapter 2 gets you started with Step 1 of the planning process: mapping the extended value stream for your organization.

Summing Up: Key Points

Lean manufacturing is a proven system for reducing inventory and lead time, improving productivity and quality, increasing customer satisfaction, and improving employee morale and involvement. The lean organization achieves these benefits by eliminating waste and non-value-adding activities using a set of tools and principles. Some of the key tools they employ include value-stream mapping, the 5S system, one-piece flow, cellular manufacturing, kanban and pull systems, Total Productive Maintenance (TPM), and the Single Minute Exchange of Die (SMED) system.

Benefits of Extending Lean to Suppliers

Using these tools, many organizations have implemented lean manufacturing to achieve lean internal value streams. Given the highly outsourced business models of most of today's organizations, extending lean can greatly magnify the benefits of implementing lean internally. There are two key reasons for implementing lean across the entire supply chain:

1. If most of the value stream for a given product is made up of supplier operations rather than internal operations, then improving the *entire* value stream will have a much greater effect on the overall cost of the value stream than improving the *door-to-door* value stream alone.

2. Without improving the extended value stream, an organization's suppliers will be building in "mass-production" style, which ultimately prevents suppliers from successfully supplying lean customers with the quality, pricing, quantity, and timeliness required. In other words, nonlean suppliers who supply lean customers do not have the tools to succeed in the long run.

On the lean implementation timeline, extending lean to suppliers and customers is dependent on the organization's business model and its size. In general, lean should be extended after the company has worked through its door-to-door value streams and completed an initial lean implementation. If an organization has a highly outsourced model, it should begin extending lean to its suppliers early, about one to two years after lean implementation has begun. For more vertically integrated organizations, extending lean should be done later.

Implementing Lean to Suppliers: 8 Key Steps

The key steps to extending lean are:

1. Map extended value streams.
2. Define core competencies.
3. Develop an implementation plan.
4. Identify new suppliers and contract with new and existing suppliers.
5. Work with suppliers and customers to map their door-to-door value streams.
6. Work with suppliers and customers to implement their future-state plans using process kaizen.
7. Develop a supplier association to sustain, improve, and expand lean.
8. Find creative ways for additional improvement through supplier process co-location and supplier involvement in product design.

Applying This Information to Your Organization: Questions to Help You Get Started

1. Where is your organization on the lean implementation timeline?

2. What type of business model does your business have? Is it highly outsourced, vertically integrated, or somewhere in the middle? To help answer this question, find out what percentage of the typical product cost is material versus internal labor.

3. When would be an appropriate time to begin extending lean to suppliers for your organization?

Chapter 2

Mapping the Extended Value Stream, Current State

Getting Started

As we stated in Chapter 1, value-stream mapping allows organizations to target the right areas for process kaizen and to track, measure, and demonstrate the effects that process kaizen improvements will have. Instead of making spot improvements that do not demonstrate benefits to a company's bottom line, value-stream mapping improves the entire system so that overall lead time can be reduced dramatically.

This chapter will teach you how to create a *current-state* value-stream map for an extended value stream. There are three things you will need to understand before you can identify your value stream:

1. What is value?

2. What is a value stream?

3. What is the significance of value and the value stream?

Let's begin with the answers to these three questions.

First, *value* is that which gives a product worth *in the eyes of the customer*.

Second, the value stream is the set of all the actions required to bring a product to the customer, including information and material flow. In the value stream, there are actions that create value and actions that create no value. *Value-creating actions* are actions that change a product such that value is added; for example, carving a piece of wood into a piece of furniture is value-added. Customers pay much more for a piece of furniture than for the same amount of wood. Therefore, the carving activity is value-creating.

On the other hand, non-value-creating actions do not increase the worth of a product in the eyes of the customer. They generally fall into one or more of the "seven wastes" discussed in Chapter 1. Using the same furniture example above, suppose that the furniture is moved to a warehouse and stored for several months before shipping to the customer. Storing and transporting product to a warehouse does not create value in the eyes of the customer (although the customer ultimately pays for these non-value-creating activities).

15

Among the actions that do not create value, some are unavoidable due to current technology or logistical circumstances, and others can be eliminated with short-term changes. For example, if an organization has separate buildings, neither of which is large enough to manufacture a complete product, the organization may have to move product from one building to another between operations. This is clearly non-value-creating; however, due to current circumstances, it cannot be eliminated in the short-term. However, the organization can eliminate, for example, multiple moves between the buildings by changing the order of operations or layout. This can be done in the short-term.

A technology-driven example might be an injection-molding process. Injection-molding equipment is made for batch production. Although it is possible to minimize changeover time and reduce batch size, it is not possible to make whatever is needed one unit at a time. Thus, injection-molding equipment will produce work-in-process (WIP) inventory, which is non-value-creating. Because the technology is such that this is unavoidable, injection molding is a good example of a non-value-creating but necessary process. Metal-stamping equipment would be another similar example. Figure 2-1 illustrates how to evaluate whether an action creates value, and what to do about it if it does not.

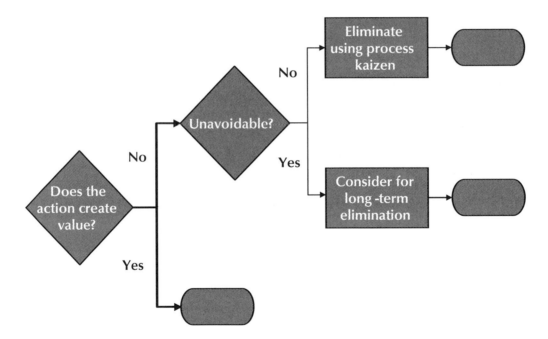

Figure 2-1. Evaluating Value-Stream Actions

Third, let's consider the significance of a value stream. A very small percentage of a value stream consists of value-creating time; most of the time is non-value-creating. Eliminating actions that create *no value* is significant because it will have a dramatic effect on profits. A lean value stream creates shorter lead times, less inventory, better responsiveness to customers, lower product costs, and increased quality. All of these lead to better top-line and bottom-line performance.

Figure 2-2 illustrates the lean transformation to shorter lead time. By eliminating non-value-creating time, total lead time is dramatically decreased. Lead time approximates the amount of inventory in the system; if, for example, 100 days of inventory exist between raw materials and the end customer, then there are approximately 100 days of lead time. If lead time is cut in half, inventory is cut in half, resulting in significant cost savings. In fact, inventory-holding costs are usually estimated to be at least 20 percent per year. If inventory is reduced from, for example, $2 million to $1 million, this represents a cost savings of at least $200,000 per year!

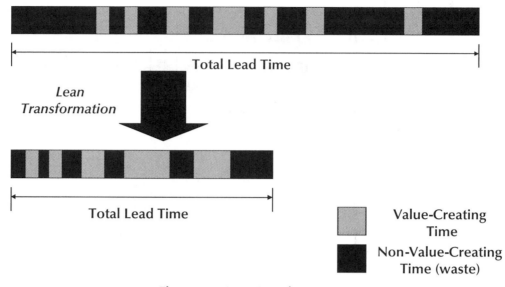

Figure 2-2. Lean Transformation

Identifying and Selecting Value Streams

How do you begin to identify the value streams in your business? Use these three major steps to identify your value streams:

1. Group your products into product families.

2. Select one of your products or product families to be analyzed.

3. Walk through the value stream from the customer back to materials in receiving.

Let's look at each of these steps in detail.

Step 1: Group Your Products

Grouping your products is usually a simple process. Make a table like Table 2-1. Along the left column, list all of your products. Along the top row, list all of your processes/equipment. Place an "X" in each cell where a product uses a process. In doing this, you will begin to see patterns which will indicate process families. For example, Table 2-1 shows that products A & C might be a product family. Although you will likely need to make adjustments, you will make progress in identifying your product families.

Tables like 2-1 work well in situations where many finished good part numbers

Table 2-1. Process Versus Product Matrix

Product	Process Step					
	1	2	3	4	5	6, 7, 8...
A	X		X	X	X	
B		X	X		X	
C	X		X	X	X	
D		X	X		X	
E, F, G...						

need to be analyzed. For example, in the aerospace industry, tier one suppliers often have thousands of finished goods part numbers. In such cases, value streams may not be obvious. In other cases, however, product families and value streams are obvious. In such cases, much less analysis is needed.

Step 2: Select a Product Family to Analyze

The criteria you use for selecting the first product family to be analyzed depend on your business situation. Following are some criteria you might consider:

1. *Highest product volume in terms of revenue.* Potentially, this can have the largest impact on the bottom line.

2. *Highest product volume in terms of units produced.*

3. *Products with the highest defect rates.* Although this can have a great impact in terms of cost reduction, it may take a long time to demonstrate results for improving high-defect-rate value streams versus taking on value streams with an average amount of defects. This is because it is necessary to create a stable process before one-piece flow is possible.

4. *Products with the highest customer return rate.* As with high-defect-rate products, products that are returned often will take a considerable amount of time to improve. Thus, these may not be the best choice for an initial value stream.

5. *Products that visit the most processes.* You will find that most changes you will make in value-stream analysis of a product will apply to many products and product families. The first value-stream-mapping exercise will take the longest; the others will be much easier.

It is important to select a value stream initially that will have the greatest impact and will have the greatest chance for success. This will generate the necessary momentum to expand to other product lines and value streams.

Step 3: Make an Initial Walk-Through of Product Flow

When you make your initial walk-through, begin with your customer and work backwards. As you walk through, consider the questions and issues listed in Exhibit 2-1, and begin to take some initial notes.

Exhibit 2-1. Questions and Issues to Consider When Conducting Your Product Flow Walk-Through

1. Think about the transmission and receipt of customer orders throughout the value stream. How is information transferred from your customer to your tier one supplier to your tier two supplier, etc.?

2. Think about the relationship between a customer order and production activity in the factory. How does each production area know what to produce? For extended-value-stream analysis, ask: How do key suppliers run their production in an extended value stream?

> **3.** Think about where a product becomes tied to a specific customer order for the end customer. This is often a final assembly, packaging, or shipping area. However, there are many other possibilities. It can also be a process further upstream, such as a paint process, where a customer-specific color is applied.
>
> **4.** Think about how orders are transmitted up the value stream. How do upstream suppliers know what to make? How do purchasing agents know what to order? Is everything driven by material requirement planning (MRP), or is there some form of signaling in place?
>
> **5.** Think about the supply of materials from suppliers and upstream processes. How often are they supplied, and how are they supplied?
>
> **6.** Think about the frequency and method of transmission of products from your organization to your customer. How often are products shipped?

After walking through and thinking through the above questions, you will be well on your way to identifying and gaining a rudimentary understanding of your value stream. Whether you are mapping an *extended* value stream or an *internal* value stream, the process of identifying a value stream is very similar.

However, when considering the *extended* value stream, it is rarely possible to physically walk through the entire process, because suppliers are often located too far away. Therefore, instead of physically walking through, you can do a *virtual walk-through* by means of a teleconference with key suppliers, as they explain the answers to each question. When doing a virtual or physical walk-through, your goal is to begin thinking about how things are done. This information will be used later in current-state mapping. The purpose of this activity is not to obtain precise data or to develop solutions. This will be done during the mapping exercise.

Let's look at how our case-study company, EVS, followed these three steps.

Case Study:
How EVS Identified and Selected Its Value Streams

EVS Corporation has more than 300 different finished-goods part numbers, but its managers realize that they do not have 300 value streams. Table 2-2 shows part of EVS Corporation's value-stream-identification matrix.

NOTE: Workstations are "CXY" where X is the cell number, and Y is the station letter of the cell.

Based on the analysis shown in Table 2-2, EVS has three value streams:

- 4400A–Q (including the 4400 and 4400 A–Q)

- 4400XYZ

- 7700

Because 4400A and 4400B make up a large percentage of overall revenue, EVS has decided to select the 4400A–Q value stream for analysis. EVS had actually performed this part of the analysis when it mapped the company's internal value streams.

The company had to revisit the walk-through to extend the thought process across its suppliers. EVS did this by meeting with representatives of its key suppliers to understand their processes. This gave EVS an initial understanding of its extended value stream.

(Continued on next page)

(Continued from previous page)

Table 2-2. EVS Product Versus Process Matrix

Product	Workstations													
	C1A	C1B	C1C	C1D	C1E	C2A	C2B	C2C	C2D	C3A	C3B	C3C	C3D	C3E
4400	X	X	X											
4440A–J	X	X	X		X									
4400K–Q	X	X	X	X										
4400X	X	X	X	X		X	X	X	X					
4400Y	X	X	X	X	X	X	X	X	X					
4400Z	X	X	X	X	X	X	X	X	X					
7700A										X	X	X		
7700C–M										X	X	X	X	X
7700C–M										X	X	X		X
7700N–Q										X	X	X	X	

What EVS Learned

In thinking through the questions, EVS listed some of its more interesting observations:

- There are major information breakdowns. In talking with suppliers, EVS determined that communication between EVS and its suppliers is not effective.
- Customer orders are not driving production.
- EVS's products do not become customer specific until the final step in the process at EVS (i.e., during final assembly and test).
- Order transmission up the value stream is inefficient and probably results in far too much inventory.

EVS Corporation realizes that there is great potential for improvement. As the company progresses through the extended value-stream-mapping exercise, it will discover just how much improvement is possible and, more importantly, the practical steps it will need to take to achieve such improvement.

Now that we've seen how to identify and select a value stream to analyze (as well as how one company, EVS, did this), let's look at how to create an extended current-state map of that value stream.

Creating an Extended Current-State Map

Forming the Mapping Team

For extended value-stream mapping, the following individuals will create the current-state map and should be represented on the team:

- *The Plant or Operations Manager or Director of Operations.* It is important that a management-level operations person be on the team. This person may also be the team leader.

- *An industrial engineer(s) or continuous improvement personnel.* Industrial engineers with lean knowledge or people working in a kaizen or lean management office will be instrumental in identifying improvement opportunities as well as performing the actual mapping.

- *A lean champion.* If your organization has a lean champion or a person in charge of a lean management office or kaizen office, that person should be involved in initial extended value-stream mapping efforts.

- *Representatives from key suppliers.* Each key supplier should be represented on the team; it is important never to assume how information and material flow through a supplier's organization. As you will see later in this chapter, the current-state mapping exercise itself is eye opening, particularly when it comes to identifying communication breakdowns.

- *Representative(s) from key customer(s).* If customer processes are involved in the extended mapping exercise, key customers or their representatives must be involved. If an organization has one or two key customers who make up a majority of demand, then it makes sense to include them. Otherwise, it may be useful to include a representative from sales or marketing instead.

Although some organizations might be resistant to including suppliers and customers, it is important to invite representatives from key supplying organizations and customers to gain a full understanding of how the value stream operates. This will allow each party to begin to communicate in a new way, considering not only a piece of the value stream but the *entire* value stream. This alone will spark "breakthrough" ideas for improving the extended value stream.

Physical Mapping of Information Flow and Material Flow

You will need the following items before you begin:

1. Pencil and eraser (Always map using a pencil because you will make mistakes.)
2. 11″ × 17″ paper

Begin mapping with your customer(s) and work backwards through suppliers. Map physical material flow first, and then map information flow. Note that material flows from left to right on the bottom of the map, and information flows from right to left at the top of the map, as shown in Figure 2-3.

Step 1. *Map end customer in the upper-right-hand side.* If there are many customers and the customers' processes will not be individually considered, map only one box that shows the aggregate demand expressed in units per day or units per week (see Figure 2-4). In special situations where there are very few customers, it may make sense to list them and their demand individually. Otherwise, one box representing the customer is adequate.

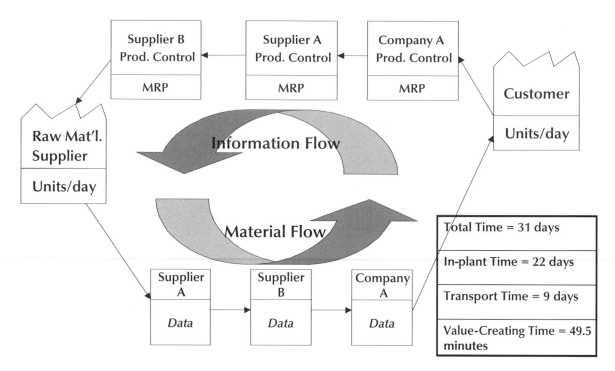

Figure 2-3. General Current-State Value-Stream Map

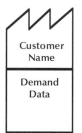

Figure 2-4. Customer or Supplier Box

Step 2. *Create a process box representing your own organization.* The process box represents an entire facility and typically includes the following information (see Figure 2-5):

- *Value-creating time (actual hands-on or processing time).* This is the amount of time that the product is worked on. This should not be an estimate such as: "It takes about a day to get through the assembly process." Instead, it needs to be precise, usually expressed in minutes or even seconds. For example, for a metal stamping process, the processing time is often 1 or 2 seconds. For an assembly process, it may be 120 minutes or more.

- *Inventory of each type: raw material, WIP, and finished goods.* This should be a snapshot of the amount of inventory expressed in units or days. Very often, value-stream-mapping teachers discourage students from using data "in the system" for inventory count. However, if inventory is relatively accurate in the system, it may suffice to use data from the system. It is unnecessary to spend days counting inventory when a close estimate can be had from data in an enterprise resource planning (ERP) system.

- *Lead time.* Lead time is approximated by the number of days of inventory. To validate this truth in your mind, imagine a piece of raw material inventory that has just arrived at a factory. If you were to mark this piece of material and wait for it to travel through all processes and arrive as a finished unit at the shipping dock ready to be shipped to the end customer, it would wait in queue for each stage of inventory to be consumed between each process. First, all raw material of its kind would need to be worked through. Then, each pile of WIP at various stages of production would be processed. Finally, it would wait for finished goods to be processed before shipping. Of course, if the raw material were expedited, it would be much quicker. However, the average lead time would be equal to the number of days of inventory.

- *Shipping/transportation time.* This is generally expressed in terms of days. Many times, it will be an approximation or average.

- *Defect rates (usually first-pass yield).* You may note yields through individual processes in a separate supporting document; however, this number will estimate the percentage of product that makes it through the entire facility defect-free.

- *Operating parameters.* Operating parameters should include how many shifts per day and how many hours per shift are running in the factory.

Figure 2-5. Extended Value-Stream Process Box

Step 3. *Create processes boxes representing suppliers to be analyzed.* Data included will be identical to that of Step 2. For large assemblies with long bills of materials, this step presents a problem. Often there are many suppliers. However, this step should only include *key suppliers of key items.*

For example, let us suppose that there are three key subassemblies that go into a product supplied by three suppliers. There may also be dozens of other parts going into the product. An organization may choose to include only the three suppliers that supply the key subassemblies. Mapping every single part that goes into an assembly is unmanageable and of little value.

Step 4. *Create a box or boxes representing raw material suppliers.* These will not be analyzed. The only data that will be shown will be the transportation time from the raw material supplier to its customer. The icon should be the same as the customer icon (refer back to Figure 2-4).

Step 5. *Begin information-flow mapping.* Map boxes representing the information-processing portion of your organization and that of each of your key suppliers. Usually, these boxes represent production control departments. In some instances, there are separate organizations that process orders and then feed the information to production control. If this is so, you may map those separately. (These boxes generally do not show processing information because the internal information flow processes should be mapped separately. This will be covered later.)

Figure 2-6. Company Production Control Icon

Step 6. *Beginning with the customer, map the information flow from right to left.* This will show the order frequency from the customer to your organization to your suppliers and between suppliers.

Step 7. *Map the flow of information from the production control departments of each organization to the process boxes.* This will show how the facilities are scheduled. For example, production control at a supplier might be a weekly schedule and a daily priority list sent to the factory floor.

Step 8. *Calculate the following metrics across the bottom of the value-stream map:*
- Value-creating time
- In-plant time
- Transportation time
- Total time

Mapping Considerations

As you map the current-state value stream map, keep in mind that value-stream mapping is not an exact science. While all the data you would like to have will probably not be available, it is important to move through the value-stream mapping exercise relatively quickly with the data you do have. Current-state mapping should take only a few days to complete.

Too often, partial current-state maps are as far as an organization progresses in value-stream mapping because it spends months just trying to *collect* the data. Use the tool to accomplish your goal; try to keep the exercise as simple as possible. Develop a common set of icons to use in your company so you have a common language with which to express ideas.

Another issue to consider is software. Although some lean practitioners claim that hand-drawn value-stream maps work best, for long-term use and distribution value-stream maps should be transposed to a computer system. There are several value-stream-mapping software providers; however, most practitioners use standard programs, such as Microsoft Visio.

One potential pitfall to avoid is spending too much time on the software piece of the exercise. The most valuable part of the mapping exercise is the hands-on mapping; software should be used for documenting it more permanently.

Current-State Metrics: Definitions and Explanations

The following metrics are computed for the current-state extended value-stream map:

- *Value-creating time.* Within a value stream, this is the time the material or product is physically being changed in such a way that value is added to the product.
- *In-plant time.* Within the extended value stream, this is the time the material or product is in the factories or plants (but not necessarily being physically worked on).
- *Transport time.* Within the extended value stream, this is the time the material or product is moving between facilities.
- *Total time.* This is the total lead time from raw materials to the end user.

    Total time = in-plant time + transport time

- Value % of time. This is the percent of total time that is value-creating.

    Value % of time = value-creating time/total time × 100 percent

- *Inventory turnover.* This is the ratio of annual sales to average inventory, which measures the speed that inventory is produced and sold.

    Inventory turnover = cost of goods sold / average inventory

- *Product travel distance.* This is the total physical distance that the product travels (between facilities) in a lean extended value stream.

Let's look at how EVS created its current-state map: how it selected its team to make the map and how that team made the actual map by calculating EVS's information flow and material flow times.

Case Study: How EVS Selected Its Mapping Team and Created Its Current-State Map

EVS put together a small team consisting of the following personnel:
- EVS Director of Operations
- EVS Sr. Industrial Engineer
- EVS Director of Marketing and Sales
- San Simeon (supplier) Plant Manager
- San Simeon (supplier) Industrial Engineer
- Electronics, Inc. (supplier) Plant Manager
- Key EVS Customer (Purchasing Agent)

EVS then created a current-state extended value-stream map for its 4400A–Q product line (Figure 2-7). This map was put together as described in the following sections:

Step 1: The Team Began with the Customer and Customer Demand

In the upper-right-hand corner (of Figure 2-7), we show a customer demand of 120 units/day. Eighty percent of this demand is overseas; 20 percent is domestic.

(Continued on next page)

(Continued from previous page)

Step 2: EVS Created Its Mapping Process Boxes

On the EVS map, there are four major process boxes. For each process box, EVS shows the value-creating time (sometimes called "hands-on" time). EVS also shows the lead-time through each factory by adding together the number of days of raw material, WIP, and finished goods. Finally, EVS shows the yield for each factory and the operating parameters (number of shifts) for the organizations described in the following sections.

EVS Itself:

- *Inventory.* The team observed 1 day of work-in-process inventory, 2 days of raw material inventory, and 2 days of finished goods inventory onsite at EVS.
- *Lead time.* The lead time of 5 days is based on the sum of the days of inventory (2 days of raw material + 1 day of work-in-process + 2 days of finished goods = 5 days).
- *Value-creating time.* The well-documented process of assembling and testing takes 60 minutes.
- *Yield.* The yield through the factory is 99.5 percent.
- *Number of shifts.* There are 2 shifts in EVS Corporation's factory.

San Simeon Assembly. This supplier supplies all subassemblies:
- *Inventory.* The team observed 60 days of raw materials, 9 days of work in process, and 15 days of finished goods.
- *Lead time.* The lead time of 84 days is based on the sum of the days of inventory.
- *Value-creating time.* Based on time studies of each step in the process, the team discovered that there is a total of 360 value-creating minutes.
- *Yield.* The yield is only 72 percent. Many products are reworked or scrapped.
- *Number of shifts.* San Simeon runs a 2-shift operation.

Trotsky metals. This company supplies the majority of the machined components:
- *Inventory.* Because Trotsky is located 3,000 miles from EVS, the team did not travel to Trotsky's location. Instead, EVS asked Trotsky to provide data. Trotsky reported 60 days of raw materials, 21 days of work-in-process, and 60 days of finished goods.
- *Lead time.* The lead time of 141 days is based on the sum of the days of inventory.
- *Value-creating time.* Based on Trotsky's documented machine cycle times for each step in the process, the team discovered that there is a total of 210 value-creating minutes.
- *Yield.* The yield is only 89.2 percent. Many products are reworked or scrapped.
- *Number of shifts.* Trotsky runs a 3-shift operation.

Electronics, Inc. This company supplies the majority of electronics components:
- *Inventory.* The team observed 60 days of raw materials, 14 days of work-in-process, and 45 days of finished goods.
- *Lead time.* The lead time of 119 days is based on the sum of the days of inventory.
- *Value-creating time.* Based on documented machine cycle times for each step in the process, the team discovered that there is a total of 3 value-creating minutes.
- *Yield.* The yield is reported at 92.6 percent.
- *Number of shifts.* Electronics, Inc., runs a 3-shift operation.

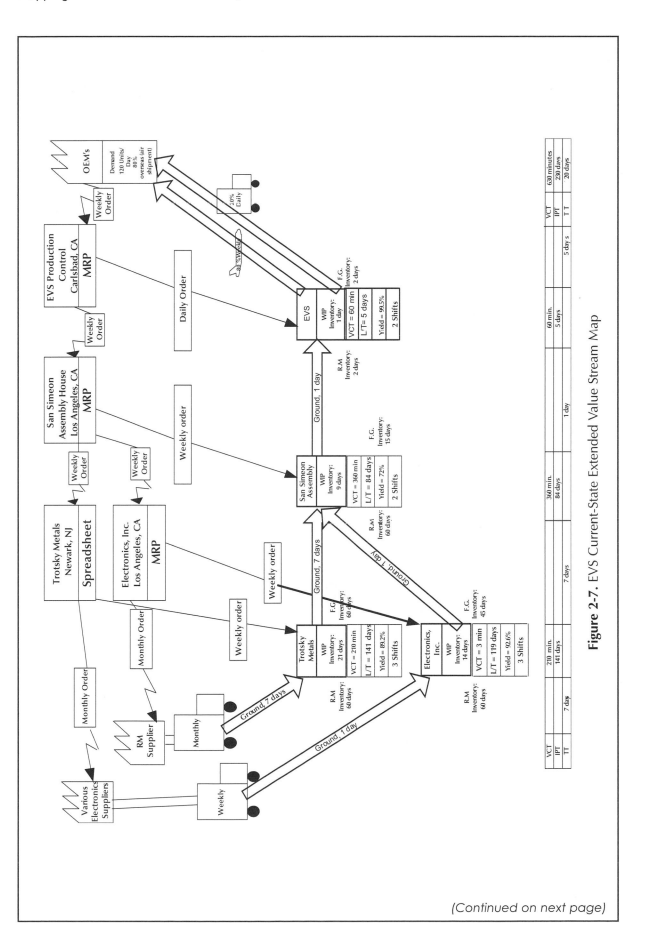

Figure 2-7. EVS Current-State Extended Value Stream Map

(Continued on next page)

(Continued from previous page)

Step 3: EVS Shows the Raw Material Suppliers in the Upper-Left-Hand Corner

Because EVS is not going to analyze or improve these organizations, the team does not show any factory data for these suppliers.

Step 4: EVS Connects Each Factory with an Arrow

This process shows how material gets transported:

- Between San Simeon Assembly and EVS, product travels via next-day ground shipment.
- Between Trotsky and San Simeon, machined components travel via ground for 7 days.
- Between Electronics, Inc., and San Simeon, electronic assemblies travel via ground for 1 day.
- Between the metal raw materials supplier and Trotsky, there is a 7-day ground shipment.
- Between the electronics suppliers and Electronics, Inc., there is a 1-day ground shipment. These suppliers are actually distributors that are local to Electronics, Inc.

Step 5: EVS Moves on to the Information Flow

Again beginning with the customer, EVS maps each production control box for each factory. This will illustrate two aspects of material flow:

- Material flow from customer to supplier (how often orders are placed)
- Material flow from production control to factory floor (how work is scheduled).

Step 6: The Key Metrics Are Summed Along the Bottom of the Map

In this case, the key metrics work out, as shown in Table 2-3.

Table 2-3. EVS Current-State Map Metrics

Metric	Value
Value-creating time	630 minutes
In-plant time	230 days
Transport time	20 days
Total time (transport + inplant)	250 days
Value % of time	0.175%
Inventory turnover (precalculated by EVS)	1.8
Total distance traveled	4,136 miles

Inventory turnover is rarely considered for an entire supply chain. Usually, it is only calculated for a specific organization by dividing cost of goods sold by ending inventory. This same calculation can be made by including all inventory in the supply chain. Obviously, this version of inventory turnover is not to be compared with internal inventory turnover. It will be a smaller number, because inventory from all value-stream participants is included.

How EVS Analyzed Its Current State

The metrics for EVS shown in Table 2-3 reveal some eye-opening facts:

- First, even though EVS has a lean internal value stream, the extended value stream for its product is hardly lean. Value-creating time is only 0.175 percent of total time!

- Second, EVS's suppliers hold large amounts of inventory, resulting in a low inventory turnover ratio of 1.8. EVS places delivery demands on its suppliers to support its lean operations; however, its suppliers do not have lean operations to support them. They compensate for this fact by holding large amounts of inventory. This condition is not sustainable in the long run; therefore, there are three possibilities for the suppliers in this value stream:

  - *Scenario 1:* They will go out of business trying to support EVS by building more and more inventory.

  - *Scenario 2:* They will be forced to raise their prices to pay for the extra inventory they have, ultimately resulting in lower profits for EVS. If EVS is unwilling to accept increases in price, it will be forced to find new suppliers that it can "squeeze" for a short period of time.

  - *Scenario 3:* They will become lean, will drive cost down, and will support EVS.

The last scenario is the one EVS will be pursuing. The company's goal is to lean out the entire value stream, creating a true lean supply chain for its products. This is the only viable long-term solution: to support and invest in its suppliers, resulting in a healthy supply chain in which all participants are thriving.

Detailed Process Mapping of Information Flow

In extended value-stream analysis, communication is often the cause of many other wastes. The value-stream map itself does not have enough detail to show where many of the information processing delays are. Therefore, supplemental to the current-state map, it is usually helpful to draw process maps or flowcharts showing the actual information flow-in detail between facilities. Generally, they will

- Reveal the sources of delays in the information flow; this will help in identifying problems and solutions for creating a lean future state,

- Clarify the steps that can be eliminated or greatly simplified,

- Allow the team to quantify information-flow issues, such as queues and information transfers, and

- Provide further food for thought for the idea-generation or brainstorming session (which will be addressed in Chapter 3).

Process mapping can usually be done in the form of a flowchart with as few as four very basic icons: process, data, decision, and end. Any software that supports flowcharting will work well for documentation. Let's go back to our case study and see how EVS mapped its information flow.

Case Study: How EVS Corporation Mapped Its Information Flow

Figure 2-8 shows EVS Corporation's information-flow process map.

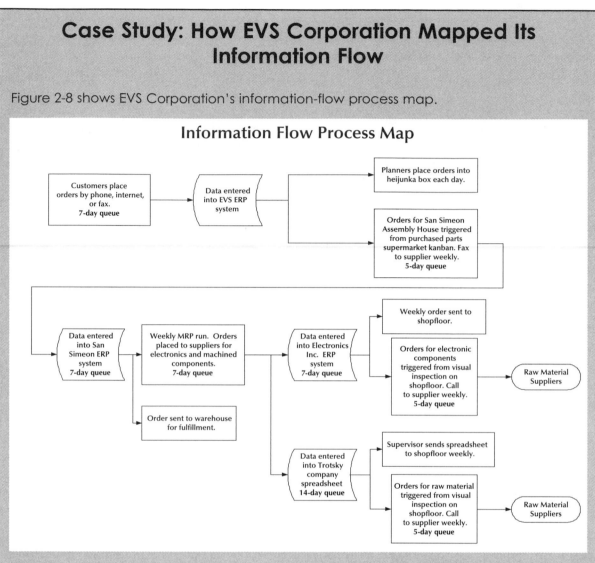

Figure 2-8. EVS Information Flow Process Map

Figure 2-8 shows the detailed path of information from customers to EVS to suppliers. From this process map, we can gather queue times and the number of information transfers. Going through step-by-step, we have the following sequence of operations:

1. EVS Corporation's customers place orders to EVS by telephoning or faxing customer service or entering orders via the Internet. These orders are entered into an ordering system and are held an average of 7 days in queue before being transferred into the ERP system. (The order-processing system is separate from the ERP system.)

2. After the orders are transferred to the ERP system and now have visibility to production control, planners schedule work on the assembly floor using a heijunka or load-leveling box. A *heijunka box* is a device that levels production by sequencing and distributing production kanban cards. For example, if a customer orders one 4400A, a card representing that order goes into an in-box. Figure 2-9 shows EVS's heijunka box; in this example, cell 1 will be running the 4400 product from 8:00 A.M. until 12:00 noon; EVS will then run 4400A–J (the card will specify the specific product); EVS will then run 4400K–Q, 4400X, and 4400 Y.

Cell 1 Heijunka Box

Product	Time Window								
	8–9	9–10	10–11	11–12	12–1	1–2	2–3	3–4	4–5
4400	/	/	/	/					
4440A–J					/	/			
4400K–Q							/		
4400X								/	
4400Y									/
4400Z									

Figure 2-9. EVS Heijunka Box

3. As parts are pulled from a purchased parts supermarket into the cell to support production, demand for orders is triggered. Specifically, when particular reorder points are reached, a colored sheet of paper indicates that a new order must be placed. Weekly, these orders are phoned in to suppliers.

4. At San Simeon, orders are entered into the ERP system. There is a 7-day delay.

5. MRP is run on a weekly basis; this triggers purchasing personnel to order electronics and machined components when certain inventory levels are reached in the system.

6. EVS orders are fulfilled in shipping because San Simeon holds inventory for EVS orders.

7. At Electronics, Inc., purchase orders from San Simeon are entered into an ERP system; a weekly production schedule is sent to the shopfloor.

8. At Trotsky, purchase orders from San Simeon are entered into a spreadsheet; the spreadsheet is sent to the shopfloor weekly.

9. Both Trotsky and Electronics, Inc., place orders from the raw materials suppliers on a weekly basis.

Table 2-4. EVS Information-Flow Process Map Metrics

Organization	Queue Time	No. of Information Transfers
EVS	12 days	3
San Simeon	14 days	2
Electronics	12 days	2
Trotsky	19 days	2
Total	**57 days**	**9**

The information transfers and queue times are summarized in Table 2-4.

According to Table 2-4, information is transferred 9 times and is in queue (therefore, *creating no value*) for 57 days. The team listed some key questions and problems observed regarding the information flow:

- Why is there a delay of 7 days before EVS customer orders are transferred to its ERP system?

- Why does EVS Corporation place orders based on reorder points only once/week?

(Continued on next page)

(Continued from previous page)

- Why is there a delay in transferring EVS order information into San Simeon's ERP system?

- Why is production scheduled at suppliers on a weekly basis? Why can't this be daily?

- Why does Trotsky use a simple spreadsheet for managing shopfloor activities? How does this remain up to date? Why is there a 14-day queue?

These observations will be used later when EVS creates its lean future state. Although the purpose of current-state mapping is not to generate *solutions*, it is useful to write down *observations*, as the team did above. Very often, the first attempt at an extended current-state value-stream and information-flow mapping will open the eyes of a team. They, like EVS Corporation's team, will see a large number of opportunities for improvement, many of which can be implemented relatively quickly and easily.

The next step for EVS Corporation's team is to begin working on a future state. We will cover that activity in Chapter 3.

Summing Up: Key Points

Value is that which gives a product worth in the eyes of the customer, and the *value stream* is the set of all the actions required to bring a product to the customer, including information and material flow. Some of the actions within a value stream are *value-creating* and some are *non-value-creating*; value-creating actions are actions that change a product such that value is added. A very small percentage of a value stream consists of value-creating time; most of the time is non-value-creating. Extended value-stream mapping enables organizations to identify opportunities for eliminating non-value-creating time within the value stream that includes all material and information flow between participants in the supply chain.

How to Map an Extended Value Stream

There are four steps to mapping an extended value stream:

Step 1. Identify and select value streams.

Step 2. Map the current state.

Step 3. Map the future state using a set of tools and principles.

Step 4. Create an implementation plan based on the future-state map.

Value-stream identification and selection involves three steps:

Step 1. *Group product families.* This is usually done using a product versus process matrix.

Step 2. *Select one of the products/product families to be analyzed first.*

Step 3. *Walk through the value stream from the customer back to materials in receiving.* For the extended value stream, the "walk-through" is usually not a physical "walk-through" but rather a mental exercise.

How to Create a Current-State Map

After a value stream is selected for analysis, a cross-functional team that includes key supplier and customer representatives and internal personnel will map the current state. There are eight steps to creating a current-state map:

Step 1. Map the end customer in the upper-right-hand side.

Step 2. Create a process box representing your own organization.

Step 3. Create process boxes representing suppliers to be analyzed.

Step 4. Create a box or boxes representing raw material suppliers.

Step 5. Begin information-flow mapping. Map boxes representing the information processing portion of your organization and that of each of your key suppliers.

Step 6. Beginning with the customer, map the information flow from right to left.

Step 7. Map the flow of information from the production control departments of each organization to the process boxes.

Step 8. Calculate the key metrics across the bottom of the value-stream map. The metrics will reveal the relatively small proportion of time that is value-creating.

Poor communication and information flow are major problems in an extended value stream; they often result in significant delays. Because the current-state value-stream map itself does not have enough detail to show where many of the information processing delays are, the value-stream mapping team should create an additional map showing information flow-in detail between supply chain participants.

After the current-state map and information-flow maps are drawn, the team is ready to create the future state, which is covered in Chapter 3.

Applying This Information to Your Organization: Questions to Help You Get Started

1. What are your organization's product lines? Can these be considered value streams?

2. If you were to select a value stream for extended value stream analysis, which would you select? Why?

3. Which of your key suppliers would be willing to go through the extended mapping process?

4. What do you suppose you will find out about your extended value stream through the mapping process? Write your answers down and compare with the actual results of your mapping process.

Chapter 3
Creating a Lean Extended Value Stream

From Current-State Mapping to Future-State Mapping

Chapter 2 described how to map the current state of your value stream; this chapter takes us to the next step, which is mapping the future state. Before you can get to that, though, you need to understand why value streams aren't already lean, and you need to know the critical elements of a lean extended value stream. Let's get started by looking at the problems and the ideal state.

The 7 Wastes (+1) of the Extended Value Stream

What differentiates lean extended value stream from a *typical* extended value stream? If I had to use one word to sum it up, that word would be *communication*. The primary reason that value streams are not lean is poor communication, and poor communication results in waste.

One key to successfully achieving a lean extended value stream is to understand the types of waste one might find in the extended value stream. "The seven wastes" is a powerful tool for implementing lean manufacturing in a facility. When analyzing the *extended* value stream, one must consider the seven wastes with a slightly different paradigm.

Waste 1: Overproduction

Overproduction simply means producing more than what is actually needed by an upstream process or customer. On the shopfloor, this generally occurs because changeover times are high, equipment is unreliable, the process is unreliable (i.e., it causes defects), and standard cost accounting metrics are used.

In the extended value stream, overproduction certainly occurs for some of these same reasons. However, one of the key causes of overproduction is poor information flow (communication) between facilities. Suppliers are often given information at the very last minute, preventing them from reacting in time. The types of information that affect the quantity of units a supplier may produce include:

- Engineering changes
- Customer order quantity changes
- Forecast changes

All of the above items are rarely communicated in a timely manner to suppliers; very often, suppliers remain "in the dark." The result is often overproduction.

Waste 2: Transportation

Moving product does not create value; this fact is amplified when examining the extended value stream. Unnecessary transportation is generally caused by making supplier selection decisions based on *single points* in a value stream, rather than seeking to optimize the *entire* value stream. Frequently, supplier selection is based purely on per-unit price. This looks great on paper; however, it results in overall higher costs in some cases. Proper selection of supplier or facility location is critical to a lean value stream.

Waste 3: Unnecessary Inventory

For the extended value stream, unnecessary inventory is generally the result of poor information flow and batch processing. Therefore, inventory is typically held for one of three reasons.

Primarily, suppliers will hold inventory to compensate for a lack of information. An obvious proof of this is the existence of finished-goods warehouses: the reason manufacturers have finished-goods warehouses is because they do not know what their customers will be ordering in the future with certainty. The less information they have about what customers want, the more inventory they need to compensate for that lack of information.

A second reason is that "mass production" suppliers often hold excess inventory to support a lean customer; this cost ultimately gets passed on to the customer in the form of higher pricing and/or poor quality. Mass producers do not function well in a lean supply chain; after all, they are set up to run in very large batches. Because they cannot support one-piece flow or small batches, they are forced to hold "just-in-case" inventory.

Finally, sometimes suppliers and their customers are holding redundant inventory. A supplier might be holding a few days' worth of inventory to handle variation in demand, and the customer may be doing the same. Extended value-stream mapping will make this obvious.

Waste 4: Inappropriate Processing

In the door-to-door value stream, inappropriate processing usually refers to using larger-scale equipment than necessary; it also refers to building rework into a process. In the *extended* value stream, it can also refer to using the wrong suppliers and/or the wrong process.

It is important to select suppliers that have the most appropriate processes for manufacturing the product. For example, companies selling low-volume products often select a low-cost supplier that is set up for high-volume production. This results in waste; the company ends up purchasing much more than it would like, and it ends up with the hidden cost of excess inventory in its factory. With regards to rework, organizations often rework parts after they come in from a supplier simply because of poor communication between facilities.

Waste 5: Waiting

This waste refers to operators waiting for machines as well as product waiting (inventory). This waste is generally the same for the extended value stream as the internal value stream; of course, it is magnified somewhat because products often wait for long periods of time prior to shipment between facilities.

Waste 6: Excess Motion

Generally, this waste applies to production personnel having to move out of their work area to locate tools, materials, etc. Like the waste of waiting, this is essentially the same for the extended value stream as the internal value stream.

Waste 7: Defects

This waste refers to defective product and information (paperwork). Its unique applications to the extended value stream are defective product moving between facilities and defective information transmitted from facility to facility. The former results in additional waste in the form of excess inventory and rework. The latter can result in many forms of additional waste. The wrong information can result in any of the following scenarios:

- *The wrong product is produced or shipped.* A supplier may manufacture the wrong product because of defective ordering information.
- *A defective product is produced.* A supplier may manufacture a defective or obsolete product because of defective design information being sent.
- *Too much product is produced or shipped.* A supplier may manufacture too much of a particular product because of defective order quantities.
- *Too little product is produced or shipped.* A supplier may not manufacture enough product because of defective order quantities.

An Additional Waste (#8): Underutilization of Employees' Minds and Ideas

For the extended value stream, this waste could be called *underutilization of suppliers' and customers' minds and/or ideas*. Organizations rarely approach their customers and suppliers to leverage their know-how with respect to manufacturing processes, information processing, and product design. This is a problematic waste of the extended value stream, and several methods for leveraging supplier and customer know-how will be addressed throughout this book.

Elements of a Lean Extended Value Stream

A lean extended value stream is one that works to eliminate the above wastes. Eliminating such wastes results ultimately in dramatically shorter lead times. Let's examine the characteristics of a lean extended value stream. Figure 3-1 provides an overview of these essential characteristics.

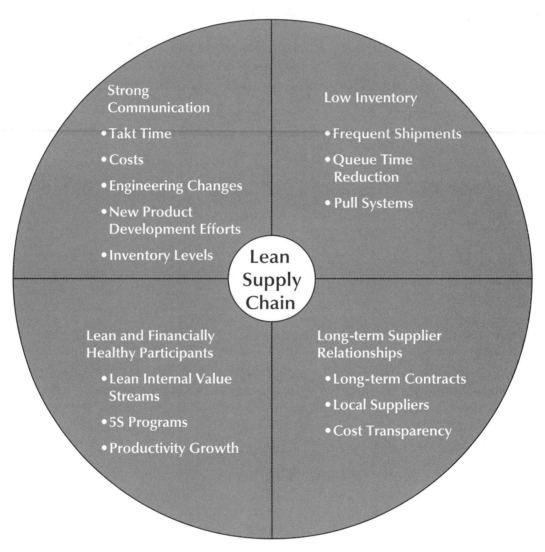

Figure 3-1. Lean Supply Chain Characteristics

Element 1: Strong Communication and Information

Each participant in the value stream has an accurate picture of the entire value stream. That is, the information described in the following sections is known throughout the value stream.

    Customer demand and product takt times. *Takt time* is a measure of customer demand in terms of available working time. It is calculated by dividing available working time by customer demand.

    Takt Time = Available work time per shift / Customer demand per shift

        Example:

        Work time / Shift = 460 minutes

Product demand/Shift = 230 units
Takt time = 460/230 = 2 minutes
The customer demands one unit every 2 minutes.

Therefore, consider that takt time may be different for each participant in the value stream because available working time may be different. Each participant should have access to its own takt time and its suppliers' and customers' takt times. When this information is missing, the result is either overproduction and excess inventory or failure to deliver product on time.

Costs and cost targets. A so-called "open-book" policy is critical to a lean extended value stream. Suppliers and customers are no longer considered adversaries; instead, they should be considered an extension of the organization. The lean organization must work closely with its suppliers and customers; this results in the lowest-cost, highest-quality value stream possible. The concept is to set cost targets and ensure that the targets can be met throughout the value stream by investing in suppliers. This will ultimately strengthen the financial health of each participant in the value stream.

Engineering changes to existing products. One of the greatest frustrations and causes of excess inventory (and consequently, higher value-stream total costs) is engineering changes. The entire value stream must be made aware of changes to products as they are made. Although many organizations struggle with communicating this information within their organizations today, the lean organization must be able to effectively communicate this information throughout the entire value stream.

New product development efforts. Suppliers should be involved from the beginning of new product development efforts. In Chapter 11, we will cover the concept of involving suppliers in the design process itself. However, at this point, it is important to understand that key suppliers need to be aware of new product development efforts because they need to anticipate changes they will need to make (e.g., freeing up capacity, purchasing new equipment, etc.). Another source of great frustration for suppliers is to be given very short notice of new products; this again results in higher costs and the potential for quality issues.

Inventory levels at each plant. Implementation of a pull-based system throughout, where each participant is aware of inventory levels at its suppliers and customers, is critical to the successful implementation of a lean extended value stream.

Element 2: Low Levels of Inventory

As a result of the first characteristic of a lean extended value stream, inventory levels must be reduced. Although some lean purists insist on *zero inventory*, in actuality, this is impossible. In a lean extended value stream or even an internal value stream, inventory levels must be set *strategically*. That is, instead of allowing inventory to accumulate in any location, the location and maximum amount of inventory must be fixed. Systems must be put in place to ensure that the inventory levels are being maintained and to adjust inventory levels as product demand shifts.

Future state inventory will be reduced based on the factors described in the following paragraphs.

More frequent shipments between value stream participants. Frequently, even local suppliers are shipping product on a weekly or even less frequent basis. More frequent deliveries result in significantly less inventory. For example, if delivery frequency changes from weekly to daily, inventory can be reduced by approximately 80 percent.

Reduction of queue times or elimination of queues, where possible. Queues in which product is waiting to be worked or information queues where information processing time result in shopfloor delays and must be eliminated. Both types of queues require a manufacturer to hold more inventory to compensate for the delays. Queues of product can usually be eliminated by implementing one-piece-flow manufacturing; information queues can usually be eliminated with information technology changes.

The implementation of pull systems where all participants have full access to information. Usually, when a company sets up a pull system with its suppliers, the suppliers are given a rule, such as, "When we fax you or e-mail you an order for replenishment, deliver it within 12 hours." The problem with this, however, is that the suppliers do not understand the underlying drivers behind the pull system. Usually, suppliers are holding more inventory than necessary to compensate for this lack of information.

Dissemination of all other information covered in the first characteristic of a lean extended value stream (above). Because inventory hides and compensates for the unexpected, disseminating information results in lower inventory levels.

Element 3: Lean and Financially Healthy Participants

Although this might seem obvious, it merits mentioning. Usually, procurement people think that the goal is to get as much from suppliers as possible for the lowest cost possible. However, this will result in unhealthy suppliers. For the lean organization, the goal is to have a lean system from raw material through to the end customer.

One major piece of the puzzle to achieving this is to convert each participant in the value stream into a financially healthy lean producer. Financially healthy lean suppliers will result in a successful value stream long term. As we will see in Chapter 5, if a particular supplier is unwilling to become lean or is simply a poor candidate, finding a new supplier may become necessary.

Element 4: Long-Term Relationships or Contracts in Place Between Participants

A lean organization must be willing to invest in its suppliers and develop trust. If an organization is unwilling to work with suppliers (or customers) based on a long-term outsourcing relationship, it can never have a truly lean supply chain. If a supplier believes that its customer may switch to another supplier at any time, it is unlikely that such a supplier will be willing to work closely with its customer to implement a lean supply chain.

On the other hand, a supplier that has a long-term contract in place with its customer will be much more willing to work closely with that customer. In Chapter 4, you will learn more about the nature of the buyer-supplier relationship.

Idea Generation: Brainstorming

How does an organization design a *future-state* extended value stream that incorporates the above characteristics of a *lean* extended value stream? At this point, the team working on the problem should have put together a current-state map. It also should have been trained in the above principles. Each member needs to have a working knowledge of lean, value-stream-mapping principles, and process kaizen principles. This knowledge is not sufficient; however, because every organization has its own unique circumstances, so creativity is needed to get from the current to the future state. The power to create a lean future state lies in the experiences and ingenuity of the team members and the collective power of the team. At this point in the process a team brainstorming session makes sense.

Before actually facilitating a brainstorming session, establish some ground rules and review the goals. The most important ground rule to communicate is that ideas should *not* be evaluated until the brainstorming session is complete.

There are several techniques for brainstorming. We have found that the most effective technique for eliciting the most ideas is the "Sticky Note" method. Each participant is given several self-adhesive notes. Set a period of time (usually 20 to 30 minutes) in which the participants are to write down as many ideas as they can (one per sticky note) to improve the current state. Participants should place sticky notes on a board in front of the room.

For brainstorming a future-state map, we recommend three brainstorming sessions, as follows:

- *Session 1.* The first session should be focused on improving information flow between facilities (and within facilities).

- *Session 2.* The second session should be focused on operational improvements; examples include changing which value-stream participant might perform a specific operation or changing the basic process to perform an operation from batch to one-piece flow.

- *Session 3.* The third and final session should be focused on logistics. The goal here is to eliminate as much transportation of product as possible.

After each session is complete, each idea is given a sequential unique number and is categorized by the team as follows:

- *Future State 1 Year (FS1).* FS1 indicates that the concept will be included in the future state and will be implemented in the first 12 months.

- *Future State 2 Years (FS2).* FS2 indicates that the concept will be included in the future state and will be implemented in the first 24 months.

- *Future State Long Term (FSLT).* FSLT indicates that the concept will not be included in the future state at this time but will be considered in the next mapping activity.

Let's take a look at how EVS handled its brainstorming sessions.

Case Study: How EVS Conducted Its Idea-Generation and Brainstorming Sessions

The team working on EVS Corporation's future-state map went through three brainstorming sessions and came up with the set of categorized ideas shown in Exhibit 3-1.

(Continued on next page)

(Continued from previous page)

Exhibit 3-1. The Results of EVS's Idea-Generation and Brainstorming Sessions

Session 1. Ideas for Improving Information Flow

FS1 Ideas	FS2 Ideas	FSLT Ideas
1. Change customer-ordering system such that orders are entered into enterprise resource planning (ERP) directly (with no delay/queue).	1. As parts are removed from EVS purchased parts supermarket and reorder points reached, send electronic signal directly to San Simeon ERP as needed.	
2. Give EVS access to entering orders directly into San Simeon's ERP system.	2. Use a better system (off-the-shelf software package) for scheduling at Trotsky rather than a spreadsheet.	
3. Automatically print orders in San Simeon warehouse on a daily basis (using ERP).		
4. Set up kanban between San Simeon and Electronics, Inc., and San Simeon and Trotsky.		
5. Set up kanban for Electronics, Inc., to order raw materials.		
6. Set up kanban for Trotsky to order from RM suppliers.		
7. Update orders more frequently on Trotsky spreadsheet.		
8. Change (from weekly) to daily orders from San Simeon to Trotsky and Electronics, Inc.		
9. Change (from weekly) to daily orders from EVS to San Simeon.		

Session 2. Ideas for Operational Improvements

FS1 Ideas	FS2 Ideas	FSLT Ideas
1. Set up one-piece-flow cell at Trotsky to run the EVS product line. 2. Set up a one-piece-flow cell at Electronics, Inc., to run EVS products. 3. Assign a team to investigate 89% yield at Trotsky and apply kaizen and/or statistical analysis tools as needed to improve. 4. Assign a team to investigate 72% yield at San Simeon and apply kaizen and/or statistical analysis tools as needed to improve. 5. Reduce 60 days of raw material at San Simeon; set up a purchased parts supermarket. 6. Set up purchased parts supermarkets at Electronics, Inc., and Trotsky, Inc.	1. As parts are removed from EVS purchased parts supermarket and reorder points reached, send electronic signal directly to San Simeon ERP as needed. 2. As parts are removed from San Simeon's purchased parts market (to be set up in year 1), electronically signal suppliers' systems as needed for replenishment.	1. Build a supplier park to support EVS by either relocating EVS to Los Angeles next to San Simeon or relocating San Simeon; Electronics, Inc., and a machining supplier to EVS' Carlsbad campus.

Session 3. Ideas for Logistical Improvements

FS1 Ideas	FS2 Ideas	FSLT Ideas
1. Find a local supplier for machined parts in Los Angeles that can supply San Simeon daily using a Kanban (to replace Trotsky). Supplier should have lean practices in place. 2. Have daily deliveries as from San Simeon to EVS and from Electronics, Inc. to San Simeon.	1. As parts are removed from EVS purchased parts supermarket and reorder points reached, send electronic signal directly to San Simeon ERP as needed.	

The EVS team has come up with some breakthrough ideas in each of its brainstorming sessions. Normally, for a group of its size, we would expect a total of about 40 to 50 unique ideas; however, for the purposes of this text, we will focus on the limited number of key ideas listed in Exhibit 3-1.

(Continued on next page)

(Continued from previous page)

Note that some of the ideas are in conflict with each other. For example, there are several ideas for *improving* Trotsky Metals, yet one idea suggests replacing Trotsky with a new supplier. This will be sorted out in the next step, in which the team will take its ideas and formulate a future state.

How EVS Created Future-State Maps

The future state is primarily a graphical depiction of a plan derived from the team's application of lean principles and creativity (brainstorming). Based on our firm's experience with clients, we are often told that teams have a hard time taking ideas from a brainstorming session and translating those ideas into a future state and action plan. We find that this often results from unstructured brainstorming (i.e., brainstorming without categorizing ideas). After a brainstorming session, the team must evaluate each idea, categorize each, and decide whether or not each idea will be implemented.

Using the ideas from the previous section, EVS created the future-state extended-value-stream map for the 4400A–Q product line (shown in Figure 3-2). Based on the FS1 and FS2 concepts, this map was created using the following steps:

1. Begin with the customer and customer demand; customer demand remains unchanged from the current state. This is not always the case in extended value-stream mapping. When it makes sense, the customer may change its order frequency. In this case, because 80 percent of EVS' customers are overseas, daily orders and corresponding daily shipments would not be feasible.

2. Next, EVS mapped its updated process boxes. On the EVS future-state map, there will again be four major process boxes. For each process box, EVS shows the value-creating time (sometimes called "hands-on" time); the value-creating time has not changed from current to future state. The lead time has changed significantly, however. EVS made the following inventory changes to reduce lead time:
   - San Simeon Assembly will now hold 2 days of raw materials. This is because there is redundant raw material inventory at Electronics, Inc. (in the form of finished goods), a new local machining supplier, and daily deliveries of raw materials made to San Simeon. San Simeon will hold 5 days of finished goods; this is approximately what the team decided was necessary to load-level San Simeon's assembly cell. During internal-value-stream mapping at San Simeon, the inventory level will be set more precisely for each subassembly. Also at San Simeon, a goal of greater than 95 percent yield was set for the future state. (Recall that yield in the current state was 72 percent.)
   - EVS has decided to replace Trotsky metals with a new machined parts supplier local to San Simeon Assembly; EVS did this because Trotsky has a very long lead time of 141 days and it is the only nonlocal supplier. The targets that the team has set for the new supplier is lead time of less than 30 days, 10 days of raw material and 5 days finished goods inventory, and 95 percent yield. In Chapter 5, which discusses implementation, EVS will go through the process of supplier selection for this supplier.
   - Electronics, Inc., will now hold 10 days of raw material and 10 days of finished goods. Because raw materials will be delivered weekly, there is no reason to hold much more than one week's worth of inventory. Ten days of finished goods was set as the target based on Electronics, Inc., delivering product daily to San Simeon Assembly and based on an amount necessary to load-level their factory. The team set a goal of greater than 98 percent yield at Electronics, Inc.; its current state yield was 92.6 percent.

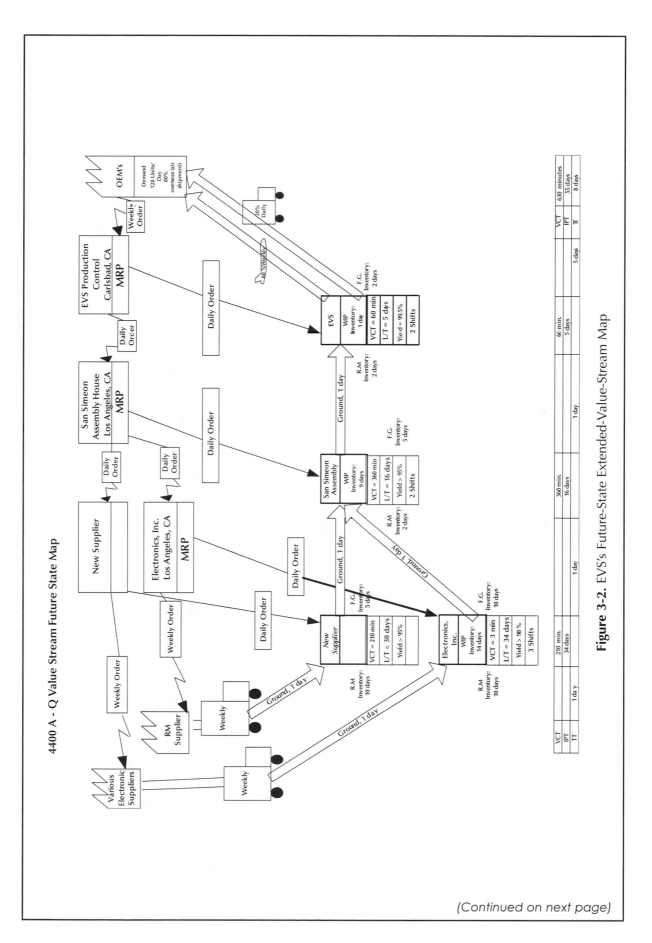

Figure 3-2. EVS's Future-State Extended-Value-Stream Map

(Continued on next page)

(Continued from previous page)

3. EVS again shows the raw material suppliers in the upper-left-hand corner of Figure 3-2. The team has decided to continue having weekly raw material deliveries to Electronics, Inc. It is also assuming weekly deliveries of materials to its new machined-parts supplier.

4. EVS again connects each factory with an arrow, showing how material gets transported. All deliveries will be one-day ground shipments. The most significant change will be having a local machined-parts supplier deliver parts to San Simeon Assembly daily.

5. Next, EVS moves on to address the future-state information flow. Again beginning with the customer, the team maps each production control box for each factory. Changes from the current state are as follows:
   - All orders placed from EVS to San Simeon and from San Simeon to its key suppliers will be placed daily. This will prevent sending batches of orders and will allow the factories to react to orders better. For example, let us assume orders were previously transmitted every Monday morning at 8:00 A.M. from EVS Corporation to San Simeon Assembly. The orders that were transmitted included items that were needed from the entire previous week. San Simeon had no awareness of what was needed on a daily basis. This lack of information requires San Simeon to hold more inventory to support the weekly orders. With the implementation of daily orders, San Simeon has much more information with which to work. Thus, it will be able to hold less inventory.
   - Electronics, Inc., will place orders to its supplier on a weekly rather than monthly basis. This will allow its orders to be more accurate; it will help achieve lower raw material inventory at Electronics, Inc. The future-state goal for raw material is 10 days, from a current state of 60 days.
   - For all factories, production control will plan daily work rather than weekly work. Planning daily work reduces the amount of expediting that occurs. If weekly orders are sent to the factory floor, they must constantly be adjusted.

6. Finally, the key metrics are summed along the bottom of the map. In this case, the key metrics work out as shown in Table 3-1.

Table 3-1. Comparison of Current State and Future State for EVS

Metric	Current-State Value	Future-State Value	% Improvement
Value-creating time	630 minutes	630 minutes	0%
In-plant time	230 days	55 days	76.1%
Transport time	20 days	8 days	60.0%
Total time (transport + in-plant)	250 days	63 days	74.8%
Value % of time	0.175%	0.694%	297%
Inventory turnover (precalculated by EVS)	1.8	Approx. 11.5	538%
Total Distance Traveled	**4,136 miles**	**Approx. 1,000 miles**	**75%**

The EVS team has planned some significant improvements to its extended-value stream; this supply chain will have less than 20 percent of the inventory it previously had and will have 187 fewer days of total time through the system. To accomplish this, the team must develop a detailed plan for implementing all of the improvements that need to be made. Before it moves on to implementation planning, the team must create a future-state information-flow map.

EVS Creates a Future-State Information-Flow Map

Figure 3-3 shows the future-state version of the detailed path of information from customers to EVS to suppliers. From this process map, EVS can measure the improvement in queue times and number of information transfers. Going through step by step, we now have the following sequence of operations:

1. EVS Corporation's customers place orders to EVS by telephoning or faxing customer service or entering orders via the Internet. These orders will now be transmitted directly into the ERP system.

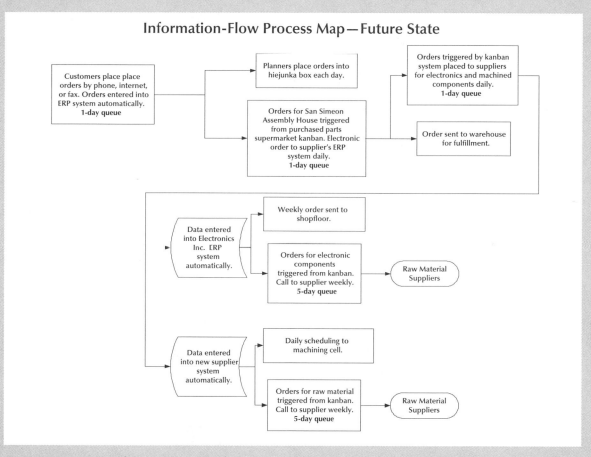

Figure 3-3. EVS Information Flow Process Map—Future State

2. Planners will continue to schedule work on the assembly floor using a heijunka or load-leveling box. This system (which was described in Chapter 2) has worked very well for EVS in keeping production level and sequence properly.

3. As parts are pulled from a purchased parts supermarket into the cell to support production, demand for orders is triggered. These orders will now be placed electronically (directly into San Simeon's ERP system) on a daily rather than weekly basis.

(Continued on next page)

(Continued from previous page)

4. A pull system will be set up at San Simeon with its suppliers; this triggers purchasing personnel to order electronics and machined components when certain inventory levels are reached in the system. These orders will be placed directly into the suppliers' ERP systems. That will mean that the new machined components supplier must have this capability.

5. EVS orders will continue to be fulfilled in shipping because San Simeon holds inventory for EVS orders.

6. At Electronics, Inc., production will be scheduled daily based on a pull system. As product is shipped from its warehouse to San Simeon, orders for product to be replenished will be sent to its production floor on a daily basis.

7. At the new machined components suppliers, production will also be scheduled daily based on a pull system.

8. Both the new supplier and Electronics, Inc., will place orders from the raw materials suppliers on a weekly basis (unless it is feasible for the new supplier to place orders for raw materials daily).

The information transfers and queue times are summarized in Tables 3-2 and 3-3.

Table 3-2. Comparison of Queue Times in the Current State vs. the Future State

Organization	Queue Time, Current State	Queue Time, Future State	% Improvement
EVS	12 days	2 days	83.3%
San Simeon	14 days	1 day	92.8%
Electronics	12 days	5 days	58.3%
Trotsky / New Supplier	19 days	5 days	76.6%
Total	57 days	13 days	77.1%

Table 3-3. Comparison of Information Transfers in the Current State vs. the Future State

Organization	No. of Information Transfers, Current State	No. of Information Transfers, Future State	% Improvement
EVS	3	2	33.3%
San Simeon	2	1	50%
Electronics	2	1	50%
Trotsky	2	1	50%
Total	9	5	44.4%

The team's brainstorming ideas have resulted in significant improvement to the information flow. A 77 percent reduction in queue time and 44 percent reduction in number of information transfers will eliminate the delays and defects in information flow that create significant waste in the extended value stream. As information is disseminated more quickly throughout the extended value stream and queue times are reduced, the ability for suppliers to make the right products is dramatically improved. This results in less inventory and faster lead times.

Let's now take a look at the process of translating a future-state map into a plan for actual implementation.

Implementation Planning: Activities That Make Your Maps *Real*

The most critical part of any value-stream-mapping activity is creating an implementation plan. Many organizations have undertaken value-stream-mapping activities. Based on my firm's experience, most organizations stop with a current-state map. Some create a future-state map. But very few create an implementation plan associated with the future state. Consequently, very few are successful. Value-stream mapping is often criticized as being a visionary activity with little basis in reality. This criticism is valid in many cases: the implementation plan is what brings reality into the activity.

For extended value-stream mapping, the implementation plan includes a diverse set of activities. Frequently, there are several major projects, including:

- *Finding and evaluating potential suppliers.* Organizations often use a "soft" approach to supplier selection; it is often based on "gut feel." This is a recipe for failure. Instead, the approach to supplier selection should be both qualitative and quantitative. An objective set of criteria and metrics must be applied as well as structured interviewing sessions. Chapter 4 covers how to develop criteria to evaluate suppliers.

- *Selecting suppliers and negotiating long-term contracts.* Selecting new suppliers is similar to hiring employees; contracting with the wrong supplier has a lasting negative effect. Supplier selection will also be covered in detail in Chapter 4.

- *Value-stream mapping at suppliers.* Value-stream mapping at other facilities almost always appears on an implementation plan for a future-state extended value stream. Chapter 5 covers the discipline of internal value-stream mapping.

- *Process kaizen activities at suppliers.* Kaizen events aimed at eliminating waste from a particular supplier process will appear on an implementation plan. Specific types of process kaizen and conducting kaizen events at supplier sites are also covered in Chapter 5.

- *Changes to information systems or new systems implementations.* Because information flow is a huge problem for the extended value stream, improvements to information systems are almost always part of future-state implementation plans.

- *Physical movement of plants or processes.* As covered in Chapter 11, co-locating supplier processes at a customer site or customer processes at a supplier site is a method for reducing lead time. Therefore, it is often a part of an implementation plan. However, usually it is not part of an implementation plan of an initial value-stream-mapping event. Usually, such moves are made later. (Note that one of the ideas developed during the brainstorming session for EVS in this chapter was to build a supplier park to support EVS by either relocating EVS to Los Angeles next to San Simeon or relocating San Simeon; Electronics, Inc.; and a machining supplier to EVS's campus. Application of supplier parks to EVS is also addressed in Chapter 11.)

- *Development of detailed plans for operational changes.*

- *Problem-solving and variation-reduction activities.* Implementation of a lean extended value stream almost always includes some form of quality improvement. Such activities are usually not suitable for kaizen events; instead, they are usually implemented using problem-solving teams or "six sigma" project teams.

- *Industrial engineering activities.* Some improvements identified on an implementation plan do not require team activities. They can often be assigned to an industrial or manufacturing engineer to implement. These may include things as simple as developing standard work charts.

Developing the Implementation Plan: Recommendations for Format and Content

Now that you know what activities should be covered in the implementation plan, let's look at what the format and content of the implementation plan should be.

Format of the implementation plan. I am often asked how to best format an implementation plan. Two problems, or mistakes, often arise in the development of an implementation plan:

- *Mistake 1.* People often get caught up in using all of the functionality of a project management computer program; that is a time-wasting mistake. Using all of the functionality of a program is not important in implementation planning, particularly not at this level.

- *Mistake 2.* When project management software is distributed to only a select few in an organization, others within the organization or other involved organizations such as suppliers cannot view the plan. If such software is used, ensure that a viewable version of the plan is accessible. A simple solution is to upload the plan in html format such that it is accessible to all key people via a secure website.

I generally recommend that the format selected is as simple to use as possible and as accessible to as many people in the organizations involved as necessary. As long as the plan has visibility and can be updated easily, it will work.

Content of the implementation plan. A useful plan includes the following information:

- *Objective.* This refers to the specific change made on the future state. For example, the objective might be to set up a long-term relationship with a new or existing supplier.

- *Goal.* The goal is what the objective is attempting to achieve. For example, if the objective is to increase frequency of shipments, the goal is to reduce inventory by a specific amount.

- *Project and major tasks.* Specifically, what is the project and what are the major tasks that need to be done to meet the objective?

- *Timing.* The plan should include the start and completion dates.

- *Team leader or responsible individual.* The plan should list who is responsible for accomplishing the task.

- *Team members.* If the task or project requires a team, the plan should list the individuals on the team. This information may not be available when the plan is initially created.

- *Status (updated regularly).* The plan should include a note on the status of the project. Often, "% Completion" is used to convey the status of a task or project; however, that is often not a meaningful number. Because at this level, the plan will not show highly detailed tasks, it is important to understand at a glance the status of major tasks and projects.

Let's look at how EVS developed its implementation plan.

Case Study:
How EVS Developed Its Implementation Plan

The team at EVS put together the implementation plan shown in Figure 3-4, based on its future state.

EVS Extended Value Stream Implementation Plan							Date: 1/7/05	
Goal	Objective	Task	Start	Finish (plan)	Finish (actual)	Team Leader	Team Members	Status Notes
Reduce machined parts inventory, travel distance, and lead time.	Select new machining supplier and set up long-term agreement.	1. Develop short list of potential suppliers.	1/1/2005	2/1/2005		Joe G.	Mary, John, Fred, James	In initial research stage, currently working down from list of 50+ suppliers.
		2. Develop criteria.	1/1/2005	2/1/2005		Joe G.	Mary, John, Fred, James	
		3. Conduct supplier audits and interviews.	2/1/2005	4/1/2005		Joe G.	Mary, John, Fred, James	
		4. Select supplier and negotiate long-term contract.	4/1/2005	6/1/2005		Joe G.	Mary, John, Fred, James	
Reduce inventory and lead time at San Simeon Assembly.	Set up pull systems and appropriate inventory levels; increase order and delivery frequency.	1. Conduct value-stream mapping internally to set appropriate inventory levels and set up pull systems.	1/1/2005	2/1/2005		Maureen	TBD	* VSM "blitz" activity to be done 1/10 – 1/14
		2. Implement future state.	2/1/2005	8/1/2005		Maureen	TBD	
Reduce inventory and lead time at Electronics, Inc.	Set up pull systems and appropriate inventory levels; increase order and delivery frequency.	1. Conduct value-stream mapping internally to set appropriate inventory levels and set up pull systems.	1/1/2005	2/1/2005		Jim V.	TBD	* VSM "blitz" activity to be done 1/17 – 1/21
		2. Implement future state.	2/1/2005	8/1/2005		Jim V.	TBD	
Reduce queue times and delays throughout value stream (information systems).	Implement future-state information flow process map.	Form team consisting of an IT person from each company.	1/1/2005	1/15/2005	1/7/2005	Mary	TBD	Team formed as of 1/7/05.
		Put together detailed project plan.	1/15/2005	2/15/2005		Mary	TBD	Team meetings to begin 1/15.
		Implement.	2/15/2005	8/1/2005		Mary	TBD	

Figure 3-4. EVS's Implementation Plan

(Continued on next page)

(Continued from previous page)

Based on its future state, EVS has decided to set four major goals and objectives:

1. The first major objective is to find and develop a long-term business relationship with a local (Los Angeles) machined-components supplier. This is critical to reducing inventory and a large percentage of the transport time in EVS's value stream. In Chapters 4 through 6, we will address a step-by-step method for developing and executing an outsourcing plan, which is what EVS will need to do to accomplish this goal. The company has set a very aggressive five-month timetable for completion.

2. The second major objective is to improve the value stream at San Simeon Assembly by reducing inventory and lead time to the levels set forth in the future-state map. EVS has set aside one month to perform the value-stream mapping and six months to implement the future state. In Chapters 7 through 9, we will address the execution of internal value-stream mapping and implementation.

3. As with the second objective, the third is to improve the value stream at Electronics, Inc., by reducing inventory and lead time. Again, a total of seven months is given to accomplish this goal.

4. The fourth objective is the information technology piece. This can be separated into several projects; however, at this level, we recommend listing one project. Several projects will be associated with this, and we recommend that one person (in this case, EVS's Information Technology Manager) be in charge of the entire project. This team will be made up of IT and operations people from each organization in the value stream.

The next step for EVS is to actually implement its plan. In subsequent chapters, we will address each of the steps required to implement. In Chapter 4, we will begin by looking at when outsourcing should and should not be used.

Summing Up: Key Points

Although communication is considered the primary waste in the extended value stream, the lean manufacturing tool known as the "seven wastes" (which has become the eight wastes) can be used to describe the waste found in the extended value stream if viewed with a slightly different paradigm.

The 8 Wastes of the Extended Value Stream

The wastes are as follows:

- *Waste 1: Overproduction.* One of the key causes of overproduction in the extended value stream is poor information flow (i.e., poor communication) between facilities.

- *Waste 2: Transportation.* This waste is amplified when examining the extended value stream due to distances between value-stream participants.

- *Waste 3: Unnecessary inventory.* For the extended value stream, unnecessary inventory is generally the result of poor information flow and batch processing.

- *Waste 4: Inappropriate processing.* In the extended value stream, this can additionally refer to using the wrong suppliers and/or the wrong process.

- *Waste 5: Waiting.* This waste has essentially the same application to the internal or extended value streams.

- *Waste 6: Excess motion.* This waste has essentially the same application to the internal or extended value streams

- *Waste 7: Defects.* The unique application of this waste to the extended value stream is defective product moving between facilities and defective information transmitted from facility to facility.

- *Waste 8: Underutilization of suppliers' and customers' minds/ideas.* The eighth waste of underutilizing employees' minds and ideas is changed for the extended value stream to apply to customers and suppliers.

A lean extended value stream is one that works to eliminate the above wastes. Eliminating such wastes results ultimately in dramatically shorter lead times.

The Characteristics of a Lean Extended Value Stream

Here are the characteristics of a lean extended value stream:

1. Strong communication and information
2. Low levels of inventory
3. Lean and financially healthy participants
4. Long-term relationships/contracts in place between participants

Based on the current-state map itself and its understanding of the key elements of the lean extended value stream, a value-stream-mapping team should go through three brainstorming sessions:

- *Session #1.* Improving information flow between facilities (and within facilities)

- *Session #2.* Making operational improvements

- *Session #3.* Improving logistics and transportation

Based on these sessions, the team should then select and categorize ideas for future-state mapping and implementation planning.

The next step is actual future-state mapping. The future state is primarily a graphical depiction of a plan derived from the team's application of lean principles and creativity (i.e., brainstorming). The steps to creating the future-state map are the same as those used to create the current-state map. After the future-state value-stream map is created, a future-state information-flow map should be created.

Developing a Future-State Implementation Plan

Based on the future-state value stream and information-flow maps, the team should create an implementation plan. The plan is the final step in the value-stream-mapping process; it will usually include activities such as:

- Finding and evaluating potential suppliers
- Selecting suppliers and negotiating long-term contracts
- Value-stream mapping at suppliers
- Process kaizen activities at suppliers
- Changes to information systems or new systems implementations
- Physical movement of plants or processes
- Development of detailed plans for operational changes
- Problem-solving and variation-reduction activities
- Industrial engineering activities

To be effective, the implementation plan should include the following information:

- The objective
- The overall goal
- Definition of the project and major tasks
- Timing
- Identification of the team leader or responsible individual
- Identification of team members
- Project status

After the value-stream-mapping team puts together its implementation plan, the teams and individuals that have been identified on the plan can begin work on their projects. The plan itself, of course, must be updated on a regular basis and made visible to the entire organization.

Applying This Information to Your Organization: Questions to Help You Get Started

1. To what extent do you observe the seven (or eight) wastes of the extended value stream in your organization's value streams?

2. Which characteristics of a lean extended value stream do your organization's value streams exhibit? Which areas need the most improvement?

3. Which of your suppliers do you envision being the keys to a successful future-state extended value stream? Do you think your future-state map will include new suppliers?

Part II

Implementation of the Lean Supply Chain

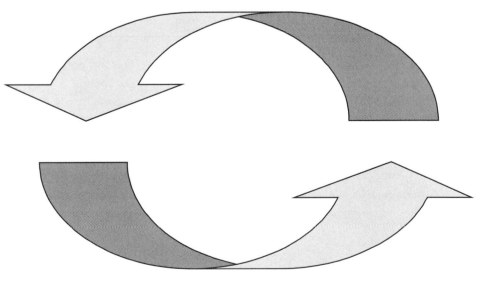

Chapter 4

Outsourcing Strategy: How to Determine When It Makes Sense to Outsource

Constructing a Framework for Make Versus Buy for the Lean Enterprise

In Chapter 3, you learned how to develop a future-state map and plan for implementation. Now, let's take a look at the implementation process itself, beginning with the question of outsourcing within the context of the lean extended value stream.

Before we discuss evaluating suppliers and negotiating long-term contracts for the lean manufacturer, we must first discuss make vs. buy considerations. Several considerations drive companies to outsource. The decision to outsource a part or assembly is often based on three primary reasons:

1. Cost reduction.

2. Lack of internal resources.

3. Refocus of core competencies.

According to outsourcing expert Michael F. Corbett, about 50 percent of executives state that reducing costs is the top reason for outsourcing.[1] Therefore, we will begin with cost considerations and treat each of the other considerations separately. This chapter also introduces several methods for determining whether or not to outsource.

Reason #1 to Outsource: Cost Considerations— The Traditional "Part-by-Part" Outsourcing Model

If you are attempting to outsource a part or assembly that is produced in-house based on lower cost, you must perform a thorough analysis. In many cases, cost can only be reduced

---

1. *The Outsourcing Revolution.* Michael F. Corbett. Dearborn Trade Publishing, 2004, p. 12.

if the supplier is going to use a more efficient process or significantly less expensive labor. You must be careful in comparing costs. Because the standard cost that you would find in an ERP system for an internally produced part includes fixed costs, comparing standard costs with the prices being quoted is not an "apples-to-apples" comparison. Unless you are going to eliminate some fixed costs, the only real cost reduction is the variable cost. If the supplier cannot produce the part for a price lower than your variable cost, you are not saving your company money.

If you are in the process of outsourcing a part or assembly in an effort to reduce cost, you should be searching for a supplier that can produce the part using a more efficient method (or a much lower labor rate) than you are currently using. This might allow them to produce the part faster and/or at a lower labor cost than you can produce the part. Even after that supplier adds in its overhead and profit, it is possible that the supplier can produce the part for less cost than you can in-house.

Usually, organizations compare the standard cost as determined by cost accounting with the price a supplier is quoting in making a make vs. buy decision. This is almost always fallacious. The standard cost includes fixed costs that will continue to be part of operations whether the product is manufactured in-house or not. In many cases, the supplier's cost will be lower than the in-house standard cost; however, the reality is that overall company costs and the costs of other products will increase if this part is outsourced; this is because fixed costs will be spread over a smaller number of units after a part is outsourced. The exception to this would be if a company shut down a portion of its operations (i.e., reduced its fixed costs) and considered outsourcing an entire manufacturing operation; in this case, it could eliminate a portion of its fixed cost and *possibly* have a lower product cost. Detailed analysis would need to be performed to determine if this is the case.

Let's take a look at how EVS evaluated its costs to see if outsourcing would save the company money.

Case Study:
How EVS Evaluated Its Costs—Traditional Model

Several years back, EVS Corporation produced many of its machined parts in-house. The company's materials manager had been tasked with reducing product cost.

He began with part A because it was the highest-volume part and had the highest potential for cost reduction. Part A had a standard cost of $2,300. The variable-cost component (labor and material) was $1,200. The fixed-cost component (overhead including machine tools, building, etc.) was $1,100. A supplier quoted the part at $1,800. Because EVS produced 3,000 of these per year, the materials manager believed he was saving the company $1.5M per year by outsourcing this part. This apparent savings is shown in Table 4-1, but the savings were not real.

The only *real* cost reduction was the variable cost reduction in this case. The company had reduced its cost by $1,200 per part, but the savings were offset by an $1,800-per-part cost to the supplier. EVS was operating at a higher cost by outsourcing this part. It had increased costs by $1.8M per year; however, in its ERP system, the standard cost of part A dropped ($1,800 vs. $2,300), as shown in Table 4-2.

The fact that costs have increased shows itself in the form of higher standard costs for all *other parts using the same facilities as part* A. This gave the materials manager incentive to outsource more parts, thus creating a cycle of increasing standard costs for in-house parts and savings on paper by outsourcing. The underlying reality of higher costs is not obvious except in the company's bottom line.

Table 4-1. Standard Costs for Part A

Standard Costs for Part A	In-House ($)	After Outsourcing ($)
Labor	1,100	
Materials	100	1,800
Fixed Costs (Overhead)	1,100	
Total (Standard Cost)	**2,300**	**1,800**
Apparent Savings per Part		**500**
Apparent Annual Cost Reduction ($3,000/year)		**1,500,000**

Table 4-2. Relevant Costs for Part A

Relevant Costs for Part A	In-House ($)	After Outsourcing ($)
Labor	3,300,000	—
Materials	300,000	5,400,000
Fixed Costs (Overhead)	3,300,000	3,300,000
Total	**6,900,000**	**8,700,000**
Actual Additional Annual Cost		**1,800,000**
Note: Fixed costs would be allocated to other parts after outsourcing		

So what does the EVS example prove? To determine if lower costs are possible by outsourcing, one must consider *all* relevant costs *in detail.* Factors that will influence whether or not lower costs can be achieved by outsourcing are process and labor costs. If a supplier has a better process for producing the part, it is possible that he can produce it for less than your organization. Also, if a supplier has lower labor costs (such as a supplier in Mexico or China), again it would be possible that he could produce the part at a lower cost. If neither of these is true, one must be skeptical that a lower cost can be achieved by outsourcing. The supplier must have some profit built into its price. Given that fact, if the supplier is using a similar process and is working with the same labor pool that you are, it is unlikely that you will save your organization money simply by outsourcing parts that you currently manufacture in-house.

Cost considerations of outsourcing to offshore suppliers. A growing trend in manufacturing outsourcing, especially over the past few years, is to switch from a local to an offshore supplier. Clearly, the driving factor behind such a move is lower cost. Based on purchase-price comparison alone, it is almost always significantly less expensive to have an offshore manufacturer produce any given component. In response to my asking why a firm has decided to do this, I have heard many a manufacturing executive say, "I can get these parts made for less than 50 percent of what we were previously paying. Our competitors are doing the same thing, so we must follow suit or go out of business."

The results, however, are usually mixed. Although on paper, it appears that a firm is saving money by purchasing a part for less than half what it had previously paid, again, the apparent cost savings does not always have a positive effect on profitability. In fact, in some cases, it actually reduces profits. Although this does not seem to add up logically, offshore outsourcing has two key problems associated with it:

Problem 1: Inventory growth. Inevitably, inventory grows at the customer site when parts are purchased from offshore manufacturers. This is because parts cannot be delivered as they are needed or on a pull-system basis. They are usually shipped in large batches of six months' or even one year's worth of product at a time. As more and more parts are sent offshore for manufacture, more space is needed at the customer site to accommodate the large batches of product. The cost of floor space and the cost of holding the inventory are hidden and, consequently, ignored.

Problem 2: Quality issues. Although the quality of offshore manufacturing is improving and is in some cases equal to or better than what can be found in the United States, no supplier ships 100 percent error-free parts. Therefore, when six months' worth of purchased parts are in the process of being consumed, unacceptable parts surface. This creates several costs, many of which are ignored:

- *The cost of scrapping the parts themselves.* Bad parts are rarely sent back to the supplier for credit; this is because it costs too much to ship parts back to an offshore manufacturer.

- *The cost of lost production.* If an entire shipment of parts is unacceptable, then valuable production time is lost while the supplier expedites production and shipment of a new batch.

- *The cost of sorting through several months' worth of product* to determine whether or not parts are good and/or rework parts. When more than a few parts are found to be unacceptable, the customer often sorts through the parts to determine if they are good and reworks them, if possible. This costs quite a bit of money, and, for the U.S. customer, all of it is in expensive U.S. labor dollars.

In some cases, it does make sense for a lean organization to utilize offshore, low labor-cost suppliers. However, it is much less often than one assumes. Detailed analysis should be done to weigh the cost savings with the increased quality, shipping, and inventory costs. I generally recommend that there must be a very significant bottom-line impact to go offshore.

There are four key factors that determine whether or not offshore suppliers make sense:

1. *Customer location.* If the customer base is in the same region as the low-cost labor supplier, a company should consider manufacturing the product offshore. For example, let us suppose that a U.S. company's customer base is in Asia. Then, the company should consider having the product manufactured completely in a low labor-cost country in Asia. This is especially true if the product has high-labor content and is a commodity.

2. *Labor content.* The amount of labor that goes into producing a product is a key indicator of whether or not offshore manufacturing should be considered. If labor content is high, offshore suppliers should be considered.

3. *Product complexity.* If a product is rather complex, it is probably not a candidate for offshore manufacturing for two reasons. The first reason is protection of intellectual property. One common problem with offshore manufacturing is the appearance of "copy cats." On the other hand, if a product is a commodity, it may lend itself to offshore manufacturing.

4. *Lead time.* If response time and lead time need to be small, offshore manufacturing may present an obvious problem.

Unfortunately, there is no simple rule for deciding whether or not offshore suppliers make sense; however, all of the hidden costs associated with offshore manufacturing need to be considered before making such a leap. Too many companies are making the leap based purely on purchase price, which is almost always a recipe for failure.

Reason #2 to Outsource: Lack of Resources

Lack of resources is another reason manufacturers choose to outsource. This is usually the simplest form of outsourcing, but one could hardly call it outsourcing in most cases. Typically, when there is a lack of resources internally in the short-term, organizations haphazardly "off-load" work to another firm. In the case of components manufacturing, this is often referred to as outsourcing to compensate for capacity constraints or is referred to as "surge capacity."

This, however, is not outsourcing. As we discuss in detail in Chapter 5, outsourcing involves a long-term business relationship that benefits both organizations. In most of these cases, suppliers are used based on their ability to respond to a short-term need; there are few, if any, other criteria applied in the selection of such a supplier.

Some cases of outsourcing due to lack of resources can form the basis for a true long-term business relationship. Startup companies, companies developing a new product, and companies experiencing major shifts in customer demand are three such cases. Let us examine each of these.

1. *Outsourcing if you are a startup company.* A company that has a "garage shop" manufacturing environment or no manufacturing resources at all cannot manufacture product in any significant volume. Therefore, if that company were to forge relationships with suppliers, this would exemplify an outsourcing relationship formed from a lack of resources.

2. *Outsourcing if you are manufacturing a new product.* If an organization has developed a new product and is unable to manufacture the product internally without significant investment, it may form a relationship with a supplier to manufacture the new product. This is often the case when a company develops a product that is very different from its typical product lines.

3. *Outsourcing if you have major shifts in product demand.* If a company experiences a major shift upward in demand (as opposed to a seasonal spike in demand), it may find itself out of manufacturing capacity. This is an ideal situation for a company to develop an outsourcing relationship with a supplier. In such cases, the company may contract a supplier to manufacture one or more particular product lines completely or a significant portion of a product line.

Lack of resources can be a valid reason for outsourcing. The lean organization that is either a startup, is developing a new product, or is experiencing a major shift in demand may choose to outsource a product line or portion of a product line in response to these changes.

Reason #3 to Outsource: Core Competency Considerations

Sometimes a company chooses to outsource a process because the process is not considered a core competency. How do we reconcile this reasoning with the earlier discussion on considering costs of outsourcing? Cost analyses like the EVS example earlier in the chapter are done everyday in manufacturing organizations throughout the world, but they do not generally apply to the lean enterprise. The lean enterprise should not be constantly searching for the *apparent* lowest cost pricing on a given component. The lean enterprise should be focused on functions or parts of a value stream, rather than on individual components. The question for the lean enterprise is "What piece of the value stream would increase long-term profitability and cash flows by outsourcing?" It is from within this framework that the lean enterprise should approach the discipline of outsourcing.

A Simple Outsourcing Test: Three Questions to Ask. In analyzing a value stream, how does the lean enterprise determine which functions are core and which are not? Outsourcing expert Michael F. Corbett uses a simple test for identifying core competencies:

1. If starting from scratch today, would we really build the capability inside?

2. Are we so good at it that others would hire us to do it for them?

3. Is this an area of the business from which our future leaders will come?

The idea is that if the answer is "yes" to each question, then it should be internally sourced. If the answer is "no" to any one of the questions, then it should be considered for external sourcing.[2] This test is a simple yet powerful tool for determining whether or not a piece of the value stream is a core competency.

Let us return to the EVS Corporation example for one moment and apply this test.

Case Study: How EVS Evaluated Whether It Should Outsource

In years past, EVS Corporation machined components themselves for all of its products rather than outsourcing to a machining supplier. If it were to ask the three outsourcing questions, what would the outcome be?

1. *If starting from scratch today, would we really build the capability inside?* If EVS were starting from scratch, it would not machine anything internally. There are many capable machine shops in southern California where EVS is located.

2. *Are we so good at it that others would hire us to do it for them?* EVS would never be asked to machine components for someone else; it did not do high-quality machining.

---

2. *The Outsourcing Revolution.* Michael F. Corbett. Dearborn Trade Publishing, 2004, pp. 81–82.

3. *Is this an area of the business from which our future leaders will come?* EVS Corporation's future leader might come from operations. Thus, in general, the answer to this question may be "yes." (A machining production manager could conceivably climb the ladder into executive operations management and perhaps further.)

The conclusion, based on the test, is that machining is not a core competency for EVS Corporation. If a function is a core competency, it should not be outsourced; however, the fact that a function is not a core competency does not indicate that the function should be outsourced. Further analysis is necessary to make such a determination. So let's look at that analysis.

Methods of Evaluating Non-Core Functions for Outsourcing

After an organization determines which pieces of a value stream are not core competencies, it then can evaluate those functions for outsourcing. A function that is being considered for outsourcing may not be outsourced in the short term; this is because outsourcing it may decrease value-stream profitability. It is likely that outsourcing a non-core function will result in lower costs when the firm follows the methods outlined in this book. Many times, firms simply "offload" parts to the lowest bidder without considering much else. As with outsourcing due to lack of resources in the short term, this is *not* a true outsourcing business relationship.

So how does the lean enterprise determine whether or not it should be outsourcing a particular non-core function within a value stream? The simplest answer is that if it can develop a long-term relationship with a supplier that specializes in that function (i.e., a supplier whose core competency is that function), it is likely that the supplier can meet cost targets for the product produced within that function while making a profit. Presumably, because this function is not core to the lean producer, it does not have the best available technology and resources to perform this function.

In contrast, if the supplier specializes in this function, then the supplier should have the best technology and resources to perform the function (thereby resulting in lower cost). Preferably, the lean producer will find a lean supplier. If not, then, as we will discuss in Part III of this book, it is in the lean producer's interest (and the supplier's interest) to ensure that the supplier will become lean.

Method 1: Calculating the Economic Benefits—The Value-Stream Cash-Flow Model

Let's suppose that an organization decides to outsource a non-core function. On the surface, it sounds reasonable to assume that a supplier that specializes in a function will ultimately be able to perform the function at a lower cost than if done internally.

This should not, however, be assumed to be true. It must be verified. We have developed a model called the Value-Stream Cash-Flow (VSCF) Model that should help evaluate the economic benefits of outsourcing a value-stream function. Let us revisit EVS Corporation to demonstrate this method.

Case Study:
How EVS Evaluated the Economic Benefits of Outsourcing a Value-Stream Function

Because we have shown that the machining function is not a core competency for EVS, let's evaluate the entire machining function within a value stream for outsourcing. The question we ask is: "What are the annual outgoing cash flows associated with this function each year, for the next five years, if we do this internally?"

Let's examine the first question. The first step is listing those resources that the value-stream function consumes: direct and indirect personnel, machines, facilities, and materials. Based on expected annual volumes and expected growth rates, these must be estimated. For EVS, we calculate all of these costs, as described in the following sections.

Calculating the Cost of Direct Personnel

At EVS, 80 people work directly on the machining function; EVS adds up the total cost (including benefits, workers' compensation insurance, salary, and any other costs directly associated with these individuals). The annual cash outlay turns out to be $6,000,000.

Based on historical data, EVS decides to use a one percent per year cost increase for each of the five years, plus a 10 percent expected growth rate. (There is actually a greater increase in cost; however, lean and continuous improvement efforts defray the increase resulting in a one percent increase.)

Calculating the Cost of Materials

EVS simply calculates the cost of materials. It turns out to be $1,000,000. Based on historical data, EVS determines that it should use a 3.5 percent cost increase per year, plus a 10 percent expected growth rate for the five-year period.

Calculating the Cost of Indirect Personnel

Currently, there are 15 support personnel including purchasing, planning, process engineering, and maintenance. The annual cash outlay turns out to be $1,800,000. Based on historical data, EVS decides to use a 5 percent per year rate of inflation.

Calculating the Cost of Equipment

The cost of repairing equipment and upgrading equipment should be estimated. Annual costs for EVS turn out to vary each year. EVS has a capital equipment plan that designates the amounts spent per year on capital equipment:

Year 1: $200,000

Year 2: $2,300,000

Year 3: $1,250,000

Year 4: $900,000

Year 5: $2,000,000

Note: Although for accounting purposes, capital equipment is depreciated over a number of years, we are interested in cash flows only at this point.

Calculating the Cost of Facilities

All the machining equipment at EVS takes up 50,000 square feet of factory floor space. This costs the company $1,500,000 per year in taxes and utilities, with a 3.5 percent increase per year. If EVS outsources this function, it could backfill this area with additional business and/or rent out the area to another business.

Consider also that it could outsource the function to a local machining operation while having the supplier purchase or lease EVS's equipment and rent this space.

Calculating Total Costs

Total cash outlays are summarized in Table 4-3.

Table 4-3. Outgoing Cash Flows

Year	Direct Personnel	Materials	Indirect Personnel	Equipment	Facilities	Total Cash Outlay
1	6,000,000	1,000,000	1,800,000	200,000	1,500,000	10,500,000
2	6,660,000	1,135,000	1,926,000	2,300,000	1,552,500	13,573,500
3	7,392,600	1,288,225	2,060,820	1,250,000	1,606,838	13,598,483
4	8,205,786	1,462,135	2,205,077	900,000	1,663,077	14,436,076
5	9,108,422	1,659,524	2,359,433	2,000,000	1,721,285	16,848,663

To calculate the net present value of the cash flows shown in Table 4-3, EVS needs to know its cost of capital. The team working on this project asks its finance department, which tells them to use 15 percent as its cost of capital. Cost of capital is the rate of return a company must earn on existing assets to meet the requirements of its shareholders and creditors. In other words, the money invested in any project must return 15 percent or better to be accepted. Based on this required rate of return, the net present value of the outgoing cash flows is $48,609,613.

We now ask: "Will the net present value of outgoing cash flows be lower than $48,609,613 if we outsource this function?" The question can be answered with reasonable certainty by analyzing all of the parts in the value stream being considered for outsourcing and considering EVS's target costs. The project costs associated with the outsourcing effort need also be considered later during the evaluation phase. Let's look first at the target-costing process.

Target Costing

Target costing means different things to different people. Some people think target costs should be based strictly on so-called *standard costs* in the system. Some suggest that they should be based on *internal processing* costs.

In actuality, target costing is a planning activity that should be part of the design of a product. Target costs are set, and then products are designed to those costs. We will address this particular topic in Chapter 11, when we discuss suppliers' roles in the design of products. In the case in which the product has already been designed, how does one set target costs for a family of parts being outsourced?

Based on experience, we have found that the best method for doing this is to have potential suppliers quote the project—not as individual parts, but as a complete project. In traditional mass production, this very idea would be sacrilege, but as we will see later in Chapter 5, traditional buyer-supplier relationships are no longer valid. Astute readers may ask, "Don't we have to go through the evaluation process first?" This is true if we do not have an existing trusted supplier to whom we can turn. Let's look at how EVS handled this situation.

Case Study:
How EVS Determined Whether or Not to Outsource

Let us assume for the moment, however, that EVS Corporation has two trusted suppliers in mind for this project. EVS Corporation can have each supplier quote the entire project. Let us suppose that the quotations turned out as follows:

- Supplier "A": $9,550,000
- Supplier "B": $9,950,000

Both of these numbers are close to the $10.5 million that it would cost internally for the first year.

The next step for EVS would be to put together a five-year cash flow based on these numbers. To be conservative, EVS will use the larger of the two numbers for analysis. Following will be the assumptions they will use:

- 10 percent volume growth rate per year

- No increases in cost per unit. In fact, on existing product, EVS will work with the suppliers to decrease cost. However, the assumption will be that per unit costs will remain the same.

Table 4-4. EVS's Five-Year Cash Flows

Year	Costs ($)
1	9,950,000
2	10,945,000
3	12,039,500
4	13,243,450
5	14,567,795

Using these simple assumptions, the five-year cash flows are shown in Table 4-4. Applying the 15 percent rate of return, the net present value of the outgoing cash flows is $39,659,087. Over five years, EVS would save $8,950,626 ($48,609,613 − $39,659,087). Outsourcing this operation clearly will be a money-saver for EVS, even after applying very conservative assumptions.

Having trusted suppliers allowed EVS to perform this analysis and determine that outsourcing makes sense for EVS. There are, however, cases in which no known trusted supplier exists; this is true especially for companies that are outsourcing manufacturing for the first time. In such cases, is there another method to determine whether or not outsourcing a family of parts will have economic benefit? Certainly, any lean organization would want to avoid the waste of going through the entire supplier evaluation process before deciding whether or not to outsource. (It is possible that after spending time evaluating potential suppliers, a company would discover that it would make better economic sense to keep the process in-house.) Fortunately, there is a method that can help determine if outsourcing will bring economic benefit without going through the evaluation process. Let's take a look at that method.

Method 2: Researching Process Technologies

This method is fairly straightforward in application. Earlier in this chapter, we mentioned that if a supplier does not have superior processes, it is unlikely that the supplier can produce a part at a lower cost. Using this same line of thinking, the types of processes that can be applied to existing products must be thoroughly researched: if better processes are available, outsourcing may very likely bring economic benefit. Frequently, new technologies exist that can increase productivity dramatically. Sometimes, radically different processes can be used to manufacture a product at much lower costs: for example, casting instead of machining, plastic injection molding instead of machining (requires changing materials), metal injection molding instead of machining, and water-jet instead of drilling, to name just a few.

It is fairly easy to research processes. Some suggestions for how to research include:

- *Using the Internet.* The Internet has many resources: articles, websites, and potential suppliers. One can find a plethora of information on process technologies.

- *Talking to existing suppliers.* This can lead to new process technologies. Good suppliers are often aware of new process technologies. Unfortunately, they are rarely consulted.

- *Talking to consultants and other professionals.* Plenty of consultants have process knowledge. They can help with the research as well as researching and locating suppliers.

- *Going to trade shows.* In the past, trade shows were the way to find out about new technologies. They are still a good way to find them; however, because of the Internet, they are less important.

Usually a process engineer, manufacturing engineer, or industrial engineer is best suited to do this type of research because such engineers are well versed in the technical aspects of manufacturing. Showing potential suppliers that perform a particular process sample parts and/or drawings will generally lead to determining whether or not the process can be used on a particular product.

If the process can be used and research shows that there is a significant cost advantage, then the outsourcing project should be pursued. At that point, a team can begin working on evaluating potential suppliers, which is the subject of Chapter 5.

Summing Up: Key Points

Reasons to Outsource

For most organizations, the decision to outsource a part or assembly is often based on one of the following reasons:

- Cost reduction
- Lack of internal resources
- Refocus of core competencies

Analyzing the Costs of Outsourcing

Cost analyses are almost invariably done by comparing the standard cost "in the system" with a supplier's quotation; but this fallacious method does not consider several *hidden* costs. In actuality, unless a supplier can produce a part using a more efficient method or a much lower labor rate, overall costs will more likely be *higher* by outsourcing. In all but a few cases, outsourcing due to lack of resources is not a true outsourcing relationship; it is an "off-loading" process done out of necessity rather than strategy. Outsourcing a process because it is not an internal core competency is the approach that the lean enterprise should use.

Determining the Profitability of Outsourcing

If a process is determined not to be a core competency, then it should be outsourced if it is profitable to do so. The Value-Stream Cash-Flow (VSCF) model—which considers the present value of future incoming and outgoing cash flows—should be used to determine whether or not outsourcing a process will be profitable. Another method for determining whether or not outsourcing a family of parts will have economic benefit is to research new processes. If a superior manufacturing process can be used and research shows that it provides a significant cost advantage, then an outsourcing project should be pursued.

Applying This Information to Your Organization: Questions to Help You Get Started

1. Think of some outsourcing decisions that have been made at your organization in the past. What were the primary drivers behind the outsourcing decisions? What type of analysis was done?

2. Think of an outsourcing relationship in which your organization is currently engaged. Would you consider the relationship to be successful? Why or why not? Does the supplier provide all of the process expertise, personnel, and technology needed?

3. What are your organization's core competencies? What processes are done internally that are not core competencies?

Chapter 5

Evaluating Current and Potential Suppliers for the Lean Extended Value Stream

Why Supplier Evaluation Often Fails

Once you've decided to outsource (the subject of Chapter 4), you need to evaluate potential suppliers. Supplier evaluation is a critical discipline that almost every manufacturing organization practices. At medium- to large-size organizations, there are often employees who are dedicated to evaluating, auditing, and developing suppliers, a testimony to the fact that supplier performance is critical to customer success.

But although almost every company *claims* to carefully evaluate suppliers, many continue to be plagued with supplier quality and delivery problems. Why is this the case? Based on observing clients throughout the years, there are two key reasons:

1. *Lack of training.* Evaluating suppliers is not a simple matter; in most cases, those individuals who are evaluating suppliers have not received any training. They usually have either purchasing or manufacturing engineering experience, and although this is certainly helpful, it is no substitute for learning the discipline of supplier evaluation.

2. *Lack of an evaluation system.* Most organizations do not have a system for supplier evaluation. Consequently, the selection of a new supplier is based on personal relationships or "gut feel." Although it is important to have a good working relationship with a new supplier, it is at least as important for the supplier's track record to prove its worth. Numbers do not lie. The criteria and methods discussed in this chapter will help readers formulate a system for their own organizations.

It is worth noting that a small percentage of people who make a living evaluating and auditing suppliers are simply people who like to travel, eat free meals (paid for by his/her own company or their suppliers), and be treated well in exchange for protecting their own interests. This results in having those suppliers who treat buyer representatives well receive continued business, regardless of their performance. This situation can be avoided by using a team approach, training the team, and having the team apply a system.

How can we set up a system that will accurately evaluate both potential and current suppliers on an ongoing basis? Based on our experience, we will cover in detail an effective method for evaluating current and potential suppliers. The process begins with selecting a team.

Selecting the Evaluation Team

It is important to use a cross-functional team rather than a single individual to evaluate potential suppliers. The team approach avoids several common pitfalls:

- The team approach prevents a supplier from being selected based on "gut feel" or a personal relationship. It is important to have several perspectives when selecting suppliers. In any important hire, an organization will have several people interview a candidate. So why wouldn't this same logic be used for selecting a key supplier?

- The team approach ensures that all key aspects of the evaluation are scrutinized. If one person were to do the evaluation, he or she would likely focus the evaluation on his or her area of expertise.

The evaluation team should consist of the individuals described in the following sections.

Manufacturing Engineers by Value Stream

Instead of having supplier quality engineers or procurement engineers who work "for purchasing," there needs to be a manufacturing engineer responsible for each value stream. This individual will be involved in identifying, evaluating, and ongoing auditing of suppliers. Because this engineer will be responsible for value-stream improvement, he or she will work to ensure good supplier performance. The engineer's bonus should be tied to specific value-stream metrics such as value-stream profitability, quality metrics, and productivity improvement metrics. We will address specific metrics in detail later in this chapter.

Outsourcing Manager

The outsourcing manager (or outsourcing project manager) should also be involved in the evaluation process. The outsourcing manager is the individual who manages the contract with the provider organization. We call this person an *outsourcing manager* rather than a "buyer" or "purchasing agent" because the primary responsibility of this individual is not to buy products but to *manage a relationship* with an outsourcing provider. As we will see in Chapter 6, the transactional aspects of buying in the lean enterprise should be based on a kanban system in most cases; the traditional purchasing model no longer applies.

Quality or Regulatory Representative

Quality is a key piece of a supplier evaluation: although manufacturing engineers certainly can provide expertise in this area, some organizations should have a quality or regulatory representative involved in supplier evaluation. For example, if a company is a medical device manufacturer, it would be helpful to involve such an individual in the evaluation and auditing processes to ensure compliance. This can be done in conjunction with regular evaluations or audits or can be done separately.

Product Design Representative

Eventually, many manufacturing outsourcing relationships turn into design outsourcing opportunities. Even if an organization does not plan on outsourcing any part of its design, a good supplier will at least be able to provide input to design. In either case, it is important to have product design represented on the team. (Supplier involvement in design will be covered in Chapter 11.)

The Evaluation Process for New Suppliers

When considering new suppliers, the evaluation process needs to consider three types of key attributes:

1. *Financial and operational.* This part of the evaluation looks at the way a company operates and its financial health. Key operational metrics such as lead time, inventory turnover, and on-time delivery need to be evaluated. Key financial metrics and ratios are analyzed as well. Obviously, even if a supplier has the right technological solution, it must be financially healthy and operationally sound.

2. *Technical and/or process expertise.* This part of the evaluation looks at the types of process technology employed, in both information flow and material flow. This includes the types of information systems that may be interfacing with those of the buyer, the types of manufacturing equipment employed, and the level of expertise of employees in the organization. It may also include product design expertise and technology (e.g., software).

3. *Business relationship.* This part of the evaluation is the one that determines the fit in terms of the business relationship, how the company relates to its employees and customers. In any potential supplier evaluation, this is critical. Interviewing a potential supplier is analogous to interviewing a job candidate: it will help determine whether or not they are a good fit. Sometimes, even if a supplier has scored well in terms of the technical, financial, and operational aspects of the evaluation, it can be the wrong supplier. This is why there must be a qualitative analysis of the potential business relationship.

Figure 5-1 provides an overview of these three evaluations, and the next sections of this chapter describe each evaluation in more detail.

Evaluation #1. Finances and Operations

This is the largest part of a supplier evaluation. This evaluation analyzes many of the same items that a value-stream-mapping activity would, plus several additional items, described in the following sections.

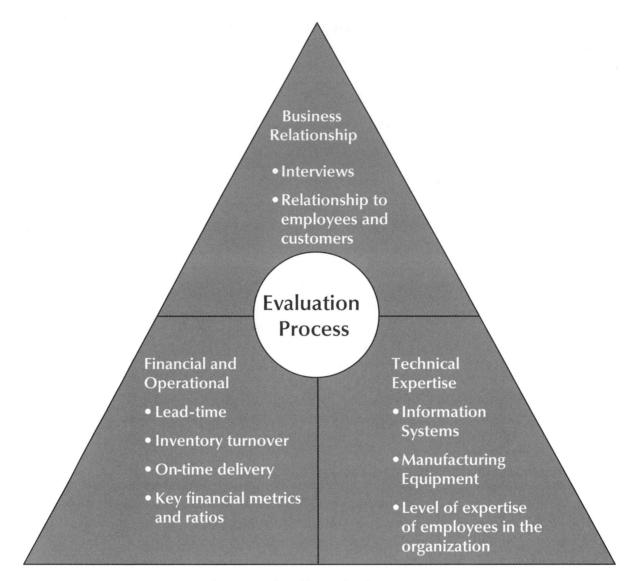

Figure 5-1. Supplier Evaluation Process

Evaluating the order-processing system. The order-processing system interfaces directly with the buyer and can have a negative effect on overall lead time. Frequently, there is a long queue time between order entry and actual production. Audit questions should include:

- How are orders received from customers (e.g., via Internet, phone, fax, etc.)?
- How quickly are orders entered into the production control system (i.e., what is queue time)?
- What is the response time for acknowledgment of corrective action requests and engineering change orders?

Evaluating the information management system. The way information is managed within an organization directly affects the responsiveness to its customers. Audit questions should include:

- What is the relationship between the orders and factory floor activity?
- What type of system(s) is (are) used (e.g., enterprise resource planning (ERP), material requirement planning (MRP), Manufacturing Execution Systems (MES)?

Evaluating the scheduling system. The scheduling methods a company uses will tell you a great deal about the type of company with which you are dealing. Effective scheduling usually indicates an organized company that can adapt; haphazard scheduling usually indicates trouble. The amount of work-in-process (WIP) inventory on the floor also indicates the effectiveness of the scheduling system. Audit questions should include:

- How is shopfloor activity scheduled?
- Is an MRP/ERP system used to schedule daily activities?

Evaluating maintenance. Poor equipment maintenance creates waste in the form of excess inventory and poor quality. Without an effective preventive maintenance program, any supplier is going to have great difficulty implementing lean manufacturing. A lean company intending to extend lean to its entire supply chain should not consider a supplier without a good preventive maintenance program (unless there are no other viable alternatives). Audit questions should include:

- Is there a preventive maintenance or Total Productive Maintenance program in place?
- Are there regular audits to ensure compliance and effectiveness?

Evaluating customer relationship management. It is critical that a supplier have a program in place for interfacing with its customers. A dedicated program manager should almost always be required; it is important in any outsourcing relationship to have one key point of contact. Open-book costing is also important for true value-stream improvement. Audit questions should include:

- Is there a dedicated program manager for each major account?
- Is there a policy for transparency (i.e., open-book costing and/or processes)?
- What systems are in place for customer management?

Evaluating supplier management. How a supplier manages its own suppliers is an indicator of how it will handle its customer's requirements as well. Audit questions should include:

- What systems are in place for supplier management?
- What types of relationship exist between you and your key suppliers?

Evaluating material flow. Although it is not always possible to find a lean supplier, if a potential supplier has good material flow through its factory and with its suppliers, this is an advantage. On the other hand, if a supplier has huge amounts of inventory, it is going to be more time-consuming and difficult to create a lean extended value stream. Audit questions should include:

- What type of system is in place for replenishment of material from internal processes?
- What type of system is in place for replenishment of material from suppliers?
- How is material transferred throughout the plant?
- What percentage of material flow is continuous flow versus pull systems (or FIFO lanes) versus push?

Evaluating 5S implementation and maintenance. A 5S system is a good foundation for lean implementation. If a potential supplier has an effective 5S system, it will have the discipline in place to implement more advanced aspects of lean manufacturing. Audit questions should include:

- Is there a 5S system in place?
- What ongoing activities are in place to sustain 5S?
- Are there regular audits?

Evaluating the relationship between design and manufacturing. If a supplier has a design department, it is important that the design group and the manufacturing group work closely in developing products. If they do not, the time to develop a manufacturable product will be extended with many design iterations. Realize that almost all suppliers *claim* to have "design-for-manufacturability" in place; nevertheless, it is important to look for evidence. Audit questions should include:

- To what degree and in what stage are manufacturing personnel involved in the product development process?
- What is the average time to develop a product?

Evaluating the quality system. Although almost all organizations have some form of quality statement or manual, it is important to verify that there is an effective system in place. Audit questions should include:

- Is a quality system in place and documented?
- If so, how effective is the system in each part of the value stream (i.e., supplier management, customer management, factory management, and information management)?

Evaluating financial metrics. Several key financial metrics and ratios indicate the financial health of a company; they can also help determine if a company is indeed implementing lean. Often so-called lean companies have similar inventory turns to a company that has not implemented lean. This usually indicates that they are lean in name only. Metrics to calculate and analyze include:

- *Return on equity (ROE).* ROE measures the efficiency with which the company employs invested capital. It is the most popular measure of financial performance.

$$ROE = Net\ income/Shareholders'\ equity$$

- *Return on assets (ROA).* ROA is a basic measure of the efficiency of resource management.

$$ROA = Net\ income/Assets$$

- *Fixed-asset turnover ratio.* This measures the sales generated per dollar of assets; it indicates how effectively a company is utilizing its assets.

$$Fixed-asset\ turnover\ ratio = Sales/Net\ property,\ plant,\ and\ equipment$$

- *Inventory turnover vs. industry average.* This key lean measurement measures how effectively a company manages its supply chain.

$$Inventory\ Turnover = Cost\ of\ goods\ sold/Average\ inventory$$

- *Current ratio.* The current ratio is an indicator of the liquidity of a company's assets relative to its liabilities.

$$Current\ ratio = Current\ assets/Current\ liabilities$$

Evaluating nonfinancial metrics. These include the following:

- *Lead time.* This measures the efficiency of the supply chain. Lead time is proportional to inventory. If there is less inventory in the system, lead time will be smaller. The number of days of inventory in a facility approximates the lead time. One way of visualizing lead time is to imagine a person placing a mark on incoming raw material and counting the time from the placement of that mark until the finished product containing the marked part ships out of the facility.

- *Average quoted lead time.* This indicates how long customers typically wait from order placement to fulfillment.

- *Average quotation turnaround time (and standard deviation).* This tells how quickly and consistently a company responds to a request for quotation from its customers.

- *Productivity growth rate.* Productivity growth rate indicates how an organization is progressing on its lean journey. Although other factors contribute to productivity growth, if productivity is growing at 10 percent or more per year, the company is doing very well. A 10 percent productivity growth rate means that a company can grow at 10 percent per year in sales without significantly increasing its workforce.

- *Rate of absenteeism.* This generally indicates how well employees are treated and valued by the company. A truly lean company values its employees. In fact, they are the only appreciating assets a company has.

- *Average first-pass yield.* This is an indicator of the robustness of internal processes. If a supplier's first-pass yield is low, then there is likely a hidden factory within that supplier's facility. Such hidden factories add significantly to cost and lead time.

- *Customer return rate.* The percentage of products that are returned by customers is an indicator of outgoing quality.

- *Equipment percentage availability.* Equipment uptime indicates how well equipment is being maintained; poor equipment availability makes lean implementation difficult.

$$\text{Equipment availability} = \frac{\text{Total working time} - \text{Unplanned downtime}}{\text{Total working time}}$$

Exhibit 5-1 is a checklist of the audit questions you should ask and the metrics you should examine when evaluating a potential supplier's finances and operations.

Exhibit 5-1. Checklist of Questions to Ask and Metrics to Examine When Evaluating a Potential Supplier's Finances and Operations

Evaluating the Order-Processing System

❏ How are orders received from customers (e.g., via Internet, phone, fax, etc.)?

❏ How quickly are orders entered into the production control system (i.e., what is queue time)?

❏ What is the response time for acknowledgment of corrective action requests and engineering change orders?

Evaluating the Information Management System

❏ What is the relationship between the orders and factory floor activity?

❏ What type of system(s) is (are) used (e.g., ERP, MRP, MES)?

Evaluating the Scheduling System

❏ How is shopfloor activity scheduled?

❏ Is an MRP/ERP system used to schedule daily activities?

(Continued on next page)

(Continued from previous page)

Evaluating Maintenance

❑ Is there a preventive maintenance or Total Productive Maintenance program in place?
❑ Are there regular audits to ensure compliance and effectiveness?
❑ Evaluating Customer Relationship Management
❑ Is there a dedicated program manager for each major account?
❑ Is there a policy for transparency (i.e., open-book costing/processes)?
❑ What systems are in place for customer management?

Evaluating Supplier Relationship Management

❑ What systems are in place for supplier management?
❑ What types of relationships exist between you and your key suppliers?

Evaluating Material Flow

❑ What type of system is in place for replenishment of material from internal processes?
❑ What type of system is in place for replenishment of material from suppliers?
❑ How is material transferred throughout the plant?
❑ What percentage of material flow is continuous flow versus pull systems (or FIFO lanes) versus push?

Evaluating 5S Implementation and Maintenance

❑ Is there a 5S system in place?
❑ What ongoing activities are in place to sustain 5S?
❑ Are there regular audits?

Evaluating the Relationship Between Design and Manufacturing

❑ To what degree and in what stage are manufacturing personnel involved in the product development process?
❑ What is the average time to develop a product?

Evaluating the Quality System

❑ Is there a quality system in place and documented?
❑ If so, how effective is the system in each part of the value stream (i.e., supplier management, customer management, factory management, and information management)?

Evaluating Financial Metrics

❑ **Return on Equity (ROE):** ROE = Net income / Shareholders' equity
❑ **Return on Assets (ROA):** ROA = Net income / Assets
❑ **Fixed-Asset Turnover Ratio:** Fixed asset turnover ratio = Sales / Net property, plant, and equipment
❑ **Inventory Turnover vs. Industry Average:** Inventory turnover = Cost of goods sold / Average inventory
❑ **Current Ratio:** Current ratio = Current assets / Current liabilities

Evaluating Nonfinancial Metrics

❑ Lead time
❑ Average quoted lead time
❑ Average quotation turnaround time (and standard deviation)

❑ Productivity growth rate
❑ Rate of absenteeism
❑ Average first-pass yield
❑ Customer return rate
❑ Equipment percentage availability: Equipment availability = (Total working time – Unplanned downtime)/Total working time

Evaluation #2. Process Expertise

This part of the analysis audits detailed process technologies, which are described in the following sections.

Evaluating manufacturing technologies. A key reason for outsourcing manufacturing is to take advantage of advanced manufacturing processes and technologies. Therefore, it is important to determine how effectively a supplier is utilizing key technologies. Questions should include:

- Based on the research done, how long have you been employing enabling manufacturing technologies?

- Is there a system in place to review current technologies and search for newer enabling technologies to improve?

Evaluating software and systems technologies. E-commerce is either presented as the panacea to all communication problems within a supply chain, or it is completely dismissed as an ineffective tool. In fact, although an e-commerce system alone cannot solve all communication problems in an extended value stream, it greatly contributes to improved information flow. Having a supplier with this capability is advantageous. Audit questions should include the following:

- What kind of ERP/MRP system is used, if any? Does it have e-commerce capability?

- Do you have any automated ordering set up with current customers?

Evaluating design expertise and technologies. If the supplier may be considered for product design outsourcing, you should consider three factors:

1. Type of design software used.

2. Type of product data management (PDM) software used.

3. Engineering expertise.

System-wise, it is highly desirable that the buyer's system and the supplier's system can "talk to each other." Audit questions should include:

- What kind of design software is used? Is it compatible with that of the buyer?

- Is there a product data management software used? Is it compatible with that of the buyer?

- What type of engineering expertise exists in terms of experience and education levels and specific disciplines (e.g., mechanical, electrical, etc.)?

Exhibit 5-2 is a checklist of questions you should ask when evaluating a supplier's process expertise.

Exhibit 5-2. Checklist of Questions to Ask and Metrics to Examine When Evaluating a Potential Supplier's Process Expertise

Evaluating Manufacturing Technologies

❏ Based on the research done, how long have you been employing enabling manufacturing technologies?

❏ Is there a system in place to review current technologies and search for newer enabling technologies to improve?

Evaluating Software and Systems Technologies

❏ What kind of ERP/MRP system is used, if any? Does it have e-commerce capability?

❏ Do you have any automated ordering set up with current customers?

Evaluating Design Expertise and Technologies

❏ What kind of design software is used? Is it compatible with that of the buyer?

❏ Is there a product data management software used? Is it compatible with that of the buyer?

❏ What type of engineering expertise exists in terms of experience and education levels and specific disciplines (e.g., mechanical, electrical, etc.)?

Evaluation #3: The Business Relationship

The objective of this part of the audit is to determine what it would be like to do business with a potential supplier. This part of the process closely resembles the "soft" side of a hiring process. Just as an employer would like to determine what a potential employee is like, a buyer needs to determine what it would be like to work with a potential supplier.

Because it is important that each potential supplier is considered equally, the same interview questions should be asked of each candidate. This part of the audit includes the activities described in the following sections.

Conducting interviews with key personnel. This round of interviews should be with the supplier program manager, production management people, key engineers, and executives. Although interview questions will vary depending on the buyer's preferences, interview questions should uncover several key issues:

• How does the potential supplier view its competitive advantages? In other words, does the potential supplier know why customers do business with them?

• How does the potential supplier solve problems with its customers? (In any buyer–supplier relationship, problems will arise; a buyer should know how such problems will be resolved.)

• How willing is the potential supplier to receive assistance from its customers? (To successfully implement a lean extended value stream, suppliers must be willing to receive assistance.)

• What types of relationships does the potential supplier have with its customers? How closely is the potential supplier willing to work with its customers?

- Does the potential supplier understand lean manufacturing? Is the potential supplier willing to implement lean?

- Has the potential supplier successfully assisted its customers in reducing cost? (If the supplier has success stories in this area (that can be verified by its customers), then it is a rare find. Although almost all suppliers claim to help their customers reduce cost, few actually do.)

- What is the potential supplier's vision for its future? (If a company's top management has no vision, it will almost inevitably fail. This is not the type of supplier to bring into a lean supply chain effort.)

Conducting interviews with several customers (by telephone). Interviews with customers will help the evaluation team to determine if the potential supplier's view of itself aligns with that of its customers. At a minimum, customers should be asked the following questions:

- Why do you do like to do business with this supplier?

- How would you characterize the business relationship with this supplier?

- What types of problems have arisen? How are the problems resolved?

Exhibit 5-3 is a checklist of the questions you should ask about the business relationship between potential suppliers and some of their current customers.

Exhibit 5-3. Checklist of Questions to Ask About the Business Relationship Between Suppliers and Their Customers

Interviewing Key Supplier Personnel (e.g., managers, engineers, executives)

❑ How does the potential supplier view its competitive advantages? In other words, does the potential supplier know why customers do business with them?

❑ How does the potential supplier solve problems with its customers?

❑ How willing is the potential supplier to receive assistance from its customers?

❑ What types of relationships does the potential supplier have with its customers? How closely is the potential supplier willing to work with its customers?

❑ Does the potential supplier understand lean manufacturing? Is the potential supplier willing to implement lean?

❑ Has the potential supplier successfully assisted its customers in reducing cost?

❑ What is the potential supplier's vision for its future?

Interviewing Customers of Potential Suppliers

❑ Why do you do like to do business with this supplier?

❑ How would you characterize the business relationship with this supplier?

❑ What types of problems have arisen? How have these problems been resolved?

Now that you know the basics of supplier evaluation, let's look at a case study example of how EVS handled its supplier evaluations. The rest of this chapter describes this in detail.

Case Study:
How EVS Evaluated Potential Suppliers of Machined Components

Based on its future-state value-stream plans, one of EVS Corporation's major projects is selecting a replacement for Trotsky Metals to supply machined components. EVS Corporation has decided to contract with two suppliers instead of only one. EVS believes that this will mitigate the risk of having only one key supplier for machined components, and EVS's volume is such that it does not want any one supplier to be too dependent on EVS for business. Each supplier selected in this process will be responsible for half of EVS's 4400A–Q line volume, but each must be capable of manufacturing any of EVS's machined components.

How EVS Selected Its Supplier Evaluation Team

To find, evaluate, and select the new suppliers, EVS has put together a team consisting of the following individuals:

- *Outsourcing manager.* This individual will be responsible for leading the team, negotiating contracts, leading interviews, leading the audit, and evaluating financial and operations metrics. EVS Corporation's outsourcing manager has extensive lean manufacturing experience; if this manager did not, the team would likely include an additional individual whose expertise is lean.

- *Manufacturing engineers (2).* These individuals will be responsible for identifying key process technologies and evaluating suppliers with regards to their technical competencies. They also have extensive lean manufacturing experience, which will complement that of the outsourcing manager.

- *Quality manager.* This individual will be responsible for evaluating key quality audit items.

How EVS Identified Its Supplier Selection Criteria

The team then began work by developing a set of criteria for a list of potential suppliers. Their list includes the following factors:

- *Location.* Supplier must be within 50 miles of San Simeon Assembly location. This is important because EVS Corporation wants the capability to maintain at least once-daily if not twice-daily deliveries. This is not feasible with EVS's current supplier, which is located about 3,000 miles away.

- *Size.* Any candidate must have at least 50,000 square feet of manufacturing floor space. EVS has decided that it does not want to do business with a small machine shop; it also does not want to be an overwhelming percentage of the supplier's business. (This does not mean that a small machine shop is never a good choice; this is merely EVS Corporation's preference.)

- *Process technology.* Each supplier must have high-speed drilling and machining capability. EVS process engineers discovered that many components can be manufactured much faster with this capability; EVS's current supplier, Trotsky, does not have this capability. EVS believes that this capability will significantly reduce its costs for machined components.

- *Process technology (2).* Each supplier must have light-assembly capability. This is necessary because there are some machined components that can be put together prior to sending them to San Simeon Assembly. (In almost all cases, if a supplier is manufacturing components that will be assembled together, it is worth considering that supplier for assembling the components it has manufactured.)

- **Lean methodologies.** The company must have applied lean concepts to its operation; this does not mean that it has completely embraced lean at this point, but it must have at least applied some of the tools successfully. At a minimum, EVS desires that any candidate have a 5S program in place.

Based on these criteria, the team researched (via the Internet) many organizations in the Los Angeles area. Based on telephone interviews, the company identified ten companies in the Los Angeles area that meet the criteria; all of them are within 25 miles of San Simeon Assembly. Here are the potential suppliers:

1. Alpha Machining Specialists
2. Beta Machine Company
3. Kappa Company
4. Gamma Products
5. Lambda Precision
6. Phi Engineering and Manufacturing
7. Sigma Six Production
8. Tau Metalworking
9. Theta Machine and Tool
10. Omega Manufacturing

To evaluate each of the above ten organizations, the EVS team developed an audit and interview form based on its criteria. Before visiting the potential suppliers for the audit, the team requested preaudit documentation; this would allow the team to calculate key metrics for discussion at the audits. The documentation the team required was as follows:

- 3 years of financial statements: balance sheets, income statements, statements of cash flows—these can be used to calculate all of the financial metrics.
- Value-stream or process maps (if any).
- Quality manual (if any).
- Partial list of current customers and references.

Each of the ten candidate suppliers was then audited using EVS Corporation's audit forms, which are shown in Figures 5-2, 5-3, and 5-4. For each of the evaluation forms shown in these figures, EVS applies the key shown in Figure 5-5.

EVS Corporation Supplier Selection Audit Metrics

Item	Calculation	Score
Return on equity (ROE)	ROE = Net income / Shareholders' equity	
Return on assets (ROA)	ROA = Net income / Assets	
Fixed-asset turnover ratio	Fixed asset turnover ratio = Sales / Net property, plant, and equipment	

Figure 5-2. EVS's Metrics Form for Evaluating Potential Suppliers

(Continued on next page)

(Continued from previous page)

Item	Calculation	Score
Current ratio	Current ratio = Current assets / Current liabilities	
Inventory turnover vs. industry average	Inventory turnover = Cost of goods Sold / Average inventory	
Average lead time		
Average quoted lead time		
Average quotation turnaround time		
Std. deviation quotation turnaround time		
Productivity growth rate		
Constant sales/Employee		
Rate of absenteeism		
Average first-pass yield		
Equipment percentage availability	Equipment Availability = (Total working time – Unplanned downtime)/Total working time	
Rate of employee turnover		

Figure 5-2. EVS's Metrics Form for Evaluating Potential Suppliers (*continued*)

EVS Corporation Supplier Selection Audit
Operations Evaluation (Part 1)

Question	Answer/Supporting Documentation	Score
Order-Processing System		
How are orders received from customers (Internet, phone, fax, etc.)?		
How quickly are orders entered into the production control system (queue time)?		
What is the response time for acknowledging corrective action requests and engineering change orders?		
Information Management System		
What is the relationship between the orders and factory floor activity?		
Scheduling System		
How is shopfloor activity scheduled?		

Figure 5-3a. EVS's Form for Evaluating a Potential Supplier's Operations (Pt. 1)

Question	Answer/Supporting Documentation	Score
Is an MRP/ERP system used to schedule daily activities?		
Maintenance		
Is there a preventive maintenance or Total Productive Maintenance program in place? Are there regular audits to ensure compliance and effectiveness?		
Customer Relationship Management		
Is there a dedicated program manager for each major account?		
Do you have a transparency policy ("open-book" costing)?		
What systems are in place for customer management?		

Figure 5-3a. EVS's Form for Evaluating a Potential Supplier's Operations (Pt. 1) (*continued*)

EVS Corporation Supplier Selection Audit
Operations Evaluation (Part 2)

Question	Answer/Supporting Documentation	Score
Supplier Relationship Management		
What systems are in place for supplier management?		
Material Flow		
What type of system is in place for replenishing material from internal processes?		
What type of system is in place for replenishing material from suppliers?		
How is material transferred throughout the plant?		
What percentage of material flow is considered continuous flow?		
What percentage of material flow is considered push?		
What percentage of material flow is considered pull or utilizes FIFO lanes?		

Figure 5-3b. EVS's Form for Evaluating a Potential Supplier's Operations (Pt. 2)

(Continued on next page)

(Continued from previous page)

5S Implementation and Maintenance		
Is a 5S system in place? Are there regular audits?		
Relationship Between Design and Manufacturing		
To what degree and in what stage are manufacturing personnel involved in the product development process?		
Quality System		
Is there a quality system in place and documented? If so, how effective is the system in each part of the value stream (supplier management, customer management, factory management, information management)?		

Figure 5-3b. EVS's Form for Evaluating a Potential Supplier's Operations (Pt. 2) (*continued*)

EVS Corporation Supplier Selection Audit
Process Technologies

Question	Answer/Supporting Documentation	Score
Manufacturing Technology		
Based on the research done, how long have you been employing enabling manufacturing technologies?		
Is there a system in place to review current technologies and search for newer enabling technologies to improve?		
Business Systems		
What kind of ERP/MRP system is used, if any?		
Does the system have e-commerce capability?		
Design Software		
What kind of design software is used?		
What type of engineering expertise exists in terms of experience and education levels and specific disciplines (mechanical, electrical, etc.)?		

Figure 5-4. EVS's Form for Evaluating a Potential Supplier's Process Technologies

Key	
0	None or ineffective, undocumented practice
1	Document, no practice
2	Document practice not effective
3	Document practice effective
4	Best practice

Figure 5-5. EVS's Audit Scorecard Key

How EVS Interviewed Suppliers and Their Customers About Business Relationships

EVS Corporation's interview questions are as follows:

1. ***Why should EVS Corporation do business with you?*** All interviewees would be asked this question. Although it's simple, it actually gives a wealth of information including the following:
   - It determines whether employees have a common vision for customer relationships and service.
   - It communicates what the potential supplier values most, and it accomplishes this more effectively than a mission or vision statement might. Often, a mission or vision statement does not reflect the true values of an organization.

2. ***What does your company do best?*** This question is actually a variation of the first question. It will help EVS Corporation determine how employees view their company. At an organization with strong leadership, all employees will know what makes their company excellent.

3. ***What are some problems that you encounter with current customers? What do you do to resolve these problems?*** This has a twofold purpose:
   - This question exposes some problems that current customers have. These are many of the same problems that EVS Corporation may have unless it puts systems in place to prevent them.
   - This question also exposes the process by which an organization solves customer problems. EVS Corporation will find out if the emphasis is on creating value for the customer.

4. ***What is your definition of lean manufacturing?*** This question will tell EVS Corporation a lot about the culture of the organization:
   - It will tell EVS whether employees understand lean and its importance to company success.
   - It will tell EVS whether the company is serious about lean. Is it a fad to them? Or is it part of the culture?
   - It will tell EVS whether the supplier's lean system is customer focused. A true lean system is focused on creating value for the customer and eliminating waste that a customer is not willing to pay for.

5. ***What are the company's plans with regards to lean manufacturing?*** Would you be willing to receive our help to accomplish these goals? This will tell EVS how willing the organization is to pursue lean further and how willing they are to work with EVS in the pursuit of lean.

(Continued on next page)

(Continued from previous page)

6. ***What is it like working at your organization? Tell me what you like and dislike.*** This will tell EVS the type of environment that the supplier has. There will always be things that any given person dislikes about his or her company; however, if most people are generally unhappy working there, it is probably not the type of company with which EVS Corporation would want to do business.

7. ***What is the company's vision for the future?*** This question relates to the effectiveness of the leadership of the company. As a potential employee would be asked to speak about his or her vision for the future, a potential supplier should be asked the same question.

8. ***Give me an example of a time in which you have contacted a customer and made a significant design or process change suggestion that resulted in a cost reduction. How often do you review designs and processes to identify improvements?*** This speaks to the potential supplier's ability and willingness to help EVS Corporation improve overall value-stream profitability through process or product improvement.

EVS Corporation also interviewed several customers of each of the ten suppliers. These interviews were intended to validate the supplier's answers to interview questions. The evaluation team asked customers the following questions:

1. Why do you like to do business with this supplier?

2. What one word best describes the business relationship you have with the supplier?

3. Give us an example of a problem that has arisen between you and this supplier. How was it resolved? Has it repeated again?

EVS's Supplier Evaluation Results

Using the forms and interview questions it developed, EVS Corporation's team evaluated each of the ten potential suppliers selected earlier. The results of the evaluation are shown in Figure 5-6.

Item	Alpha	Beta	Kappa	Gamma	Lambda	Phi	Sigma	Tau	Theta	Omega
Return on equity (ROE)	11.8%	10.4%	14.6%	8.1%	20.7%	8.8%	15.3%	16.2%	16.9%	16.1%
Return on assets (ROA)	3.8%	3.7%	6.9%	3.5%	10.9%	6.8%	9.0%	8.1%	8.5%	9.0%
Fixed-asset turnover ratio	7.5	7.1	9.2	6.5	12.5	7.1	13.5	11.8	11.6	12.1
Current ratio	1.8	1.5	3.3	1.9	3.9	1.7	3.7	3.8	3.5	3.8
Inventory turnover vs. industry average	0.8 × Avg	0.7 × Avg	1.5 × Avg	6 × .Avg	2.8 × Avg	0.9 × Avg	2.0 × Avg	2.2 × Avg	2.6 × Avg	2.7 × Avg
Average lead time (days from raw material arrival to shipment)	75	86	40	100	21	67	30	27	23	22
Average quoted lead time (days)	45	45	30	45	15	45	15	15	15	15
Average quotation turnaround time (days)	10	10	8	9	3	10	2	3	3	4
Std. deviation quotation turnaround time	3.3	2.1	2.5	2.1	.5	2.5	.3	.4	.4	.5

Item	Alpha	Beta	Kappa	Gamma	Lambda	Phi	Sigma	Tau	Theta	Omega
Productivity growth rate	0.8%	0.7%	3.3%	0.5%	6.8%	1.1%	5.5%	4.1%	6.9%	6.5%
Constant sales/Employee	$105K	$100K	$115K	$95K	$180K	$88K	$145K	$170K	$170K	$185K
Rate of absenteeism	2.5%	3.1%	3.5%	3.0%	0.5%	2.9%	0.6%	0.5%	0.5%	0.6%
Average first-pass yield	85.5%	87.5%	84.7%	86.5%	96.7%	91.5%	98.5%	97.5%	98.0%	98.1%
Equipment percentage availability	85%	84%	80%	86%	98%	94%	99%	99%	95%	98%
Employee turnover	15%	7.5%	8.5%	9.5%	2.5%	10.5%	2.1%	3.0%	2.9%	2.7%

Operations Evaluation Summaries

Item	Alpha	Beta	Kappa	Gamma	Lambda	Phi	Sigma	Tau	Theta	Omega
Order-Processing System	**2**	**2**	**2**	**2**	**3**	**2**	**3**	**3**	**4**	**3**
How are orders received from customers (Internet, phone, fax, etc.)?	2	2	2	2	3	2	3	3	4	3
How quickly are orders entered into the production control system (queue time)?	2	2	1	1	3	1	3	3	3	3
What is the response time for acknowledgment of corrective action requests and engineering change orders?	0	0	0	1	3	1	4	4	4	3
Information Management System	**0**	**0**	**0**	**0**	**3**	**0**	**3**	**3**	**2**	**3**
What is the relationship between the orders and factory floor activity?	2	2	2	2	3	2	3	3	2	3
Scheduling System	**2**	**2**	**2**	**2**	**3**	**2**	**3**	**3**	**2**	**3**
How is shopfloor activity scheduled?	2	2	2	2	3	2	3	3	2	3
Is an MRP/ERP system used to schedule daily activities?	No	No	No	No	No	Yes	No	No	No	No
Maintenance	**0**	**0**	**0**	**3**	**3**	**3**	**2**	**3**	**3**	**3**
Is there a preventive maintenance or Total Productive Maintenance program in place? Are there regular audits to ensure compliance and effectiveness?	0	0	0	3	3	3	2	3	3	3

Figure 5-6. EVS's Supplier Evaluation Results Summary

(Continued on next page)

(Continued from previous page)

Operations Evaluation Summaries *(continued)*

Item	Alpha	Beta	Kappa	Gamma	Lambda	Phi	Sigma	Tau	Theta	Omega
Customer Relationship Management	**2**	**2**	**2**	**3**	**3**	**2**	**3**	**4**	**4**	**3**
Is there a dedicated program manager for each major account?	2	2	2	3	3	2	3	4	4	3
Do you have a transparency policy ("open-book" costing)?	No	No	Yes	Yes	Yes	No	Yes	Yes	Yes	Yes
What systems are in place for customer management?	2	2	2	2	2	3	2	3	3	3
Supplier Relationship Management	**1**	**1**	**1**	**2**	**2**	**3**	**2**	**3**	**3**	**3**
What systems are in place for supplier management?	1	1	1	2	2	3	2	3	3	3
Material Flow	**1**	**1**	**1**	**3**	**3**	**4**	**4**	**4**	**4**	**4**
What type of system is in place for replenishment of material from internal processes?	0	0	0	3	3	3	4	4	3	4
What type of system is in place for replenishment of material from suppliers?	0	0	0	3	3	4	4	4	4	4
How is material transferred throughout the plant?	2	2	2	3	3	3	4	4	3	4
What percentage of material flow is considered continuous flow?	20%	20%	20%	20%	40%	40%	40%	50%	40%	45%
What percentage of material flow is considered push?	80%	80%	70%	80%	0%	40%	20%	0%	0%	0%
What percentage of material flow is considered pull or utilizes FIFO lanes?	0%	0%	10%	0%	60%	20%	60%	50%	60%	55%
5S Implementation and Maintenance	**2**	**2**	**2**	**2**	**3**	**3**	**4**	**4**	**4**	**4**
Is a 5S system in place? Are there regular audits?	2	2	2	2	3	3	4	4	4	4

Figure 5-6. EVS's Supplier Evaluation Results Summary *(continued)*

Operations Evaluation Summaries (*continued*)

Item	Alpha	Beta	Kappa	Gamma	Lambda	Phi	Sigma	Tau	Theta	Omega
Relationship Between Design and Manufacturing	**0**	**0**	**0**	**0**	**0**	**0**	**0**	**3**	**3**	**3**
To what degree and in what stage are manufacturing personnel involved in the product development process?	0	0	0	0	0	0	0	3	3	3
Quality System										
Is there a quality system in place and documented? If so, how effective is the system in each part of the value stream (supplier management, customer management, factory management, information management)	1	1	1	2	2	2	3	3	4	3

Process Technologies Evaluation Summaries

Item	Alpha	Beta	Kappa	Gamma	Lambda	Phi	Sigma	Tau	Theta	Omega
Manufacturing Technology	**2**	**2**	**2**	**2**	**4**	**3**	**3**	**4**	**3**	**3**
Based on the research done, how long have they been employing enabling manufacturing technologies?	3	3	3	3	4	3	3	4	3	3
Is there a system in place to review current technologies and search for newer enabling technologies to improve?	0	0	0	0	3	3	3	3	3	3
Business Systems	**0**	**0**	**0**	**0**	**2**	**3**	**2**	**3**	**2**	**3**
What kind of ERP/MRP system is used, if any?	0	0	0	0	3	3	3	3	3	3
Does the system have e-commerce capability?	0	0	0	0	0	3	0	3	0	3
Design Software	**3**	**3**	**3**	**3**	**3**	**3**	**3**	**3**	**3**	**3**
What kind of design software is used?	3	3	3	3	3	3	3	3	3	3
What type of engineering expertise exists in terms of experience and education levels and specific disciplines (mechanical, electrical, etc.)?	3	3	3	3	3	3	3	3	3	3

Figure 5-6. EVS's Supplier Evaluation Results Summary (*continued*)

(Continued on next page)

(Continued from previous page)

Summaries of EVS's Evaluation of Ten Potential Suppliers

Based on the scores shown in Figure 5-6 and the interview Q & A, EVS put together the following summaries of each organization.

Potential Supplier #1: Alpha Machining Specialists—No longer a candidate

Operations and financial metrics. Alpha scored relatively poorly in each of the metrics compared to the other organizations studied. Specifically,

- It had low financial numbers in terms of return on equity, return on assets, and inventory turnover.
- It had long lead time and quoted lead times.
- Its employees have high turnover rates and absentee rates.
- Its equipment has a large downtime percentage.

Ratings in key areas. Alpha also scored low in each of the key areas rated:

- Its order-processing system is ineffective; it does not effectively process corrective action requests from customers. This is particularly important to EVS.
- Its scheduling system is not effective; it primarily runs a push system.
- It has no preventive maintenance system.
- It does not have "open-book" costing. This is an EVS requirement.
- It does little or nothing with regards to supplier management.
- Its 5S program is not audited and merely consists of surface questions.

Interview questions. The EVS team and outsourcing manager developed a good rapport with Alpha, and Alpha employees answered EVS's questions well. Alpha's customers also appeared to enjoy doing business with Alpha.

Decision. In spite of the positive interview, due to the company's inadequate performance, Alpha will be dropped as a potential candidate for this project.

Potential Supplier #2: Beta Machine Company—No longer a candidate

Operations and financial metrics. Beta also scored relatively poorly in each of the metrics compared to the other organizations studied. Similarly to Alpha,

- It had low financial numbers in terms of return on equity, return on assets, and inventory turnover.
- It had long lead time and quoted lead times.
- Its employees have relatively high turnover rates and absentee rates.
- Its equipment has a large downtime percentage.

Ratings in key areas. Beta scored low in each of the key areas rated:

- Its order-processing system is also ineffective. Auditors found that Beta had many requests for corrective action, but Beta's response in each case was to increase inspection rather than determining root cause.
- Also running a primarily push system, Beta schedules mainly using expediting. Most jobs being worked on at the time of the audit had a red "hot" ticket on them, indicating that they needed to be expedited.
- It has no preventive maintenance system.

- It does not have "open-book" costing. This is an EVS requirement.
- It does little or nothing with regards to supplier management.
- Its 5S program consists of a daily cleanup; however, there is no evidence that a true 5S program was ever implemented.

Interview questions. The interview with Beta went very poorly. The Beta team seemed unprepared, and it did not understand the importance of the company's customers. Interviews with Beta's customers validated this concern. For example, two of the customers characterized their business relationship with Beta as "competitive."

Decision. Based on the poor interviews and the fact that customers characterized their business relationship with Beta as "competitive"—which is not the type of relationship EVS desires—Beta is no longer a candidate.

Potential Supplier #3: Kappa Company—No longer a candidate

Operations and financial metrics. Kappa scored well in some of the metrics compared to the other organizations studied but poorly in others. If EVS Corporation were to do work with Kappa, EVS would need to help Kappa implement lean. Here's what EVS found out about Kappa:

- It had very strong financial numbers in terms of return on equity, return on assets, and inventory turnover.
- It had fair lead time and quoted lead times.
- Its employees have high turnover rates and absentee rates.
- Its equipment has a large downtime percentage.

Ratings in key areas. Kappa scored low in many of the key areas rated:

- Its order-processing system is the most ineffective of all companies. Kappa also did not have a system in place for handling requests for corrective action.
- Kappa also runs a push system.
- It has no preventive maintenance system.
- It does little or nothing with regards to supplier management.
- Its 5S program needs to include regular audits and an incentive system.

Interview questions. The interview with Kappa went well. EVS Corporation's team left the interview process impressed with Kappa's organization. The organization seemed willing to accept EVS Corporation's ideas and lean manufacturing system. Kappa's customers also had very positive words for Kappa, describing the company as a "helpful" supplier.

Decision. Based on the fact that Kappa scored low in many of the key areas, it will no longer remain a candidate.

Potential Supplier #4: Gamma Products—No longer a candidate

Operations and financial metrics. Gamma was the weakest overall among all organization in terms of the metrics:

- It had poor financial numbers in terms of return on equity, return on assets, and inventory turnover.
- It had long lead time and quoted lead times.
- Its employees have high turnover rates and absentee rates.
- Its equipment has a large downtime percentage.

(Continued on next page)

(Continued from previous page)

Ratings in key areas. Gamma scored low in many of the key areas rated:

- Its order-processing system is among the most ineffective of all companies. Gamma has a system in place for handling requests for corrective action, but it does not employ it.
- Gamma also runs a push system.
- It has a preventive maintenance system, but it has not been in place long enough to bring the equipment availability up to what they would like.
- It does little or nothing with regards to supplier management.
- Its 5S program needs to include regular audits and an incentive system.

Interview questions. The interview with Gamma went poorly. EVS Corporation's team left the interview process wondering how Gamma maintains a customer base. Gamma's financial performance confirms this concern. EVS Corporation opted not to spend time interviewing Gamma's customers.

Decision. Gamma will no longer remain a candidate.

Potential Supplier #5: Lambda Precision

Operations and financial metrics. Lambda had the best overall financial performance and was among the best in terms of all metrics:

- It had the strongest financial numbers in terms of return on equity, return on assets, and inventory turnover.
- It had the shortest lead time and quoted lead times.
- Its employees have low turnover rates and absentee rates.
- Its equipment has a small downtime percentage.

Ratings in key areas. Lambda scored exceptionally well in many of the key areas rated:

- Its order-processing system was among the most effective of all companies studied. It had an effective corrective action system in place that actually works to eliminate the root cause of errors.
- Lambda has an effective system for scheduling production; it utilizes FIFO lanes and continuous flow. Consequently, it has very low inventory levels.
- Lambda has a Total Productive Maintenance system in place; based on the results, the system is working very well.
- Lambda has a system for supplier management: it maintains frequent deliveries with suppliers.
- Lambda has a good 5S program in place that is regularly audited.

Interview questions. The interview with Lambda went very well. EVS Corporation's team left the interview process impressed with Lambda's organization. The organization had strong financials, a good lean manufacturing system in place, and a strong customer relationship management system. Customers verified that Lambda was one of their best suppliers. EVS Corporation's team developed a good rapport with Lambda.

Decision. Lambda remains a strong candidate.

Potential Supplier #6: Phi Engineering and Manufacturing—No longer a candidate

Operations and financial metrics. Phi scored relatively poorly in each of the financial and operations metrics:

- It had poor financial numbers in terms of return on equity, return on assets, and inventory turnover.
- It had long lead time and quoted lead time.
- Its employees have high turnover rates and absentee rates.
- Its equipment has a 94 percent average uptime percentage; this is about average for the companies studied.

Ratings in key areas. Phi scored low in most of the key areas rated:

- Its order-processing system is among the most ineffective of all companies. Phi has a system in place for handling requests for corrective action, but it does not employ it.
- Phi runs a hybrid of push, pull, and FIFO lanes. Phi's poor inventory and lead-time metrics show that its system is not effective.
- It has a preventive maintenance system, which has resulted in improved equipment uptime.
- It has an effective supplier management system and scored well in this area.
- Its 5S program is effective; the auditors were impressed with the consistency of the audits.

Interview questions. The interview with Phi went well. EVS Corporation's team developed a good rapport with the Phi team. Phi's customers also described their relationship with Phi as very positive. However, Phi would require a significant amount of work from EVS Corporation to bring it up to speed.

Decision. Phi will no longer be considered.

Potential Supplier #7: Sigma Six Production

Operations and financial metrics. Sigma Six ranked among the best in overall financial performance and overall operations performance:

- It had very strong financial numbers in terms of return on equity, return on assets, and inventory turnover.
- It had reasonably good lead time and quoted lead times.
- It had the best average quotation turnaround time at two days.
- Its employees have low turnover rates and absentee rates.
- Its equipment has a 99 percent uptime.

Ratings in key areas. Sigma Six scored exceptionally well in many of the key areas rated:

- Its order-processing system was among the most effective of all companies studied. It has a very effective corrective action system in place.
- Sigma Six has an effective system for scheduling production: it utilizes a hybrid system of FIFO lanes, push, and continuous flow. This results in lower-than-average inventory levels.
- Sigma Six has a preventive maintenance system in place: although its equipment uptimes are excellent, the record-keeping is not completely accurate.
- Sigma Six has a system for supplier management: it maintains frequent deliveries with suppliers.
- Sigma Six has a strong 5S program in place that is regularly audited.
- It did not have a strong design-for-manufacturability system in place.

(Continued on next page)

(Continued from previous page)

Interview questions. The interview with Sigma Six did not go very well, according to EVS Corporation's team. EVS Corporation's team left the interview process feeling like Sigma Six did not have enough of a customer focus. Sigma Six's customers indicated that Sigma Six's work was high quality; however, a few said that Sigma Six was not very adaptable to change.

Decision. Based on its strong performance in terms of metrics, it remains a strong candidate.

Potential Supplier #8: Tau Metalworking

Operations and financial metrics. Tau ranked among the best in overall financial performance and overall operations performance:

- It had very strong financial numbers in terms of return on equity, return on assets, and inventory turnover.
- It had reasonably good lead time and quoted lead times.
- Its employees have low turnover rates and absentee rates.
- Its equipment has a 99 percent uptime.

Ratings in key areas. Tau scored exceptionally well in many of the key areas rated:

- Its order-processing system was among the most effective of all companies studied. It has a very effective corrective action system in place.
- Tau has an effective system for scheduling production: it utilizes a hybrid system of FIFO lanes, push, and continuous flow. This results in lower-than-average inventory levels.
- Tau has a preventive maintenance system in place: although its equipment uptimes are excellent, the record-keeping is not completely accurate.
- Tau has a system for supplier management: it maintains frequent deliveries with suppliers.
- Tau has a strong 5S program in place that is regularly audited.
- Tau is one of three of the companies under consideration that has a strong design-for-manufacturability system in place.

Interview questions. EVS Corporation's team was impressed with Tau's team during the interview. The EVS team developed a great rapport with Tau's team, and Tau's team made the EVS evaluators feel like the two companies could work very well together successfully. Tau's customers had very positive comments on their relationship with Tau; most indicated that Tau was their top supplier.

Decision. Tau remains a very strong candidate.

Potential Supplier #9: Theta Machine and Tool

Operations and financial metrics. Theta ranked among the best in overall financial performance and overall operations performance:

- It had very strong financial numbers in terms of return on equity, return on assets, and inventory turnover.
- It had low lead time and quoted lead times.
- Its employees have low turnover rates and absentee rates.
- Its equipment has a respectable 95% uptime.

Ratings in key areas. Theta scored exceptionally well in many of the key areas rated:

- Its order-processing system was the best of all companies studied. It also has a very effective corrective action system in place.
- Theta has an effective system for scheduling production: it utilizes a hybrid system of FIFO lanes, push, and continuous flow. This results in lower-than-average inventory levels.
- Theta has a preventive maintenance system in place, but although its equipment uptimes are excellent, the record-keeping is not completely accurate.
- Theta has an effective system for supplier management: it maintains frequent deliveries with suppliers, and Theta has a kanban system in place with its own suppliers.
- Theta has a strong 5S program in place that is regularly audited.
- Theta is one of three of the companies under consideration that has a strong design-for-manufacturability system in place.

Interview questions. EVS Corporation's team felt that Theta's team was adequate during the interview; however, the EVS team did not develop a great rapport with Theta's team. But Theta's customers' comments were almost all very positive, and Theta's scores are excellent.

Decision. Theta remains a candidate.

Potential Supplier #10: Omega Manufacturing

Operations and financial metrics. Omega ranked among the best in overall financial performance and overall operations performance:

- It had very strong financial numbers in terms of return on equity, return on assets, and inventory turnover.
- It had low lead time and quoted lead times.
- Its employees have low turnover rates and absentee rates.
- Its equipment has 98% average uptime.

Ratings in key areas. Omega scored exceptionally well in many of the key areas rated:

- Its order-processing system was the best of all companies studied. It also has a very effective corrective action system in place.
- Omega has an effective system for scheduling production: it utilizes a hybrid system of FIFO lanes, push, and continuous flow. This results in lower-than-average inventory levels.
- Omega has a preventive maintenance system in place, but although its equipment uptimes are excellent, the record-keeping is not completely accurate.
- Omega has an effective system for supplier management: it maintains frequent deliveries with suppliers, and Omega has a kanban system in place with its own suppliers.
- Omega has a strong 5S program in place that is regularly audited.
- Omega is one of three of the companies under consideration that has a strong design-for-manufacturability system in place.

(Continued on next page)

(Continued from previous page)

Interview questions. Leaving the interview process, many of EVS Corporation's team members felt that the Omega team was the best among all candidate organizations. The EVS team felt that Omega was the best fit based on the interview. Omega's customers responded with very positive feedback on their relationships with Omega.

Decision. Omega emerged from the audit process as the strongest candidate.

How EVS Made the Final Supplier Selections: The Decision Process

Several strong candidates remained after the audit and interview process; EVS Corporation's team wanted to review all evaluations and go through a formal decision process. Based on the ratings and interview questions, EVS first narrowed its decision to the following five organizations:

1. Lambda Precision
2. Sigma Six Production
3. Tau Metalworking
4. Theta Machine and Tool
5. Omega Manufacturing

Each team member then independently ranked the five organizations. Then, as a team, they agreed on the following ranking of the five organizations:

1. Tau Metalworking
2. Omega Manufacturing
3. Lambda Precision
4. Theta Machine and Tool
5. Sigma Six Production

Most team members had initially ranked Omega and Tau in the top two; the question of which should be the #1 choice among these two organizations led to the most debate. However, because the team's task was to identify two organizations with which to contract, the decision was easily made: EVS would pursue contracts with both Tau Metalworking and Omega Manufacturing.

How to Handle More Complicated Supplier Selection Processes

As shown in the case study, EVS was able to make a fairly easy decision after performing the evaluation of these ten potential suppliers. However, not all supplier evaluations end with such a relatively simple final selection process. Often, the question of which supplier or suppliers to choose does not have so obvious an answer. Two scenarios can complicate the selection process:

1. *If several candidates rate highly.* After auditing and interviewing the candidates, it may be the case that many of them rated equally high. In this scenario, a team may find difficulty selecting one or two good candidates if there are ten. This is a sign that the evaluation process was done well. The team can develop additional criteria as a team to apply to the candidates. For example, if two of the ten are located

within a mile, the evaluation team could make the case that those two candidates should be selected because delivery frequency could be multiple times per day.

2. *If most candidates rate poorly.* After auditing and interviewing the candidates, it may be the case that none are acceptable to the team. That is, although they met the criteria initially set prior to the audit, they performed poorly in the audit. This is not a common scenario; however, it does occasionally happen.

   This is usually the result of inadequate preaudit criteria. In such cases, the team should develop more rigorous criteria and identify additional candidates to audit. Although this may be costly, it is more costly to select a substandard supplier that could cause many years of added cost.

These two scenarios can happen. The first scenario is not much of a problem: a company can never have too many good candidates. The second scenario, on the other hand, can be avoided by spending time to develop good criteria up front. The EVS case study shows a well-thought-out process of developing criteria; the result was a smooth evaluation and selection process. Once this process is complete, organizations can deermine the nature of their buyer-supplier relationships—which is the subject of Chapter 6.

Summing Up: Key Points

After an outsourcing project is identified, a team must be assembled to evaluate potential s uppliers. The team should consist of the following members.

1. Manufacturing engineers by value stream
2. Outsourcing manager
3. Quality or regulatory representative
4. Product design representative

How to Evaluate Potential Suppliers

The team should develop an evaluation system that considers three major components.

1. *Financial and operational.* This part of the evaluation examines the way a company operates and its financial health. It is the largest part of the evaluation, and will include many financial and nonfinancial metrics. It should also include questions regarding order processing, information management, scheduling, maintenance, customer relationship management, supplier relationship management, 5S, quality, and design for manufacturability.

2. *Technical and process expertise.* This part of the evaluation looks at the types of process technology employed, in both information flow and material flow. This includes manufacturing technologies, software and systems technologies, and design expertise and technologies.

3. *Business relationship.* This part of the evaluation is the one that determines the fit in terms of the business relationship. This is the "softer" side of the evaluation; it includes a series of interviews with key personnel. The objective of this part of the audit is to determine what it would be like to do business with a potential supplier.

Applying This Information to Your Organization: Questions to Help You Get Started

1. What is your organization's procedure for evaluating and selecting suppliers? What types of metrics should be included that are not currently being used?

2. Who are your key suppliers? Calculate some of the key metrics presented in this chapter. How would you characterize your suppliers' performance based on the metrics?

Chapter 6

Buyer-Supplier Relationships in the Lean Enterprise—Contracting

Managing the Outsourcing Relationship

Once the supplier evaluation process is complete (as covered in Chapter 5), the next consideration for the lean enterprise is the nature of the buyer–supplier relationship. The traditional purchasing model has buyers and suppliers as adversaries or at least competitors. The supplier is trying to bid just low enough to get a contract while the buyer is looking for the lowest price. In contrast, the lean buyer–supplier model is one of cooperation. The buyer and supplier are partners: if the buyer succeeds, the supplier succeeds. The supplier's organization is an extension of that of the buyer. What does such a relationship look like?

A manufacturing executive once told me that he expected to increase his professional staff by about as many shopfloor people as he was planning to decrease due to outsourcing; he felt that he needed about that many people to manage the effort. Although there certainly needs to be someone managing the outsourcing effort, it should not be a large group. If a large group is needed to manage an outsourced function, then the organization did not do their homework. It clearly must have chosen the wrong provider if the provider needs to be managed that closely. This scenario offers little or no economic benefit.

Typically, one or two people are needed internally to manage a large outsourcing function. For smaller outsourcing efforts, one person can manage two or more suppliers. The supplier should be providing all dimensions of expertise needed:

- *Process expertise.* The supplier needs to be the process expert. If the buyer is sending manufacturing engineering support to help the supplier solve process problems, the buyer has likely chosen a supplier that does not have process expertise. (We will show in Chapters 7 through 9 that a lean customer must help its suppliers in lean implementation and other disciplines; however, the buyer should not be providing day-to-day process support.)

- *Human resources.* The supplier needs to provide all of the personnel required to support the operation.

- *Technology/Capital resources.* The supplier needs to provide the technology—the capital resources that the buyer does not have.

These three elements make an outsourcing relationship successful. If the supplier cannot provide all three of these, the relationship will not succeed long-term. The buyer will end up providing resources it should not provide in such a relationship. The idea is that the supplier has complete ownership of the outsourced function; this is what many "outsourcing" relationships lack. To ensure that the supplier will have ownership of the outsourced function, three key tasks need to be done:

1. *Select an appropriate supplier.* This task was described in detail in Chapter 5.

2. *Develop an appropriate long-term contract* with the supplier that has been selected. This is covered in this chapter.

3. *Set up a supplier association for continuous improvement.* This topic is covered in Chapter 10.

Negotiating the Contract

After an organization has identified and selected a key supplier for the lean enterprise, the organization must negotiate a contract that:

- Delineates the purpose of the relationship and how the relationship will be managed

- States the responsibilities of each party

- Identifies the scope of services

- Identifies the quality, productivity, and other metrics by which the supplier will be measured

- Defines the compensation plan for the supplier, including standard terms and incentive programs

Let's look at each of these topics in detail.

Delineate the Buyer–Supplier Relationship and the Supplier's Responsibilities

Frequently, outsourcing relationships fail because the buyer organization ends up doing more than it originally thought it would be doing. That is, it ends up giving its supplier a significant amount of support. Part of this problem should be addressed through the selection process described in Chapter 5. The other critical element that will prevent this problem from occurring is negotiation of an effective contract.

I've often heard that the contract should be nothing more than a general agreement outlining the relationship at first. However, if the contract is too general, it will not serve any purpose other than to make both parties have a good feeling about the relationship. A key purpose of a contract is for both parties to fully understand what their responsibilities are. Therefore, the contract needs to clearly identify what the buyer and supplier responsibilities are. Exhibit 6-1 is a checklist of questions that should be answered in your contract with your suppliers.

Exhibit 6-1: Questions That Your Contracts with Your Suppliers Should Answer

❏ What resources will be provided by whom?
  • Design engineering resources
  • Manufacturing/industrial engineering resources
  • Equipment
  • Tools, dies, molds, etc. (Who owns them?)
  • Training
❏ What will be the costs for support resources provided by the supplier above and beyond the price of components? Specifically, this applies to "one-time" items like design engineering, tool making, and the like.
❏ Who is responsible for maintaining, repairing, and upgrading equipment? Occasionally, the buyer will provide equipment. When equipment breaks down or needs to be upgraded, whose responsibility is it to repair or purchase new equipment?
❏ What project management resources will be provided from each organization and what are their specific responsibilities?
❏ What will be the types of meetings in which the organizations will participate? For example, will the supplier be participating in kaizen events, design reviews, or training sessions at the buyer site?
❏ How often will supplier audits occur, and what is expected of each party during an audit?

Describe the Services Provided by the Supplier and the Metrics of Evaluation

This part of the contract will describe the scope of work that the supplier will provide to the buyer. This part of an agreement should be very detailed as well; it should clearly delineate the expectations of what the supplier will be providing.

This will avoid another common problem in outsourcing relationships, that of "scope creep." Scope creep occurs typically in one of two ways:

• The buyer demands increasingly more reports, changes, etc., that were not addressed in a contract. This is the most common form of "scope creep."

• The supplier asks for resources from the buyer that the buyer expected the supplier to provide as part of the agreement.

To avoid any form of "scope creep," a contract must be detailed enough such that any independent third party could understand the responsibilities of the buyer and supplier in the contract.

Associated with the *scope of services* are the *standards of performance*. Some of the key metrics discussed in Chapter 5 should be discussed as key performance metrics or standards for the contract. At a minimum, these would include lead time, on-time delivery, and quality measures.

Determine a Pricing and Incentives Plan

The next key piece of the contract outlines the pricing and incentives plan. Although cost is not the only consideration, as mentioned previously, entering an outsourcing relationship must create value for both the supplier and buyer. To accomplish this, it is important that the supplier be given the tools and incentives to succeed.

First, "open-book" or transparent costing must be in place. That is, the buyer should be able to know how much it costs the supplier to produce components. The buyer's goal is no longer to maximize its own profits and minimize the profits of the supplier. Instead, both organizations must work toward increasing total value; this will ultimately maximize profits for both organizations.

The contract need not specify the pricing on each item that the supplier will provide; but it should specify the method by which prices will be determined. The buyer and supplier need to gain agreement on pricing. Initial pricing can be based on supplier cost plus a reasonable percentage of profit. Generally speaking, pricing on existing products should be expected to decrease. The buyer must challenge the supplier to decrease pricing through productivity improvements, and the buyer must ensure that the supplier has the tools to accomplish such improvements. Assisting the supplier with lean and other tools will be covered in Chapters 7 through 9.

Some form of gainsharing should be specified. That is, the supplier should receive a portion of any additional savings beyond the expected pricing decrease through improvements made. For example, suppose a given product costs $100 in year 1, and the target for year 2 is a 5 percent decrease ($95). Suppose also that the supplier is able to improve its process so that it can decrease costs by 10 percent instead of 5 percent. Assuming that there is a 75/25 split such that the supplier receives 75 percent of the additional savings beyond the 5 percent it is expected to save, the supplier will charge $93.75 per unit ($95 less 25 percent of the additional savings). The supplier will receive 75 percent or $3.75 of the additional savings per unit.

Now that you know the basics of what information a supplier contract should include, let's look at how EVS handled its contract negotiation process with its suppliers.

Case Study:
How EVS Negotiated Contracts with Its Suppliers

EVS Corporation negotiated new contracts with Tau Metalworking, Omega Manufacturing, and its existing key suppliers for the 4400A–Q value stream, San Simeon Assembly and Electronics, Inc. EVS Corporation met with representatives of each of these suppliers and worked on agreements. As a group, responsibilities were determined as follows:

- **Resources:** Who will provide what resources? EVS determined the following:
  - **Design engineering resources.** Design engineering resources would be addressed as needed in separate contracts.
  - **Manufacturing/Industrial engineering resources.** Each supplier would provide a manufacturing engineer at least 50 percent dedicated to EVS product lines.
  - **Equipment.** Equipment would be 100 percent owned, maintained, and upgraded by suppliers.
  - **Tooling.** All tooling would also be 100 percent owned, maintained, and upgraded by suppliers.
  - **Training.** EVS Corporation would provide consulting and training on an as-needed basis to its suppliers throughout year 1 to assist with lean implementa-

tion. This would be at no charge to the suppliers. Beyond year 1, a supplier association would be in place to provide training, consulting, and additional assistance, also free of charge.

- **Cost of support resources.** Suppliers would provide support resources such as design engineering and tool making using their regular hourly rate based on separate quotations and/or contracts as needed.
- **Project management.** Each supplier would have a project manager for EVS Corporation (not necessarily 100 percent dedicated); the project manager would be the key point-of-contact. EVS Corporation would have its Outsourcing Manager manage each key account.
- **Kaizen event support.** EVS Corporation, as part of the training provided, would require suppliers to send participants to kaizen events at EVS at no charge. Likewise, EVS Corporation would provide resources at kaizen events at supplier sites as needed, also at no charge.
- **Meetings.** EVS would conduct monthly outsourcing meetings; these meetings would require participation from project managers, and the meetings would be no longer than 60 minutes. The purpose of the meetings would be to update resolution status of any major problems and to communicate any major changes in forecasted demand.
- **Audits.** EVS would conduct quarterly supplier audits lasting no longer than one day. The project manager would be required for the entire time. Other personnel such as manufacturing engineers, quality personnel, and supervisors would be required to provide information as needed.
- **Reports.** EVS would require each supplier to provide quality reports, key metrics, 5S audit results, and productivity reports in general for their facilities on a monthly basis. Metrics to be reported would include lead time, inventory turnover, on-time delivery, and process yields. Additionally, quality reports for EVS Corporation's products produced would be required.
- **Pricing.** It was agreed that EVS Corporation would set initial pricing based on each supplier's internal cost to produce, plus a reasonable profit percentage. All of the parties agreed to a 5 percent pricing decrease per year and a 50/50 split of additional savings, where the supplier would keep 50 percent of any additional savings achieved. (Note that EVS Corporation would be helping suppliers achieve the pricing decrease by providing lean consulting and training.)

Buyer–Supplier Relationships in the Lean Enterprise— Managing Operations

The next part of the relationship is the operational aspect. After the parties agree to a contract, the lean organization and its suppliers do not proceed with a traditional purchasing model of operating—that is, instead of a buyer ordering large quantities of product based on MRP triggers, the buyer implements a pull system that allows parts to be produced and delivered by suppliers when they are needed. The future-state extended value-stream map and implementation plan should identify where pull systems are needed. The rest of this chapter covers the basics of setting up pull systems with suppliers.

Kanban-Controlled Pull Systems Versus MRP

Using a traditional material requirement planning (MRP) system for scheduling a factory, every production area is scheduled independently. There is no link between customer orders and actual production on the factory floor, and there is no link between production in one manufacturing area and the need of the next downstream process.

In contrast, in lean manufacturing, kanban systems are used to remedy this problem; items are scheduled based on *actual consumption* rather than forecast. *Kanban* is a Japanese word meaning "signboard" or "sign." A kanban signal, usually a card, is used to provide instructions to withdraw parts from a supermarket (warehouse) or produce parts. Because parts are made or are moved only when a signal is given, kanban systems prevent over-production and excess inventory.

The "nuts and bolts" of kanban systems are rather simple in concept. When a part or set of parts has been consumed in a manufacturing cell, a card or other signal is used to instruct material handlers to withdraw parts from a supermarket to replenish the cell. This is called "withdrawal kanban" because the kanban is used to instruct a material handler to withdraw parts. When a part or set of parts has been consumed from a supermarket, a card or other signal is used to instruct an upstream manufacturing process to produce additional parts to replenish the supermarket. If the upstream process is a continuous flow-manufacturing cell, the card or signal would represent one unit (or one shipment size). If the upstream process is a batch process, there is not one card per unit or bin but rather one card per standard batch size; when a certain number of units is consumed, a single signal is sent to the upstream process. This type of kanban is called "production kanban."

Let's compare traditional MRP forecast scheduling with kanban system scheduling.

Scheduling with MRP. We will begin with an MRP-based system. Let's suppose we have a factory that molds plastic components and assembles them into products. The products go to a finished goods inventory warehouse until they are shipped to a customer. They have injection-molding machines and assembly cells. Using MRP to schedule, the injection-molding machines receive a weekly schedule, and the assembly cells each receive a weekly schedule. The schedules are based on forecasted demand from customers. Customers actually place orders, and the orders are filled in shipping. In this scenario, there is no relationship between production in each of the manufacturing areas. Thus, there is no control over the amount of inventory that accumulates. The result is that *the warehouse has too much of what is not needed and not enough of what is needed.*

Scheduling with kanban pull systems. Now if we were to consider the same manufacturer using a kanban-controlled pull system, we would have a very different outcome. This is illustrated in Figure 6-1. As customers place orders, product is shipped from the finished goods warehouse to fill the orders. As product is removed from the shelf, kanban cards are sent to the assembly cells to instruct them to produce product to replenish the shelves. As plastic components are consumed in the assembly cells, kanban cards are picked up by material handlers; the cards instruct the material handlers to replenish the material in the cells. As material handlers remove components from the warehouse to replenish the manufacturing cells, production kanban cards are sent to the injection-molding process to instruct that process to replenish the warehouse. In this scenario, the amount of inventory is controlled. Production is based on actual customer demand instead of a forecast. If a kanban system is set up properly, *there are far fewer shortages and far less inventory.*

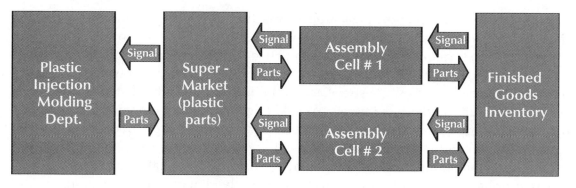

Figure 6-1. Pull System

Setting up Supplier Kanban Systems

One of the most common questions purchasing and operations managers ask is how to set up kanban system with their suppliers that work. Many have endeavored to set up kanban systems with suppliers, but few have succeeded. This section will concentrate on the factors critical to successful supplier kanban systems.

The principles behind a kanban system for suppliers are the same as those for the production kanban for an internal operation. As parts are consumed from a purchased parts warehouse, production instructions are sent to the supplier to replenish the parts. This is similar to production instructions being sent to the injection-molding machines in the previous example. To make the analogy clearer, let us suppose that the manufacturer in the previous example did not have injection-molding equipment. (See Figure 6-2.) Instead, injection-molded parts were purchased from a supplier. As injection-molded parts are consumed from the warehouse and delivered to the assembly cells, a signal would be sent to the injection-molding supplier to replenish the warehouse. The signal might be sent once per day and the quantity may vary, or the signal may be sent when a certain level of inventory is reached (reorder point).

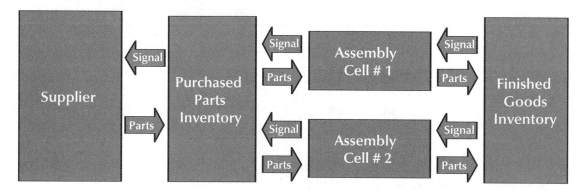

Figure 6-2. Pull System Including Suppliers

Step 1: Determine Your Ideal Delivery Frequency

The first consideration in setting up a pull system with a supplier is the delivery frequency. Is the supplier overseas? If so, a traditional kanban system will not work because the lead time will be too long; it is not feasible to have long-distance suppliers delivering frequently.

For example, one of my clients had a supplier in China delivering six months' worth of parts at a time; setting up a kanban system with such a supplier will not work because delivery is far too infrequent and the time to deliver is too long.

The purpose of a kanban system is to have only the inventory that is needed delivered at the time it is needed. Ideally, a supplier should be within driving distance and should make daily or multiple daily deliveries. Weekly or even monthly deliveries, though certainly not as desirable, can work with a kanban system as well. Less frequent deliveries are generally not conducive to a kanban system.

Not all parts must be on a kanban system; in some cases, it makes sense to have an overseas supplier for particular parts; in other cases, there may be custom components that must be engineered to order. In such cases, it is acceptable to set up a kanban system for most parts, while treating the others as exceptions.

Step 2: Choose Your Kanban Signal Method

The next consideration is how to signal suppliers using kanban. Setting up a kanban with a supplier involves one of two possibilities:

- *Option 1:* When a particular level of inventory is reached, the supplier is notified to send a fixed amount of product to the buyer to replenish the buyer's purchased parts supermarket. This is called a *fixed-quantity kanban.*

- *Option 2:* At a particular time each day (or week), the supplier is notified to send a variable amount of product to replenish the buyer's purchased parts supermarket. This is called a *fixed-interval kanban.*

In internal manufacturing, usually a card is used to signal another internal process to produce additional product (*production kanban*) or to withdraw product from a stockroom or supermarket (*withdrawal kanban*). The card is physically placed in a kanban accumulation post. Although it is possible to send cards to suppliers with their deliveries, in most cases, this is impractical. The most widely used methods for signaling suppliers are as follows:

Method 1: *Fax kanban.* Instead of a card, the signal is a sheet of paper that can be faxed to the supplier indicating the part number, quantity required, delivery time (lead time), and delivery address (see Figure 6-3). At a particular time each day, a fax is sent to the supplier specifying the quantity needed (this is fixed-interval kanban). The quantity would be based on the number of containers used since the last fax. This can be based on an accumulation of cards (one per container used) or based on visually checking the quantities on a rack in the warehouse. The supplier fills the order and delivers it in the agreed-upon time. Alternatively, faxes can be sent as soon as a set amount of inventory is reached (this is fixed-quantity kanban).

Method 2: *E-mail kanban.* Instead of a fax, an e-mail is sent to the supplier with essentially the same information as the fax would have.

Method 3: *Electronic kanban.* Instead of using a manual system (either a fax or e-mail), an electronic signal is sent to the supplier. There is no physical card. An e-mail or other electronic notification is automatically generated and sent to the supplier; the signal would specify the number of parts needed. The quantity will be based on usage, which is usually tracked using a bar-coding system. This system is the most complicated to implement because it usually requires implementation of a custom system or customization of a standard ERP system. It works well particularly for large companies that need to manage many part numbers.

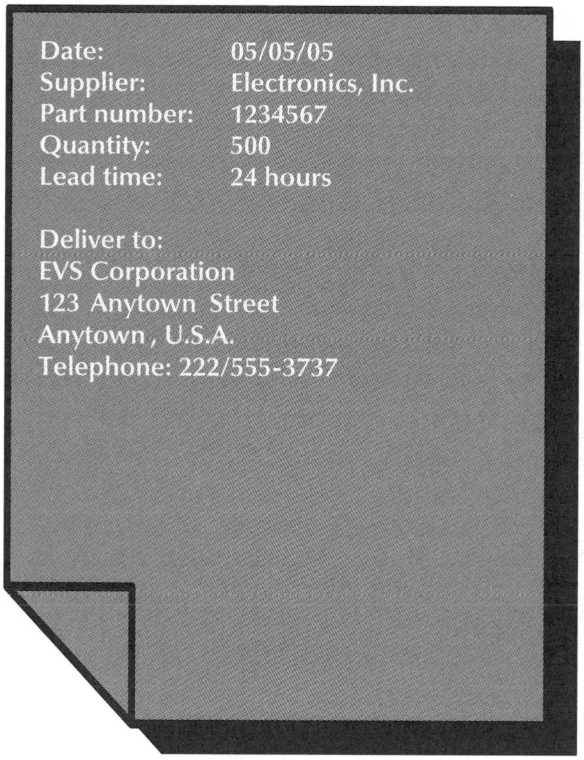

Date: 05/05/05
Supplier: Electronics, Inc.
Part number: 1234567
Quantity: 500
Lead time: 24 hours

Deliver to:
EVS Corporation
123 Anytown Street
Anytown, U.S.A.
Telephone: 222/555-3737

Figure 6-3. Sample Fax Kanban

Step 3: Determine the Container Size for Parts

The third consideration is the container size for each part to be included in the kanban. Most companies tend to utilize the containers that suppliers use, but these are almost always too large. Instead, containers should be sized based on their usage.

For example, let's suppose that an organization uses a two-bin type system in its manufacturing cells. That is, empty bins, instead of actual cards, are used to signal a material handler that replenishment is needed. If hourly replenishment is desired on the manufacturing line, then each bin should hold one hour's worth of materials. If practical, the organization should have its suppliers supply the parts in the same container or bin size. This would eliminate the extra work of *transferring* the parts from a large container to a smaller container for use in manufacturing.

Step 4: Calculate Your Desired Maximum Inventory Level

After containers are sized, the maximum inventory level must be calculated; this is used to properly size purchased-parts supermarket racks and square footage. The maximum inventory level is the maximum amount of inventory that should be on purchased-parts supermarket shelves for any given part number. Confusion surrounds this subject; however, it is a rather simple calculation to determine the maximum inventory level:

Max inventory level = Replenishment cycle stock + buffer stock + safety stock

where

- *Replenishment cycle stock* = Replenishment cycle (days) × average usage/day. Replenishment cycle stock is based on the average usage over the replenishment cycle.

- *Buffer stock* = Confidence factor standard × deviation of daily usage replenishment cycle (in days). Buffer stock is the amount of extra stock that compensates for variation in daily usage on the factory floor.

- *Safety stock* = Safety percentage × (replenishment cycle stock + buffer stock). The safety percentage should be based on supplier reliability, quality, and delivery performance. The safety stock is the amount of extra stock that compensates for delivery or quality issues.

Most spreadsheet programs have the capability of calculating standard deviation for the buffer stock calculation. The confidence factor is based on confidence interval levels for a normal distribution. In Table 6-1, we have listed various levels of confidence, ranging from 90 to 99 percent. These confidence levels roughly correspond to probabilities of a stock-out based on production variation. Additional confidence levels can be found in any standard statistics textbook.

Table 6-1. Confidence Factors for Calculating Buffer Stock

Confidence Level	Confidence Factor (for calculating buffer stock)
99%	2.326
97.5%	1.960
95%	1.645
92.5%	1.440
90%	1.282

Step 5: Calculate the Amount of Warehouse Space Needed

After the maximum inventory level has been calculated for each purchased part in the supplier kanban system, the amount of necessary rack square footage should be calculated. This will be used for determining the amount of space needed in a purchased-parts supermarket to accommodate the maximum inventory.

The final consideration is sizing the purchased-parts supermarket. This is a simple matter of calculating the number of parts containers at the maximum inventory level, calculating the amount of square footage that the containers will consume, and calculating the number of racks necessary to accommodate the bins. Let's walk through each step:

1. **Calculate the number of containers:**

   Number of containers = Maximum inventory level of parts / parts per container

2. **Calculate square footage that the containers will consume:**

   Rack square footage = Container length × container width × number of containers

3. **Calculate the number of racks that will be needed:**

   Number of racks = Total rack square footage needed / square footage per rack

Summary of the Key Elements of the Kanban System

At this point, all of the key elements of the kanban system have been addressed:

1. Delivery frequency
2. Type of signal (and whether it will be a fixed-interval or fixed-quantity signal)

3. Container size
4. Maximum inventory levels
5. Purchased-parts supermarket sizing

Vendor-Managed Inventory

Vendor-Managed Inventory (VMI) is a system by which a supplier manages the inventory with no intervention from the customer. Typically, suppliers fill inventory in designated locations throughout a plant at time intervals ranging from multiple times per day to weekly. An open purchase order is usually in place, and the supplier invoices the customer against the open purchase order, based on what is consumed by the customer. VMI should be put in place for low-cost items such as fasteners and low-cost electronic components. This eliminates the waste of having personnel spend time ordering, stocking, and moving very inexpensive parts around the factory floor. VMI has also successfully been used for regular items; however, in such cases, the vendor should deliver to the purchased-parts supermarket, not directly to the factory floor.

VMI is essentially a kanban system with more supplier responsibility. Instead of customer personnel stocking the purchased parts market, suppliers do it directly. The signal may be a visual check of inventory by the supplier or an automatically generated signal.

Let's see how EVS set up kanban systems with its suppliers.

Case Study:
How EVS Set up Its Kanban Systems with Its Suppliers

Recall that EVS Corporation has put in place new contracts with Tau Metalworking, Omega Manufacturing, and its existing key suppliers, San Simeon Assembly and Electronics, Inc. EVS Corporation now has the task of implementing the "nuts and bolts" of those agreements. Let's consider the kanban system that San Simeon Assembly will be operating with Tau Metalworking, following all of the steps just described.

Step 1: EVS Determines Its Ideal Delivery Frequency

San Simeon Assembly and Tau Metalworking agreed that Tau would deliver parts once daily to San Simeon Assembly.

Step 2: EVS Determined the Type of Signaling System It Will Use

San Simeon and Tau agreed to a fixed-interval system with fax signaling. San Simeon would fax Tau orders each day at 8:00 am, and Tau would deliver parts to San Simeon each day at 3:00 PM.

Step 3: EVS Determined Its Container Size

San Simeon Assembly would like to size containers such that one container will equal two hours' worth of material; this corresponds to the material delivery frequency on its factory floor. (Material handlers deliver parts to assembly cells every two hours.) They agreed that San Simeon would purchase the containers necessary to accomplish this; Tau would fill the containers with parts and ship them and would pick up empty containers when they deliver parts.

(Continued on next page)

(Continued from previous page)

Step 4: EVS Determined Its Maximum Inventory Levels

Let's review the calculations required to set up a kanban system for one particular part, part number 105113, which is a machined component that Tau Metalworking will be producing. Table 6-2 shows the daily production usage data for a 6-week period:

Table 6-2. Production Usage for EVS Part Number 105113

Day/Week	1	2	3	4	5	6
Monday	45	51	47	61	57	56
Tuesday	50	58	52	57	54	46
Wednesday	49	49	53	52	47	60
Thursday	61	52	55	51	49	57
Friday	47	60	46	61	51	62

Based on the data in Table 6-2, the average production usage is 53.2 and the standard deviation is 5.2. The replenishment cycle stock is then calculated:

Replenishment cycle × average daily usage = 1 day × 53.2 units/day
= **54 units (rounded up)**

Based on a 97.5 percent confidence level (see Table 6-1), the buffer stock calculation is as follows:

Buffer stock = Confidence factor × standard deviation of daily usage ×
replenishment cycle
= 1.96 × 5.2 units × 1 day
= **11 units (rounded up)**

It was decided that although Tau's data suggest excellent quality and delivery reliability, an additional 20 percent safety stock factor would be used at first. Safety stock would be calculated as follows:

Safety stock = Safety stock percentage (buffer stock + replenishment cycle stock)
= 20% × (54 + 11)
= **13 units**

The maximum planned inventory to be held in San Simeon Assembly's purchased-parts inventory will be:

Replenishment cycle stock + buffer stock + safety stock = 54 + 11 + 13
= **78 units**

Step 5: EVS Determined the Necessary Space Required for Purchased-Parts Inventory Racks

We will again work through the calculation for part number 105113 only. There will be 3 parts per container and the container will be 8" long and 6" wide. First, EVS needs to calculate the number of containers it will need:

Number of containers = Maximum inventory level of parts/parts per container
= 78/3
= 26

Next, EVS calculates the square footage that the containers will consume:

Rack square footage = container length × container width × number of containers

= 8" × 6" × 26

= 1248 in^2

= 8.67 ft^2

Finally, EVS needs to calculate the number of racks it will need for this part. Racks contain 4 shelves that are 18" deep and 96" long. Each shelf is 12 ft^2 in area. Assuming that we arrange the containers of part number 105113 two deep on the rack, the rack has 16" × 96" × 4 shelves of available square footage, or 42.7 ft.^{2}

Number of racks = Total rack square footage needed/square footage per rack

= 8.67 ft^2/42.7 ft^2

= .203

Thus, about 20 percent of one rack will be needed to accommodate part number 105113.

A similar calculation would need to be made for each part number to determine the total number of racks needed to accommodate all of the purchased machined parts.

How EVS's Supplier Kanban System Will Work in Practice

Now, let's review how the kanban system will work in practice:

- Each day at 8:00 AM, San Simeon faxes an order to Tau to be delivered at 3:00 PM. The quantity of parts to be delivered each day will be equal to the previous day's consumption.

- Each day at 3:00 PM, Tau delivers parts to San Simeon.

For example, let us assume that on Monday, 51 units of part number 105113 were consumed by San Simeon's assembly process. Here's what will happen next:

- On Tuesday morning at 8:00 AM, San Simeon will fax an order for 51 units.

- Tau will deliver 17 containers of parts (3 parts per container) and pick up the empty containers at 3:00 PM.

EVS has now determined its supplier's delivery frequency, the type of signaling system it will use, the container size for each part, the maximum inventory level for each part, and the necessary space required to accommodate the inventory. The next step for EVS will be to help its suppliers improve their internal operations to support the overall value-stream improvement goals. We will cover the first step in this process, value-stream mapping at supplier sites, in Chapter 7.

Summing Up: Key Points

After suppliers have been selected, the next consideration for the lean enterprise is to establish the nature of the buyer-supplier relationship. Outsourcing relationships fail often because suppliers need too much support from the buyer's organization. A successful outsourcing relationship is one in which the supplier provides all dimensions of expertise needed:

- The supplier needs to be the process expert.

- The supplier needs to provide all of the personnel required to support the operation.

- The supplier needs to provide the technology.

Negotiating the Buyer-Supplier Contract

To accomplish this, the buyer needs to develop an appropriate long-term contract with the suppliers it has selected. The contract must

- Delineate the purpose of the relationship and how the relationship will be managed
- State the responsibilities of each party
- Identify the scope of services
- Identify the quality, productivity, and other metrics by which the supplier will be measured
- Define the compensation plan for the supplier including standard terms and incentive programs

Setting Up a Pull System to Facilitate Buyer-Supplier Operations

The next part of the relationship is the operational aspect. After the parties agree to a contract, the lean organization and its suppliers should *not* proceed with a traditional purchasing model of operating—that is, instead of a buyer ordering large quantities of product based on MRP triggers, the lean enterprise must implement a *pull system* that allows parts to be produced and delivered by suppliers when they are needed. Usually, such pull systems involve signaling of suppliers using e-mail, fax, or other electronic kanban. The steps to setting up such pull systems are as follows:

- Determine delivery frequency
- Determine type of signaling system
- Determine container sizes
- Determine maximum inventory levels
- Calculate the amount of warehouse space needed

Applying This Information to Your Organization: Questions to Help You Get Started

1. What types of long-term contracts does your organization have with its suppliers? What changes do you think need to be made?

2. Among your organization's current supplier base, which suppliers do you think might be able to supply product based on a pull system? Which type of kanban system do you think would work best?

Chapter 7

Value-Stream Mapping at Supplier Sites

Identifying Internal Improvements at Supplier Sites

Once you've set up a working relationship with your suppliers (as described in Chapter 6), you should consider how you can improve the value stream that now encompasses those suppliers. Value-stream mapping is the primary tool for identifying, planning, and tracking key improvement projects that will contribute to overall value-stream improvement. In Chapters 2 and 3, we covered the tool of extended value-stream mapping, which identifies improvements to the entire supply chain. This chapter will address how to identify internal improvements at supplier sites. In this case the mapping will include details about information and material flow within a supplier facility, but it will not show any details of information or product flow in other factories (i.e., those of its suppliers and customers).

Recall that *value-creating actions* are those actions that add value to a product; they are those actions for which customers are willing to pay. On the other hand, *non-value-creating actions* typically fall under the seven wastes discussed in Chapter 1. The customer would not be willing to pay for those; however, some are necessary in the short term due to current technological or logistical circumstances. For example, if a supplier's facility has multiple buildings but not enough floor space in one of the buildings to accommodate all of the manufacturing processes, then there will be a non-value-creating but necessary action of transporting product between buildings.

The current-state value-stream map will show information and material flow as it currently exists at a supplier site. The future-state map will show an attainable information and product flow with significantly less waste and shorter lead time than that of the current state. The future-state map is developed by working through a series of calculations and questions and brainstorming, similar to what was done in Chapter 3. A supplier value-stream mapping event will result in a one-year implementation plan for improving the internal value streams at each supplier facility.

Selecting the Team for Value-Stream Mapping at a Supplier Site

For internal value-stream mapping at a supplier site, the following individuals from the supplier's organization should be represented on a team:

- *Plant or Operations Manager or Director of Operations.* It is important that a management-level operations person be on the team. This person may also be the team leader.

- *Industrial engineer or continuous improvement personnel.* An industrial engineer with lean knowledge or a person working in a kaizen or lean management office will be instrumental in identifying improvement opportunities as well as performing the actual mapping.

- *Production area manager(s) or supervisor(s).* Each production area involved in the value stream should have a representative. Buy-in and input from production management is critical to implementing the future state.

- *Purchasing representative.* Delivery frequency is a process that almost always changes during future-state mapping; thus, a purchasing manager or buyer would be able to provide input and buy-in.

- *Planning representative.* Scheduling production areas is one of the key processes that the team will reengineer in the value-stream-mapping process.

- *Shipping/receiving/warehouse representative.* The shipping process as well as the issues of raw material and finished goods inventory management are included in value-stream mapping.

- *One representative from a customer and/or supplier site.* Although there will not be analysis of customer or supplier processes, customers and suppliers can provide an outsider's perspective. If the customer or supplier has implemented lean, it would be of great benefit to the team to include a representative.

Physical Mapping of the Supplier Site—In Its Current State

As in extended value-stream mapping, you will need the following items before you begin the process:

1. Pencil and eraser (Always map using a pencil because you will make mistakes.)
2. 11" × 17" paper

Figure 7-1 is a simplified illustration of a current-state value-stream map. It shows information flow from right to left at the top and material flow from left to right at the bottom. Each process box shows relevant data. At the bottom-right-hand corner are the key metrics: Value-Creating Time vs. Lead Time. Let's walk through the mapping process step by step.

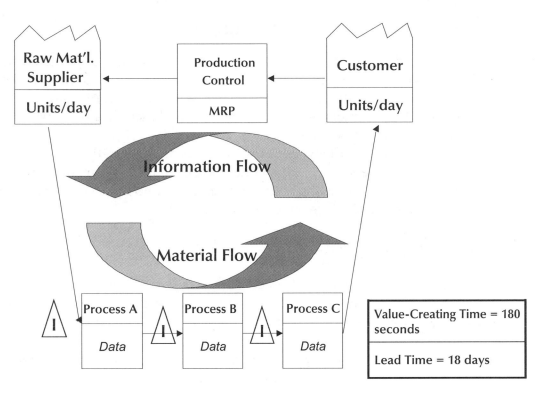

Figure 7-1. Current-State Value-Stream Map

Step 1: Begin with the Customer Box

To create a current-state value-stream map, begin with the customer box, which should appear in the upper-right-hand side of the map. The customer box should include the following data:

- *Product demand.* Each product in the value stream and its daily demand needs to be listed. If many products are demanded, simply list the aggregate demand and attach a spreadsheet showing demand by part number.

- *Number of locations.* If applicable, include the number of customer locations to which the units will be shipped. If there is only one location, it is useful to include the location name and distance from the facility being mapped.

- *Basic operating information.* Include basic customer operating information such as hours per shift, number of shifts worked per day, and days worked per week. If there are many customers, this can be omitted.

Step 2: Map the Shipping Function

The next step is to map the shipping function, moving backwards along the material-flow portion of the value stream (in the bottom section of the map). Include a process box that indicates this function. Under the shipping function, you should include whether inventory accumulates here (i.e., if there are shipping lanes) or if there is a temporary staging area. However, it is unnecessary to include other process data, such as processing times for shipment. However, no rule precludes a team from including such information, if they intend to use it for improving the shipping process itself.

Step 3: Map the Finished-Goods Inventory

Next, continuing backwards along the material-flow portion of the map, map the finished goods inventory. You can use the inventory symbol (usually a triangle) and indicate the number of days and/or the quantity of inventory held. If there are multiple part numbers, it may be useful to write the aggregate number on the map and include a spreadsheet showing details for each part number separately.

It may even be useful to group the types of inventory using the 80/20 rule. That is, if there are many part numbers, separate high volume (the top 20 percent), medium volume (the next 20 percent) and low volume (the bottom 60 percent). If no finished goods inventory exists, leave this icon out and move on to the next item.

Step 4: Map All Internal Areas of Material Flow

Next to finished-goods inventory is the last process in the material-flow portion of the value stream. Generally, this is a final assembly or packaging function; however, it may be a basic manufacturing process such as injection molding, machining, metal stamping, or electronic assembly.

The process box represents an area of one-piece flow or near one-piece flow. A manufacturing cell, though it may have many processes, would be represented by one process box if there is little or no work in process (WIP) inventory in between processing steps. In the process box, include data such as:

- *Number of operators.*

- *Working time.* Working time should be the time available minus breaks and other planned downtime, such as a planned daily or twice daily clean-up.

- *Processing time.* This is the total processing time (i.e., hands-on time) for a process to be completed. This may be different from the cycle time, which is how often a part is completed by a process. For example, a manufacturing cell might have five steps, each of which is completed in one minute. The processing time would be five minutes; the cycle time would be one minute.

- *Cycle time.* The cycle time may be included if it is different from the processing time.

- *Changeover time.* The changeover time should be the "part-to-part" changeover time; that is, the time it takes from the last good part from a run to the first good part on the next run.

- *Machine uptime.* This metric is defined as the percentage of time that a machine is not down for unplanned maintenance (i.e., repairs). If multiple machines are represented by one process box, include several values. If the entire line shuts down if one machine is down, report the uptime percentage for the line.

- *Run size or EPEi:* If there is a minimum run size of parts, list it here. This can also be expressed in terms of time. Many organizations are now using the term EPEi (Every Part Every Interval) to represent the interval at which they run high volume parts. For example, they may have a rule on an injection-molding process that they will run a given part no more than once per week. Their EPEi is one week. This means that they run a week's worth of parts once per week; it may take only a few hours or less to run these parts, but they run a batch size of one week.

- *First-pass yield.* Include the percentage of good product coming off the process.

- *Rolled-throughput yield.* If several processes are inside the process box, it may be useful to include rolled-throughput yield.
- *Pack size.* If a set number of units per package are shipped, then include that number here. For example, if products are sold in sets of four in a box, then the pack size would be four.

In between process boxes, you should map WIP inventory, again represented by the triangle icon that was used for finished-goods inventory. After mapping each process box back to first one, include an inventory icon to represent purchased parts or material to the left of the process box.

Step 5: Map Supplier Boxes

The final box in the material-flow portion is the supplier box (or boxes). If there are many suppliers, one box may be used per product type, and a spreadsheet listing each supplier and product supplied may be used to supplement the map. Alternatively, use one box per key supplier and key product supplied.

Some organizations manufacture large assemblies with huge bills of materials. In such cases, it is best to map only a few key components. Always keep in mind that the purpose of mapping is *to identify improvements*. Therefore, it is not critically important to list each part used in the production of an assembly. Attempting to create a perfectly comprehensive current-state value-stream map is often a source of frustration, and it is often the reason people give up. Do not try to create a comprehensive value-stream map. Instead, think in terms of *mapping key data only*.

Step 6: Map Information Flow

Begin information-flow mapping across the top of the map from right to left. Beginning with the customer, identify the information flow first from the customer box to the facility.

Identify what information is sent and where it is sent. If it is sent to an order-processing function, you may draw a box for that function and draw an arrow from the customer to the order-processing box. If it is sent directly into an enterprise resource planning (ERP) system, you may draw an arrow from the customer to the ERP system. Include a description of the information sent in a small box along the arrow. For example, if the customer sends a monthly forecast, show that in the box.

Step 7: Map Information Flow to Suppliers

Again, draw arrows from the production control or purchasing function to the suppliers showing the information that is sent. Information will include forecasts and orders and their frequency.

Step 8: Map the Flow of Information to the Factory Floor from Production Control

This step must answer the question, "How does each area on the floor know what to produce?" At this point, draw in arrows showing information flow from production control to each process box on the factory floor that is scheduled. Show what information is sent.

Information can include work orders, daily or weekly schedules, priority lists, etc. Lastly, identify how material is conveyed between processes in the material-flow portion of the map: push, pull/kanban, and first-in-first-out (FIFO) lane. In general, areas of push between process boxes would be anywhere production is not controlled by a FIFO lane or pull system (i.e., kanban).

Step 9: Calculate Key Metrics

After the map is complete, the team should calculate the following key metrics:

- *Estimated lead time.* This is the sum of the days of inventory observed in the factory from raw material to finished goods. If you were to mark an incoming purchased component and count the days until that component has gone through all of the processes and is to be placed in a box and shipped, this would be the lead time. The number of days of inventory approximates this lead time.

- *Value-creating time (or total processing time).* This is the total time that material is being processed (i.e., assembled, machined, molded, stamped, welded, etc.).

- *% Value-creating time.* This is the percentage of the total lead time in which product is actually being worked on:

  % Value-creating time = Value-creating time / Estimated lead time

Once the team has mapped a supplier's current state of material and information flow, the team can create a future-state value-stream map for each supplier. The next section describes that function in detail, walking you through step by step.

Creating a Future-State Value-Stream Map

Based on the data on the current-state map, the team will next create a future-state map by working through a series of four major tasks:

1. Determine opportunities for one-piece flow.
2. Identify proper systems for upstream production and inventory management.
3. Identify a system for scheduling.
4. Identify necessary process improvements.

Let's look at each of these tasks in more detail.

Task 1: Determine Opportunities for One-Piece Flow

The first principle of developing a lean future-state value stream is to create one-piece flow wherever possible. This is a two-step process.

Step 1: *Determine takt time.* The first step in achieving this principle is to calculate *takt* time, which is defined as follows:

$$\textbf{Takt time} = \frac{\text{Available working time per shift/}}{\text{Average units of product demanded per shift}}$$

Takt time tells you the rate at which the customer is buying a product or family of products relative to the working time available. For example, if the available working time per shift is 420 minutes, and 840 units per shift are demanded on average, then takt time is 30 seconds or 0.5 minutes.

Even in a make-to-order environment or an environment with volatile demand, takt time can be determined based on historical customer demand. The purpose is to set production rates to takt time and to ensure that processes can meet takt time. Strategically set inventory levels can be used to compensate for volatility in demand. Takt time should be recalculated based on shifts in demand; thus, takt time should not be adjusted too often. For example, Toyota adjusts takt time on a monthly basis for the automobile assembly operations.

Step 2: *Determine where one-piece flow is possible.* One-piece flow is achieved when processes are linked such that each process is running at approximately takt time and no WIP accumulates in between processes. The processes are usually co-located in a U-shape; this is called a one-piece-flow manufacturing cell. One would generally not include processes that run in large batch mode in a cell; however, some small-batch processes may be included if changeover times are sufficiently low. Key considerations for one-piece flow include:

- ***Highly capable processes.*** Processes must be able to consistently produce good product. If there are many quality issues, one-piece flow is impossible.

- ***Highly repeatable processes.*** Process times must be repeatable as well. If there is much variation, one-piece flow is impossible.

- ***Equipment with very high (near 100 percent) uptime.*** Equipment must always be available to run. If equipment within a manufacturing cell is plagued with downtime, one-piece flow will be impossible.

The criteria should not be applied based on *current-state* realities; rather, they should be applied based on what the team believes it can achieve in the *future* state. It may be the case that no series of processes has all three of the criteria based on current performance. The team should use its judgment to determine whether or not process capability and repeatability and equipment uptime can be improved within a one-year period after applying lean tools. After thinking this through, the team needs to identify the following:

- Which (if any) processes are candidates for one-piece flow?

- How many one-piece-flow cells will be needed and which processes and equipment will be included in each cell?

- What is the approximate number of operators required? (The number of operators should be based on achieving takt time.)

During value-stream mapping, however, the team need not actually design the manufacturing cell in detail. Designing and implementing the cell will be a task in the implementation plan.

Task 2: Identify Proper Systems for Upstream Production and Inventory Management

After the team identifies opportunities for one-piece flow, it must then determine how it will manage upstream processes and the inventory throughout the system. The team must take three major steps.

Step 1: *Determine how to schedule areas that are not candidates for one-piece flow and manage inventory in between processes.* Usually, such areas are upstream processes that can be scheduled using a pull system or, if the process is make-to-order, an alternate scheduling system. Managing inventory between upstream processes themselves and between upstream processes and one-piece-flow cells is a function of the type of system that will be used for scheduling:

- If scheduling will be pull-based, then a supermarket of parts will be installed in between processes; withdrawal from the supermarket will be based on kanban.

- If the process is make-to-order, a FIFO lane may be used for storing the inventory between processes. A FIFO lane is an area that can hold a limited quantity of parts of any type. When the maximum number of units is reached, the upstream process stops. This not only prevents overproduction upstream but ensures that products are produced in a particular sequence (first in, first out).

- Another alternative to a supermarket kanban system is to sequence processes such that a signal is sent to an upstream process to produce a part per customer order and deliver it to the one-piece cell as it is needed (with no inventory storage in between).

Let's consider a practical example. Suppose that during a value-stream-mapping activity, the value-stream mapping team identified an opportunity for a one-piece-flow assembly cell; further, we will assume that an upstream injection-molding process produces parts that go into the assembly cell. Injection molding will not go into the cell because it is by nature a batch process that cannot be scaled to run to takt time. How do we ensure that this upstream process produces what the assembly cell requires without overproducing?

The traditional lean method is to create a pull system in which parts are stored in limited quantities in a supermarket. As the parts are withdrawn from the supermarket and sent into the one-piece-flow assembly cell, orders are triggered to the injection-molding area via kanban cards or other signals. This allows the upstream process to produce only what is needed by the downstream one-piece-flow assembly cell. The inventory would be controlled by the number of kanban or signals in the system.

In some cases, however, pull systems are not practical. Let's now assume that the operation is make-to-order, with customized parts made in the upstream process, so that it is not practical to store all possible parts in a supermarket. Instead of supermarkets, a FIFO lane can be used between the injection-molding process and the assembly process. As bins of injection-molded components accumulate in the FIFO lane, they are pulled by the downstream assembly process. If the FIFO lane is full, then the injection-molding process is stopped (to prevent overproduction). In some cases, the process does not actually stop, but a full FIFO lane serves as a visual indicator that a problem exists and needs to be addressed. Instead of stopping the process, overtime might be used in the downstream process to make up the time.

Step 2: *Identify inventory management methods for purchased parts.* Purchased-parts inventory is treated similarly to inventory of parts produced from upstream batch processes. They may be stored in a purchased-parts supermarket, and a kanban system with the suppliers may also be implemented to regulate the flow of incoming purchased parts. For make-to-order parts, a FIFO lane may be implemented.

Step 3: *Identify inventory management methods for finished goods.* The team needs to decide which products to hold in finished goods and which to produce to customer order. In a job-shop environment, this is a moot point: there will be no finished-goods inventory. In other cases, the answer ranges from zero finished-goods inventory to holding some parts in a finished-goods supermarket to holding all parts in a finished-goods supermarket.

It is often impractical to hold all possible parts in finished goods, except for low-mix, high-volume manufacturers with few finished-goods part numbers. Instead, it often makes sense to hold certain parts in finished goods and make others to order. The most common method is to produce high-volume parts to stock and to make low-volume parts to order, thus managing the exceptions.

Task 3: Establish a System for Scheduling

One of the key principles of lean is to schedule only one area in the value stream based on customer orders instead of scheduling every process independently. The team must next determine the one point in the process that will be scheduled and how to level product volume and mix in this area.

Step 1: *Determine the one scheduling point in the value stream.* Instead of independently scheduling linked workcenters using material requirement planning (MRP), lean principles dictate that only one area of production should be scheduled based on customer demand. This area is usually a final assembly or final packaging area or is further upstream in the case of a custom, make-to-order operation. For most operations, it is possible to schedule the process immediately upstream from the finished-goods supermarket or shipping operation. The general rule is that one cannot schedule downstream from the process that makes a product customer-specific.

Let's consider a simple case, a traditional standard product manufacturer, rather than a highly customized manufacturer. Suppose that the manufacturer makes custom electronic equipment consisting of a powder-coated sheet metal outside and electronic components and PC boards inside. Let's suppose that all of the electronics are purchased from a supplier, but there are three internal manufacturing processes:

1. *Sheet metal fabrication*, where sheet metal pieces are cut. The size of the final products are specified by the customers; however, there are only three possible sizes.

2. *Powder-coating*, where customer-specified colors and decals are applied to the sheet metal.

3. *Final assembly*, where the final products are assembled.

In this scenario, the scheduling point would likely be the powder-coating process. It is possible to create a supermarket of sheet metal components because there are only three possible sizes. However, scheduling final assembly would not work because powder-coating is the process that makes the product customer-specific. Thus, the powder-coating process would be the ideal scheduling point. Orders would be sent to the powder-coating process. Sheet metal parts would be withdrawn from a supermarket, and powder-coated parts would then be sent into a FIFO lane in front of the final assembly area.

Step 2: *Develop a plan to level the product volume and mix within the area being scheduled.* The concept here is to ensure that each cell is running consistent volumes and producing a mix of products. For example, let's assume that five products are produced by a cell: A, B, C, D, and E. Let's also assume that product is shipped each day. The cell currently runs product A on Monday, B on Tuesday, C on Wednesday, D on Thursday, and E on Friday. More inventory must be held to support this system because each product is shipped daily.

Instead, with leveling, the cell might produce all five products each day in a level fashion, thereby limiting inventory throughout the value stream. This is easy for high-volume cells running few products through it. A simple scheduling board (i.e., a white board) can be used. You can simply list the production requirements per hour and track actual versus planned throughout the day.

However, for high-mix situations, a different method must be used. Process times are often not the same from product-to-product in such situations. A heijunka or load-leveling box may be used, but it must be modified. One of our clients uses a system in which the size of cards represents the total time that an order will take to complete. The cards are then sequenced in slots, as shown in Figure 7-2. This is more flexible than using a post-office-style scheduling box with rigid intervals. With the system shown in Figure 7-2, times can vary and the schedule can be filled accordingly. Even changeover "cards" can be inserted to represent time in between product types for a changeover.

Scheduling Board									
	Time Window								
Cell#	8–9	9–10	10–11	11–12	12–1	1–2	2–3	3–4	4–5
1									
2									
3									

Figure 7-2. Sample Scheduling Board

Task 4: Identify Necessary Process Improvements

Process improvements must be made to accomplish the future-state goals that a value-stream-mapping team has identified. Also, other waste-removing process improvements can be identified to further enhance the future state. The team should utilize a brainstorming process (as described in Chapter 3) to identify process-improvement opportunities. Each person on the team should be invited to generate improvement ideas for the value stream. Then, each of the ideas should be reviewed for inclusion in the future state.

Table 7-1 includes the types of process improvements that would be generated and the tools that would assist in implementation.

Table 7-1. Sample Process Improvements

Process Improvement	Project Tools to Employ
Improved equipment maintenance and uptime	TPM (Total Productive Maintenance), 5S
Changeover time reduction	SMED, 5S, TPM
Supplier delivery improvements	Kanban system
Scheduling improvement ideas	Kanban systems, load-leveling
Quality improvement/variation reduction	Six Sigma/statistical methods, 5S, TPM

Creating the Physical Map and Calculating Metrics

Following the brainstorming session, the team must create the future-state map that reflects all of the improvements identified: one-piece flow, upstream production and inventory management, scheduling, and other process improvements. The map should be created in a similar fashion to the current-state map (described at the beginning of this chapter):

1. Begin with the customer box, which should appear in the upper-right-hand side of the map.

2. Moving backwards along the material-flow portion of the value stream (in the bottom section of the map), map the shipping function.

3. Continuing backwards along the material-flow portion of the map, map the finished-goods inventory supermarket, if any.

4. Map all internal areas of material flow, showing the metrics as future-state goals.

5. Map supplier boxes.

6. Begin information-flow mapping across the top of the map from right to left. Beginning with the customer, identify the information flow first from the customer box to the facility.

7. Map information flow to suppliers including orders and forecasts.

8. Map the flow of information to the factory floor from production control; this should include any pull systems, FIFO lanes, or other transfer of information between processes to trigger production or withdrawal of materials.

9. After the map is complete, the team should calculate the value-creating time, estimated lead time, and percent value-creating time.

Creating an Implementation Plan

The final step for the team is to create an implementation plan that will identify projects that need to be completed to achieve the future state. It will also allow for tracking of the initiatives. A sample plan is shown in Figure 7-3.

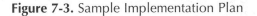

| Value-Stream Implementation Plan | | | | | Date: | | | |
Goal	Objective	Task	Start	Finish (plan)	Finish (actual)	Team Leader	Team Members	Status Notes

Figure 7-3. Sample Implementation Plan

The purpose of the implementation plan is to track the following items and make their status accessible and visible to the entire organization:

- Project current status
- Objective
- Start and end dates
- Measurable goal and actual results
- Responsible individual and/or team

Now that you've seen each step of this process, let's see how EVS did it for one of its suppliers.

Case Study:
How EVS Handled Value-Stream Mapping for One of Its Suppliers—San Simeon Assembly

EVS Corporation worked with each of its key suppliers to improve their internal value streams. Let's walk through the San Simeon Assembly value-stream-mapping project together.

EVS Selects Its Mapping Team

EVS and San Simeon put together a small team consisting of the following personnel:
- EVS Sr. Industrial Engineer
- San Simeon Plant Manager
- San Simeon Industrial Engineer
- San Simeon Purchasing Agent
- San Simeon Warehouse/Shipping Manager
- San Simeon Test and Assembly Supervisor
- Electronics, Inc., Industrial Engineer

The Team Creates a Current-State Value-Stream Map for San Simeon

The team created a current-state value-stream map for the 4400A–Q product line (see Figure 7-4). This map was put together as follows:

1. The team began with the customer and customer demand. In the upper-right-hand corner, it shows that EVS Corporation's demand is 120 units/day; this corresponds to the end customers' aggregate demand.

2. Mapping process boxes was the next step. On this current-state map, there are four major process boxes. For each process box, the team showed the relevant data including processing time, changeover time, number of operators, working time, and number of shifts. The team also indicated the inventory levels between each process. The process boxes in the material-flow portion are:
   - Shipping
   - Testing
   - Final assembly
   - Two parallel subassembly functions for "A" and "B"

3. Next, the team shows key suppliers in the upper-left-hand corner: Electronics, Inc., and machining suppliers Tau Metalworking and Omega Manufacturing. Because the team was not going to analyze or improve these organizations, it doesn't show any factory data for these suppliers. It shows only the ship frequency and method.

4. The team then connected each process box with a push arrow, showing that material is pushed from step to step in the current state.

5. Next, the team moved to the information flow. Again beginning with the customer, it mapped the information flow from EVS Corporation to San Simeon's production control department. The team then mapped the information flow from

(Continued on page 126)

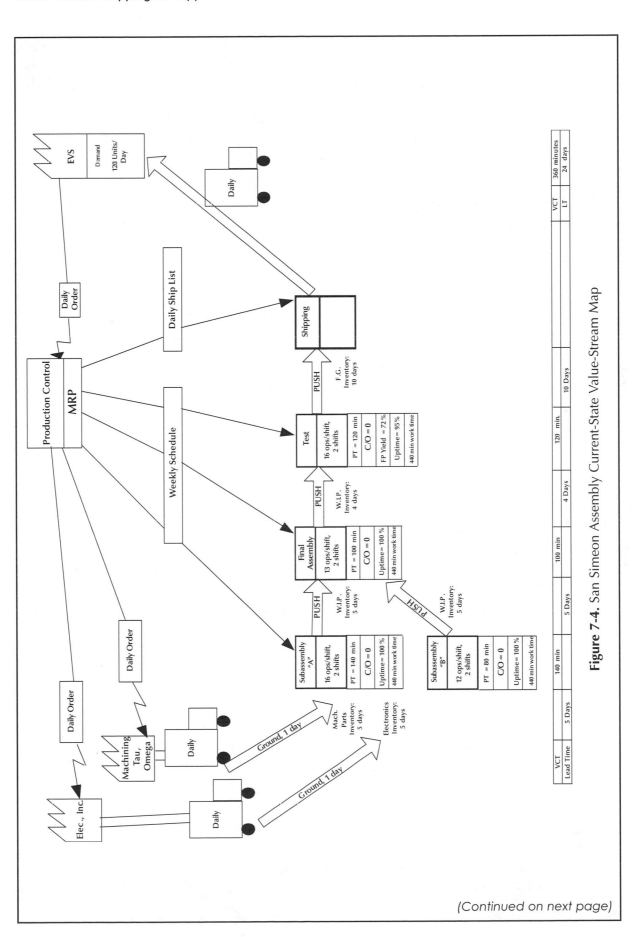

Figure 7-4. San Simeon Assembly Current-State Value-Stream Map

(Continued on next page)

(Continued from page 124)

San Simeon to its suppliers. Finally, it mapped information flow from San Simeon's production control department to each of its process areas.

6. Finally, the team summed up the key metrics along the bottom of the map. In this case, the key metrics work out as shown in Table 7-2.

Table 7-2. San Simeon Current State Map Metrics

Metric	Value
Value-creating time	360 minutes
Estimated lead time through the plant	24 days
% Value-creating time	1.04%

The EVS Team Creates a Future-State Value-Stream Map for San Simeon

The team then created a future-state map by working through the tasks discussed earlier in this chapter and by holding a brainstorming session. The team addressed each task, as described in the following sections.

Task 1: *Determine opportunities for one-piece flow with load-leveling.* First, the team calculated takt time as follows:

Available working time = 440 minutes/shift
Units demanded/Shift = 60
Takt time = Available working time per shift/Units of product demanded per shift
Takt time = 7.33 minutes

This means that the customer (EVS Corporation) is buying this product at a rate of one unit every 7.33 minutes.

After calculating takt time, the team worked to determine where one-piece flow is possible. It made a table listing each process and identifying what would need to be done to achieve one-piece flow: see Table 7-3.

Table 7-3. San Simeon One-Piece-Flow Candidate Chart

Process	Barriers to One-Piece Flow	Include in one-piece flow cell?
Subassembly "A"	Need to determine method scale process to takt time—currently would require too many people	Yes
Subassembly "B"	Same as above	Yes
Final assembly	Same as above	Yes
Test	Same as above, improve uptime improve yield	Yes

The team determined that it would like to create a one-piece flow cell that combines all four processes. There are several barriers identified to one-piece flow:

• *Scaling to takt time.* Although the takt time is 7.33 minutes, each of these processes is significantly longer. If there were one cell, too many operators would be required to run the cell. For example, the total time is 360 minutes: a back-of-the-envelope calculation for the number of operators required in the cell would indicate that almost 50 operators would be needed:

Number of operators required = Total operator time to build one unit/Takt time
$$= 360/7.33$$
$$= 49.1 \text{ operators}$$

The team has decided to create five identical cells instead of one, with a goal of reducing the work content so that only 30 total operators (six per cell) will be needed.

- *Uptime on test equipment.* Currently uptime is 95 percent; in a one-piece-flow cell, uptime should be closer to 100 percent. The team will need to address this issue later during brainstorming.

- *Yield improvement.* Only 72 percent of units pass under the current system. This will need significant improvement; again, this will be addressed during brainstorming.

Task 2: *Identify proper systems for upstream production and inventory management.* The next step after identifying areas of one-piece flow is to identify how to manage areas that cannot be one-piece flow, including inventory management throughout the value stream.

In this case, the team will attempt to create 100 percent one-piece flow; this means that the only inventory that needs to be managed is purchased parts and finished goods. The team decides that because purchased parts are delivered daily, it can reduce inventory to at most 2 days. Also, the team believes that it can reduce finished-goods inventory to 3 days. This would create a total of 5 days (given that EVS Corporation holds 2 additional days of inventory at its facility). EVS believes that eventually it can produce directly to shipping; however, the team has decided that it will not attempt that approach at this time.

Task 3: *Establish a system for scheduling.* With a set of one-piece-flow cells to schedule, the issue for the team is not where to schedule but how to level the product volume and mix within the cells. Because changeover time is zero and process times are consistent from unit-to-unit, scheduling product as needed per EVS electronic orders will level the mix well. However, the team needs to address the issue of fluctuating daily demand. This 3 days of finished-goods inventory will be used to buffer against demand fluctuation.

Task 4: *Identify possible process improvements.* The team working on EVS Corporation's future-state map went through a brainstorming session and came up with several ideas to implement. We will not describe the brainstorming process in detail here because it is covered in Chapter 3. Following are the key process improvements that the team brainstormed for the future state:

1. Do a study on test process; determine how to reduce time significantly by eliminating or modifying tests done. (Can some of the tests be done at earlier stages?)

2. Improve preventive maintenance on test equipment to improve uptime; have maintenance group work with organization that designed and manufactured equipment (i.e., custom equipment).

3. Create a pareto chart on causes for failure during test process. Put a problem-solving team together to improve first-pass yield by attacking key issues.

4. Use a daily order list to release work to the assembly and test cell.

(Continued on next page)

(Continued from previous page)

5. Implement simple automation such that the operators can be better utilized in the cell; that is, while some processes are being done automatically, operators can move on and add value in other areas of the cell.

6. Perform 5S implementation in purchased-parts market, finished-goods warehouse, and each of the assembly/test cells.

The future-state map for San Simeon, shown in Figure 7-5, now reflects the following changes:

- Five identical cells that combine all assembly and test operations. This will be much easier to manage.
- A daily order list that schedules the cells to produce on a daily basis
- Less finished-goods inventory (3 days)
- Less purchased-parts inventory (2 days)
- No WIP

Table 7-4. San Simeon Current- vs. Future-State Chart

Metric	Current-State Value	Future-State Value	% Improvement
Value-creating time	360 minutes	280 minutes	22.2%
Estimated lead time through the plant	24 days	5 days	79.1%
% Value-creating time	1.04%	3.24%	212%
# Operators/shift	57	30	29.8%

Table 7-4 demonstrates the current-state to future-state improvement. A 79 percent reduction in lead time indicates a corresponding inventory reduction. If we were to put some of the above figures into dollar values, we would do the following:

- ***Calculate the savings from operator reduction.*** (Operators will not actually be released from the company; they will be used in another area of the organization.) The savings is calculated as follows:

  27 operators/shift × 2 shifts × $35,000/year cost = $1.89 million annual savings

- ***Calculate the savings from inventory reduction.*** EVS Corporation and San Simeon agreed to use a 25 percent holding cost for inventory. Based on the 75 percent reduction in inventory, the team calculated the savings as follows:

  75% × $4.5 million × 25% = $843,750 savings

Thus, the total savings from inventory reduction and process improvement will be $2.73 million annually, a significant bottom-line improvement.

The next step is to take the value-stream mapping activity and translate it into actual results, using the tools of process kaizen. In Chapter 8, you will learn about these tools.

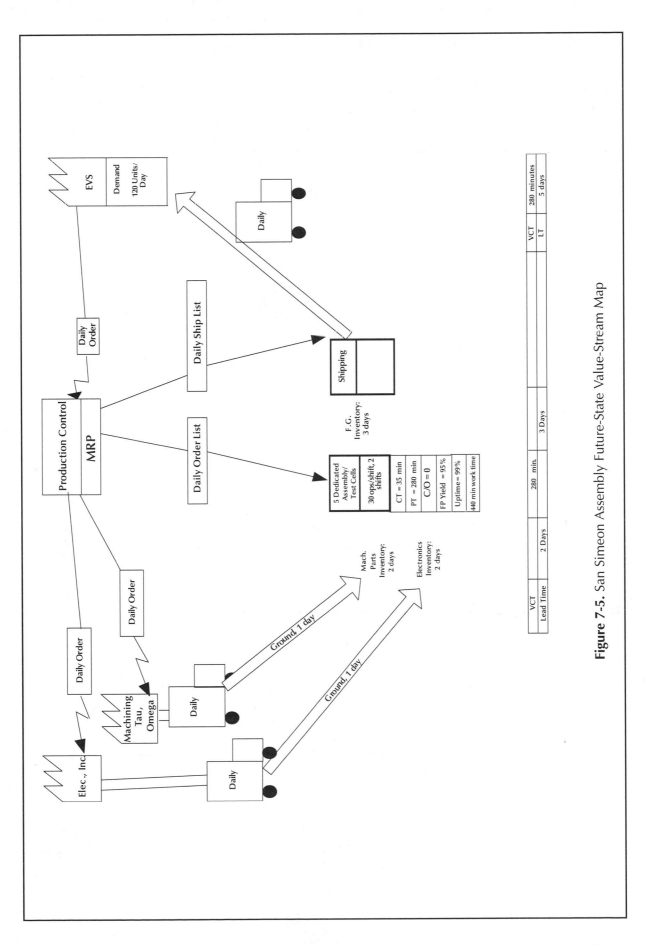

Figure 7-5. San Simeon Assembly Future-State Value-Stream Map

Summing Up: Key Points

Value-stream mapping is the primary tool for identifying, planning, and tracking key improvement projects that will contribute to overall value-stream improvement. Using a similar technique to that described in Chapters 2 and 3, a cross-functional team can create current-state and future-state value-stream maps to improve the internal value stream at a supplier site. This value stream would include door-to-door material and information flow.

Map the Current State of the Extended Value Stream, Encompassing Your Suppliers

Specifically, to create a current-state map, there are nine basic steps:

- **Step 1:** To create a current-state value-stream map, begin with the customer box, which should appear in the upper-right-hand side of the map.
- **Step 2:** Moving backwards along the material-flow portion of the value stream (in the bottom section of the map), map the shipping function.
- **Step 3:** Continuing backwards along the material-flow portion of the map, map the finished-goods inventory.
- **Step 4:** Map all internal areas of material flow.
- **Step 5:** Map supplier boxes.
- **Step 6:** Begin information-flow mapping across the top of the map from right to left. Beginning with the customer, identify the information flow first from the customer box to the facility.
- **Step 7:** Map information flow to suppliers.
- **Step 8:** Map the flow of information to the factory floor from production control.
- **Step 9:** Calculate estimated lead time, value-creating time, and percentage of value-creating time.

Map the Future State of the Extended Value Stream

After creating a *current*-state map, the team can create a future-state map by doing the following:

- Create areas of one-piece flow wherever possible.
- Determine how to manage upstream processes and the inventory throughout the system.
- Determine the one area in the process that will be scheduled and how to level product volume and mix in this area.
- Utilize a brainstorming process as described in Chapter 3 to identify process-improvement opportunities.

The team must then develop an implementation plan that captures all of the improvements of the future state; the plan will include process-improvement projects necessary to achieve the future state, which we'll describe in Chapter 8.

Applying This Information to Your Organization: Questions to Help You Get Started

1. Which of your suppliers would you choose to work with first for internal value-stream mapping? Why?

2. Who within your organization and that of your suppliers would you like to include in your first value-stream mapping activity?

Chapter 8

The Tools of Process Kaizen

Process Kaizen Eliminates Waste

We have shown in Chapter 7 that the purpose of internal value-stream mapping is to identify and plan opportunities for process kaizen. The purpose of process kaizen is to eliminate waste at the process level; unlike value-stream mapping, process kaizen tools are the tools of implementation. Process kaizen tools work to together to eliminate the 7 (+1) wastes of manufacturing, so let's begin with a review of these; then the rest of this chapter examines each key process kaizen tool and its usefulness.

Reviewing the 7 Wastes (Plus 1) of Manufacturing

Let's begin with a review of the seven wastes of manufacturing (described in detail in Chapter 1). Recall that Taiichi Ohno, the former Chief Engineer at Toyota who popularized the Toyota Production System, is credited with identifying the seven wastes of manufacturing. The following paragraphs describe the 7 wastes—plus one.

Waste 1: *Overproduction.* Overproduction is the chief waste; interestingly, it is a result or cause of each of the other wastes. Very simply, it means producing more than what is required. Overproduction is often done because of long changeover times between runs. People often think, "Why not just run this machine for another hour? We'll use the parts." If this is done often, the extra parts can end up creating a huge waste: excess inventory. Overproduction also covers up quality and equipment reliability problems.

Waste 2: *Transportation.* Moving a product around a factory does not create value for the product. Although some transportation is necessary, it must be minimized. Examples of minimizing transportation include implementing one-piece-flow manufacturing cells with effective material handling. When a one-piece-flow manufacturing cell is designed, the small space between processes and machines minimizes transportation within the cell, and properly designed material delivery routes to the cell minimize the transportation of material throughout the factory.

Waste 3: *Unnecessary inventory.* Although inventory can be used to help level production and respond to customers quickly, *too much inventory* results in significant costs such as scrap or rework due to obsolescence and engineering changes, extra floor space needed to store inventory, and dollars invested in inventory. One-piece flow and lean work to set reasonable levels of finished goods, raw materials, purchased parts, and internally produced parts inventories. Work-in-process (WIP) inventory, however, should be zero inside a true one-piece-flow cell.

Waste 4: *Inappropriate processing.* When this waste was first identified, it primarily referred to the use of large batch-and-queue equipment that could not be scaled to one-piece flow; however, this waste can refer to any inappropriate form of processing. Rework is one of the most common forms of inappropriate processing, particularly when it is built-in to a manufacturing process. Rework is often built-in to processes as a "finishing" or "QA" step.

The idea here is that the product should be manufactured correctly the first time. I once consulted with a factory that spent more labor time reworking the product than in the regular manufacturing process! The solution is to improve the manufacturing process so rework is not required. This is often referred to as "building quality in." It may be cliché by now, but building in quality is a critical part of implementing lean and one of the pillars of the Toyota Production System.

Waste 5: *Waiting.* The waste of waiting primarily refers to the misuse of people—the waste of time. For example, when operators are required to wait for a machine to cycle, this is the waste of waiting. You can eliminate this waste by creating enough automation on the machine that the operator can perform another task while a machine is cycling. Waiting can also refer to the imbalance of a production line or manufacturing cell such that the processes are not all running at takt time, resulting in processes (i.e., people and equipment) waiting for others to be completed.

Waste 6: *Excess motion.* One can observe excess motion in nearly any process involving people. The first place to look for excess motion is walking. Are operators walking to retrieve parts or tools? The second type of excess motion relates to ergonomics. Are people reaching, bending, or moving in such a way that may cause injury? The solution to excess motion is to bring all necessary items (i.e., tools, parts, etc.) for any process to their point of use.

Waste 7: *Defects.* Perhaps the most obvious of wastes, defects result in either scrapping or reworking a product. This clearly is waste and should be eliminated by improving processes. Many defects can be eliminated simply by standardizing processes and implementing standardized work.

Waste 8: *Underutilization of employees' minds and ideas.* As discussed in Chapter 1, under-use of employees' or customers' minds and ideas is the eighth waste. This waste is solved by implementation of lean manufacturing. Because lean involves people at all levels of an organization, people from the factory floor level up to the president are involved in generating continuous improvement ideas and implementing them. If lean is done properly, the eighth waste is eliminated.

Tool #1: Standardized Work

Standardizing every operation is one of the most important tools of lean. Although not usually considered a major tool in itself, having a standard work chart for every operation is absolutely critical to lean success. Even customized operations have common work elements that can be standardized. Most factories that are struggling with lean have a lack of standardization.

For example, in a manufacturing cell, each operator should have a standard work chart showing the following information:

- Operations he/she is to perform

- Takt time

- Standard times for each operation

- Graphical representation showing where each operation is to be performed

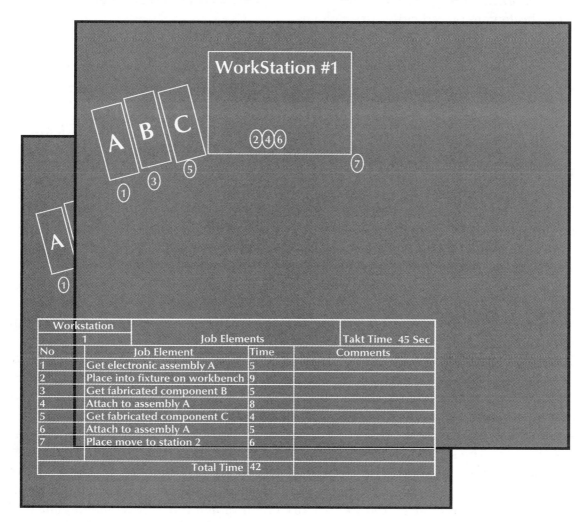

Workstation				Takt Time 45 Sec	
	1	Job Elements			
No	Job Element		Time	Comments	
1	Get electronic assembly A		5		
2	Place into fixture on workbench		9		
3	Get fabricated component B		5		
4	Attach to assembly A		8		
5	Get fabricated component C		4		
6	Attach to assembly A		5		
7	Place move to station 2		6		
		Total Time	42		

Figure 8-1. Sample Standard Work Chart

Ideally, a standard work chart should be one page. Figure 8-1 shows an example of a simple standard work chart.

Frequently, a plant manager's idea of a standard work chart is a binder full of rarely used work instructions. This is not standardized work! Standardized work charts should be used for delivery of material throughout a plant, manufacturing operations, and any other operation that can be standardized.

Standardized work charts ensure that anyone walking through a factory (or office) can tell whether or not standard work is being followed. If each employee at an organization performs an operation his/her own way, the organization *cannot* be lean. Lean success is dependent on standardization of operations, whether or not the product is standard.

Tool #2: The 5S System

Recall from Chapter 1 that the intent of 5S is to have only what is needed available in the workplace, a designated place for everything, a standard way of doing things, and the discipline to maintain it. Translated from Japanese into English the five Ss are as follows:

- *Sort.* Remove all items from the workplace that are NOT needed for current production.
- *Set in order.* Arrange needed items so that they are easy to find and put away. Items used often are placed closer to employee.
- *Shine.* Make sure everything is clean and functioning.
- *Standardize.* Using tools, maintain consistent application of the first 3S's.
- *Sustain.* Create a culture of properly maintaining correct 5S procedures and continuous improvement.

For the organization, 5S creates fewer defects, less waste, fewer delays, fewer injuries, and fewer breakdowns. These advantages translate to lower cost and higher quality.

For the operator, the 5S's create a superior working environment. They give the operator an opportunity to provide creative input regarding how the workplace should be organized and laid out and how standard work should be done. Operators will be able to consistently find things easily. The workplace will be cleaner and safer. Jobs will be simpler and more satisfying with many obstacles and frustrations removed.

Let's take a closer look at each of the 5 S's.

Sort. The first "S" requires you to distinguish between what is needed and what is not needed. Then, it requires you to discard what is not needed. This is known as *"red-tagging."* A team goes through all items (e.g., tools, equipment, material, etc.) and asks the question: "Do I need this to do my job on a regular basis?"

Items that are used rarely should be red-tagged; it is often the case that these are used for "tweaking" a nonconforming part or process. Handle these problems by finding the root cause and *solving* the problem, rather than fostering a "hidden factory" using quick-fixes such as these. After determining what is actually needed, update all documentation to reflect the needed parts.

Set in order. The second "S" requires you to organize things so that they are easy to use and label them so that anyone can find, use, and return them to the correct place easily. Visual controls should be used where practicable in this activity; a visual control is any communication device used in the work environment that tells you at a glance how work should be done. The basic requirements for setting in order usually include the following:

- Work areas should include simple, organized storage of tools and equipment with visual confirmation. (It should be obvious, at a glance, exactly where a tool belongs and if it is missing.)
- Tools and equipment used most frequently should be placed closest to the point of use.
- Workstations should have a place for each tool, with no toolboxes or drawers that interfere with visibility and require unnecessary motion to open and close.
- The floor should be taped or painted to indicate areas of operations, parts, walkways, discrepant material, and hazards.
- Standard work charts should be current and posted at the workstation.
- A signboard strategy should be in place:

- Signs indicate cell, product lines, and workstations.
- A white board indicates production goals versus actual results.
- Area information boards display key metrics (inventory, training, calibration, etc.).
- Ergonomic guidelines should be applied in the design of tools and workstations.

Shine. The third "S" involves bringing the workspace back to proper order by the end of each day. It requires the following tasks:

- Periodic (at least once daily) cleanup
- Identification of responsible person(s) for cleanup
- Establishment of cleanup/restocking methods (tools, checklists, etc.)
- Periodic supervisor inspection

The third "S" also includes any simple preventive maintenance on equipment and inspection of equipment for leaks, frayed wires, and other problems.

Standardize. The fourth "S" is the method by which an organization maintains the first three S's. Organization, orderliness, and cleanliness are maintained and made habitual by incorporating 3S duties into regular work routines. The methods need to be standardized using tools such as checklists and standard work charts for 3S activities.

Sustain. The fifth "S" allows the organization to sustain its 5S programs and create a culture of continuous improvement. This requires an executive 5S champion to ensure that 5S becomes part of the culture, regular audits with posted results, and 5S performance measurement of workgroups.

Implementation of this final S is where most companies fall back into their old ways of doing things. Frequently, 5S is thought of as an activity rather than an element of company culture; companies implement 5S for several months only to find themselves back in their previous state. To effectively sustain a 5S program, it is critical that performance be measured and that top management be visibly committed.

Tool #3: SMED/Quick Changeover

Quick changeover is an effective method for eliminating overproduction and excess inventory. The primary reason for overproduction is economies of scale. That is, when more of an item is produced, the "per-unit" cost is lower because the fixed cost of setup is spread over more parts. The concept behind quick changeover is to reduce the setup time in order to make shorter production runs feasible. As mentioned in Chapter 1, the Single-Minute Exchange of Die or SMED system, created by Dr. Shigeo Shingo, takes a three-step approach to reducing changeover time, described in the following sections.

Step 1: Separate Internal and External Setup

To do this, create a process map of each work element in the changeover process and categorize each step as external or internal:

- *External setup steps* are those that can be done outside of the machine (e.g., retrieving tools) or while the machine is running.
- *Internal setup steps* are those that require the machine to be shut down; they are generally steps that are done inside the machine itself.

Step 2: Convert Internal Setup to External Setup Wherever Possible

To convert from internal to external, revisit those steps categorized as internal and brainstorm methods for converting to external. For example, if a step such as heating a plastic injection mold is currently done inside the machine, is it possible to externalize this step by preheating the mold outside the machine prior to installation?

Step 3: Streamline All Aspects of the Setup Process

The most complicated of the three steps, streamlining requires the most creativity and analysis. First, streamline the internal setup process. This involves reviewing the internal setup process in detail and brainstorming methods for reducing the time of each work element (or eliminating work elements). Fortunately, in the book *A Revolution in Manufacturing: The SMED System,*[1] much work has been done by Shigeo Shingo and others that can be used in common manufacturing processes, especially injection molding and metal stamping.

After you have developed a plan for streamlining the internal process, work on streamlining the external process. Some streamlining of the external process can be done with 5S and layout improvements. Other types of streamlining might be a system for storing and retrieving fixtures, molds, and dies.

Quick changeover is one of the key process kaizen tools; the three-step SMED system can reduce a changeover from hours to minutes; this tool allows organizations to significantly reduce inventory.

Tool #4: Manufacturing Cells and One-Piece Flow

Since the mid-1990s, almost every factory I've visited has had or has claimed to have manufacturing cells in one form or another. I have seen everything from true continuous-flow cells to a bank of like machines brought together to form a "cell." In most cases, however, management would often admit that they haven't seen the kind of improvements they expected from implementing such cells. The next sections of this chapter examine the common types of cells:

- Functional cells
- Group technology or mixed-model cells
- Product-focused cells

We'll also explore how (and whether) they fit into a lean manufacturing environment.

Functional Cells

Functional cells are cells consisting of similar equipment. For example, a factory that does primarily machining operations might have a bank of lathes together in a "turning cell." Another example would be a cell consisting of several sets of similar test equipment. These cells are called "functional cells" because they perform a specific function (as opposed to manufacturing a complete product, assembly, etc.).

---

1. *A Revolution in Manufacturing: The SMED System.* Shigeo Shingo. Productivity Press, 1985.

Although there are exceptions, in most cases, functional cells do not fit into a lean manufacturing environment. In a factory consisting of functional cells, product often travels from cell to cell to have various operations done. Functional cells often create a haven for several types of *muda* (the Japanese term for "waste").

1. *Inventory.* WIP inventory almost always accumulates in front of the equipment and workstations in a functional cell.

2. *Transportation.* Product often moves from cell to cell throughout the factory.

3. *Waiting.* Product often waits long periods of time without being operated on.

4. *Overproduction.* Functional cells usually have large, expensive equipment. Emphasis is usually on keeping the machine running with little emphasis on quick changeover. This causes a tendency to overproduce for economies-of-scale's sake. The needs of the next downstream customer are rarely known or considered.

5. *Overprocessing.* Large, expensive equipment is often used in places where smaller equipment would be used in a one-piece flow cell.

6. *Defects.* Because operators are generally process focused and are usually not aware of the bigger picture (i.e., the completed product), quality suffers in a functional cell. Defects are often created and not detected until much later in the process.

Group Technology or Mixed-Model Cells

These are the least understood type of cells. Many people mistake group technology cells for functional cells when in fact they are most closely related to product-focused cells; this is perhaps the reason many now call group technology cells "mixed-model" cells, showing emphasis on the product.

Mixed-model cells are cells in which a series of operations for several products take place. The products are often similar, and the operations are very similar for each product (though not always identical). This type of cell *can* work well within a lean manufacturing environment, particularly if the organization is characterized by high-mix, low-volume products. In such organizations, it is rarely possible to have product-focused cells.

Product-Focused Cells

Cells that are product-focused typically run one type of product through a series of operations. These cells are most closely associated with lean manufacturing. Many people incorrectly assume that these are the only type of cells compatible with lean; however, they are ideal for low-mix, high-volume environments only.

Creating a One-Piece-Flow Manufacturing Cell

As noted, functional cells, which contain equipment that performs an identical process, are generally incompatible with lean manufacturing. On the other hand, group technology (or mixed-model) and product-focused cells work well for the lean producer. For a high-mix environment, group technology cells—which generally run product families through a series of similar operations—are more appropriate. For a high-volume, low-mix environment, product-focused cells are ideal. Whether you use product-focused or group technology cells, the most important factor is whether or not you create one-piece flow.

One-piece flow is an environment in which material moves from one value-creating step to the next, with no WIP inventory in between steps. It does not necessarily mean that products must move in batches of one; instead, small batches can be used where appropriate. Creating one-piece flow manufacturing cells includes analyzing and engineering the manufacturing steps, customer demand, equipment, labor, and physical layout. Most cells that have been set up in factories around the world do not have one-piece flow; most changes to cells have been layout changes only. That is, machines were moved in a cellular arrangement, and nothing more was changed. But a change in layout alone does not create one-piece flow.

Following are the key steps to creating a true one-piece-flow manufacturing cell.

Step 1: *Decide which products or product families will go into your cells.* Then determine the type of cell: product-focused or group technology (mixed model). Keep in mind:

- For product-focused cells to work correctly, demand needs to be high enough for an individual product.

- For mixed-model or group technology cells to work, changeover times from product to product must be kept short.

Step 2: *Calculate takt time for the cell.* Takt time, often mistaken for cycle time, is not dependent on your productivity—it is a measure of customer demand expressed in units of time. Recall the equation:

Takt time = Available work-time per shift / Customer demand per shift

Suppose the customer demands one unit every 40 seconds. What if your demand is unpredictable and relatively low volume? Typically, demand is unpredictable; however, aggregate demand (that is, demand of a group of products that would run through a cell) is much more predictable. Takt time should generally not be adjusted more than monthly. Furthermore, holding finished-goods inventory will help in handling fluctuating demand.

Step 3: *Determine the work elements and time required for making one piece.* In much detail, document all the actual work that goes into making one unit. Time each element separately several times, and use the lowest repeatable time. Do not include wasteful elements such as walking and waiting time.

Step 4: *Determine if your equipment can meet takt time.* Using a spreadsheet, determine if each piece of equipment that will be required for the cell you are setting up is capable of meeting takt time.

Step 5: *Create a lean layout.* More than likely, you will have more than one person working in your cell (this depends on takt time); however, you should arrange the cell such that one person can do it. This will ensure that the least possible space is consumed. Less space translates to less walking, movement of parts, and waste. U-shaped cells are generally best; however, if this is impossible due to factory floor limitations, other shapes will do. For example, I have implemented S-shaped cells in areas where a large U-shape is physically impossible.

When laying out a manufacturing cell, the designer must also consider the following:

- *Efficient material delivery to the cell at the point of use.* Material handlers should not interfere with production; if possible, materials should be delivered from the back side of the cell and placed at their points of use. Operators should not be walking outside the cell to retrieve parts.

- *Ergonomics.* Operators must be able to work comfortably and safely within a cell environment. Motions should be analyzed within a cell to ensure that operators are not likely to sustain injury due to things like stretching or repetitive motion.

• *Machine design.* Machines to be included in the cell should to be able to run one unit at a time to takt time. It is generally best to use machines that are small and less expensive rather than large, multitask equipment. There are, however, exceptions to this rule. For example, in industries where human handling causes problems (e.g., semiconductors), it makes sense to purchase large multitask equipment rather than less automated equipment.

Step 6: *Determine how many operators are needed to meet takt time.* Keep in mind the equation:

Number of operators = Total work content / Takt time
Example: Total work content: 49 minutes
           Takt time: 12 minutes
           Number of operators: 49 / 12 = 4.08 (4 operators)

If there is a remainder term, it may be necessary to kaizen the process and reduce the work content. Other possibilities include moving operations to the supplying process to balance the line. For example, one of our clients moved simple assembly operations from its assembly line to its injection-molding operation to reduce work content and balance the line.

Step 7: *Determine how the work will be divided among the operators.* There are several approaches:

• Splitting the work evenly between operators

• Having one operator perform all the elements in the direction of material flow

• Reversing the above

• Having one operator per station

• Using combinations of the above

Conclusion

After a team has worked through the above seven steps, it will have gathered much of the necessary data required to begin drawing and laying out a one-piece-flow manufacturing cell. The final steps involve testing and debugging the cell to ensure that it runs as designed. If a cell is being implemented during a kaizen event, the expectation should be that the cell should be running as designed with one month of the kaizen event completion.

Designing and implementing manufacturing cells at supplier sites involves significant creativity. Although the above seven steps will work for any manufacturing process, they cannot be applied without significant creativity from the team.

Tool #5: Total Productive Maintenance

Total Productive Maintenance (TPM) is used to increase machine uptime. By ensuring that equipment is properly maintained at all times, organizations can eliminate inventory and maintain consistency.

TPM is aimed at eliminating the so-called "six big losses":

1. Breakdown losses

2. Setup and adjustment losses

3. Idling and minor stoppage losses

4. Speed losses

5. Quality defects and rework

6. Startup/yield losses (reduced yield between machine startup and stable production)

Overall equipment effectiveness (OEE) is the key metric in determining how well equipment is performing with regard to the six big losses. OEE measures equipment effectiveness in terms of availability, performance, and product quality. Availability tells us what percentage of time the equipment is actually running when we need it.

OEE is calculated as follows:

$$Availability = \text{Operating time}/\text{Loading time} \times 100 \text{ percent}$$

where:

Operating time = Loading time − Downtime

Loading time: The daily or monthly time available for operation minus planned stops (e.g., breaks in the production schedule, stops for planned maintenance, meetings, etc.)

Downtime: Total time for unscheduled stops (e.g., breakdowns, retools, adjustments)

Performance is based on two factors:

1. *Operating speed rate*, which tells us how fast a machine is running compared to its designed/ideal speed.

2. *Net operating time*, which is the time during which equipment is being operated at a constant speed within a specified period.

Performance is calculated as follows:

$$Performance\ rate = \text{Net operating time} \times \text{Operating speed rate}$$

where:

Net operating time = (Units of output × actual cycle time per unit)/(Loading time − downtime) 100 percent

Operating speed rate = Ideal cycle time/Actual cycle time per unit × 100 percent

Quality rate is simply the rate of quality products or 100 percent − defect rate.

Finally, we calculate OEE:

$$OEE = \text{Availability} \times \text{Performance rate} \times \text{Quality rate}$$

After the above metrics are calculated for each piece of equipment, then equipment improvement project teams determine which losses have the greatest impact on equipment effectiveness and prioritize improvement efforts accordingly. Various types of improvement programs are described in the following sections.

TPM—Autonomous Maintenance Program

An autonomous maintenance program stabilizes equipment and halts accelerated deterioration. The program makes operators responsible for cleaning and inspection, lubrication, precision checks, and other light maintenance tasks. In carrying out these activities, operators learn more about their equipment and become better equipped to detect problems early. To implement such autonomous maintenance, operators are systematically trained in a step-by-step program.

TPM—Planned Maintenance System

Planned maintenance improvement is led by the maintenance department. The maintenance department will handle all of the planned maintenance tasks that are beyond the scope of the autonomous maintenance program. These are tasks that require special skills, significant disassembly, special measuring techniques and tools, etc. As equipment operators improve their skills, the maintenance group will perform fewer and fewer planned maintenance activities and will focus its efforts on improvements designed to reduce the maintenance required on equipment.

TPM—Maintenance Prevention Design and Early Equipment Management

Maintenance Prevention (MP) Design involves discovering weak points in currently used equipment and feeding back this information to equipment design engineers. Similar to design for manufacturability, MP Design takes the following factors into consideration:

1. Ease of autonomous maintenance (operator maintenance)
2. Ease of operation
3. Improving quality
4. Improving maintainability
5. Safety

MP Design can be applied to develop criteria for selecting "off-the-shelf" equipment as well.

Early Equipment Management is a system for dealing with problems that surface during test running, commissioning, and startup of new equipment. During this period, production and maintenance engineering people must correct problems caused by poor selection of materials at the design stage, errors occurring during fabrication of the equipment, or installation errors. In an ideal world, Early Equipment Management should not be very complicated (particularly if MP Design is properly applied at the design stage.)

All of the elements of TPM are significant parts of a foundation for lean manufacturing. Most importantly, they work together to increase OEE. Without sufficiently high OEE, lean success becomes much more difficult to achieve.

Tool #6: Six Sigma and Statistical Methods

The success of GE, Motorola, and others has prompted many an executive to declare that he or she wants "Six Sigma." Some companies view Six Sigma as their prevailing, culture-changing program and add lean tools to their Six-Sigma toolboxes. Others have lean as their program of emphasis with Six-Sigma tools as complementary. In the context of this book, we are assuming lean is the key program and Six-Sigma tools will be used where appropriate. It is not necessary to create a separate Six-Sigma program; however, it is necessary to use many of the tools of Six Sigma to achieve process improvements. Let's examine Six Sigma and its tools.

Six Sigma is concerned with reducing process variability. The goal of Six Sigma is a Six-Sigma level of quality, which is 3.4 defects per million opportunities. To accomplish this, projects are identified and prioritized based on their cost-savings potential. Then project teams attack the problems using the DMAIC method: Define, Measure, Analyze, Improve, and Control. Chapter 9 covers each phase and some tools that work well. Chapter 9 also describes problem-solving teams because these tools do not lend themselves to kaizen events very well.

Summing Up: Key Points

Implementing the future state involves process-improvement tools. Here's a recap of the tools described in this chapter:

- *Standardized work.* Standardized work should be applied to every repeatable process in manufacturing and logistics, including assembly processes, other production processes, material delivery, and inventory management. Lean success depends on standardization of operations, whether or not the product is standard.

- *5S.* The 5S system organizes and standardizes the workplace. 5S is often used as an initial step to lean implementation on the shopfloor; it is one of the most effective ways of involving employees at all levels early in the lean implementation process. The five Ss are Sort, Set in order, Shine, Standardize, and Sustain.

- *One-piece flow/Cellular manufacturing.* One-piece flow is a manufacturing method by which one piece or a small batch of product moves from operation to operation with no WIP in between steps. It is usually employed within manufacturing cells.

- *Total Productive Maintenance (TPM).* TPM is a system for improving OEE (Overall Equipment Effectiveness), a measure of equipment uptime. TPM involves operators, engineers, and maintenance personnel working together in a team environment to ensure consistent maintenance and to eliminate the so-called "six big losses."

- *Quick Changeover/ SMED.* Developed by Shigeo Shingo, the SMED system (Single-Minute Exchange of Die) is a three-step method for reducing changeover time that allows manufacturers to run smaller batch sizes.

- *Six Sigma and statistical methods.* To achieve a reduction in process variance, it is sometimes necessary to use many of the tools of Six Sigma.

Any of the above tools (other than Six-Sigma methods) can be used within the context of a kaizen event, which is a 3- to 5-day breakthrough event that includes a cross-functional team working with an in-house or outside facilitator. Within a short period, the team sets and achieves a specific goal by employing the tools of process kaizen.

Applying This Information to Your Organization: Questions to Help You Get Started

1. Based on your knowledge of some of your key suppliers, which would benefit most from implementing 5S?

2. Which suppliers have processes with long changeover times? If you were to help them reduce their changeover times, what benefits would you and your supplier derive?

3. Which of your suppliers have processes that are dedicated to your organization's products? Can one-piece-flow manufacturing cells be implemented?

Chapter 9

Facilitating Kaizen Events for Suppliers and Customers

Benefits of Kaizen Events

Now that you have a clear understanding of the tools of process kaizen (covered in Chapter 8), let's take a look at how to conduct kaizen events, which are one of the most effective ways to make rapid improvements at supplier and customer sites. A kaizen event is typically a 3- to 5-day breakthrough event that includes a cross-functional team working with an in-house or outside facilitator. Kaizen events are appropriate for new implementations as well as continuous improvement. They are used for implementing several lean tools, including:

- 5S Workplace Organization
- Visual Controls
- Mistake Proof (Poka-yoke)
- SMED (Single Minute Exchange of Die)
- TPM (Total Productive Maintenance)
- One-Piece Flow Cells/Layout
- Material Delivery/Routing

The kaizen event process generally includes the following nine elements:

1. Management kick-off.
2. Educate. Train the team in lean with emphasis on the particular tool being used.

3. Set goals.

4. Map out the current condition.

5. Brainstorm ideas.

6. Develop the future state.

7. Develop a plan to implement the future state.

8. Implement as much as possible during the event.

9. Report out and celebrate.

Each of these elements will be discussed in more detail in this chapter.

When planned properly, kaizen events produce a high return on investment (ROI); rapid, breakthrough improvements can be implemented in a short time period. Kaizen events typically eliminate the following problems:

• Bottlenecks

• Overtime

• Need to purchase capital equipment

• Need to build new facilities or expand facilities

Intangible benefits include:

• *Increase in human capital.* Participants will enhance their lean knowledge and team skills, which can be leveraged to continuously improve their work environments after the event is over.

• *Improved employee morale.* Kaizen event participants typically spread the excitement they experienced during the event.

• *More employee involvement.* Kaizen events are one of the best ways to involve employees at all levels in a lean program.

• *Improved communication.* Kaizen events are often eye-opening experiences for participants.

Finally, kaizen is flexible. It can be done anywhere on almost any process; it is not limited to the shopfloor. Because of their broad application, kaizen events are effective for improving supplier and customer processes while simultaneously teaching them lean methods.

Planning a Kaizen Event

Planning a kaizen event includes the following steps:

Step 1: Selecting the area

Step 2: Selecting team members

Step 3: Selecting the team leader and facilitator

Step 4: Preparing the area

Step 5: Obtaining the necessary background information

Step 6: Determining the event timetable

Let's look at each in detail.

Planning Step 1: Selecting the Area

When selecting the first area for a kaizen event at a supplier site, consider the following guidelines.

Use value-stream mapping. As discussed in Chapter 7, value-stream mapping is the primary tool for identifying improvements. Kaizen events are used to implement many of the improvements found on a future-state value-stream plan.

Select a highly visible, big impact area. It is often best to select a big impact area particularly for a first kaizen event. This will help build momentum for future improvements by persuading people at the supplier site of the power of kaizen and lean.

Select an area that is guaranteed to succeed. It is critically important that the first kaizen event succeed, especially if you are facilitating the event for a supplier. Failure will be a major roadblock to further implementation. If it succeeds, it will provide the necessary momentum for the supplier to continue the lean journey.

Do not select a politically charged issue. Politically charged issues usually result in gridlock, just as they so often do in national politics. Politically charged issues cannot be worked out in a one-week period.

Select an area with a lot of WIP (work-in-process) inventory. If significant inventory must be reduced, this will have a big impact on cash flow. Therefore, an area with a lot of "low hanging fruit" would be an ideal place to begin kaizen.

Planning Step 2: Selecting Team Members

The kaizen team makeup is one of the most important success factors in a kaizen event. Work closely with your supplier in selecting team members for an event. Consider the following guidelines:

- *Fifty percent or more of the team members should be from* **outside** *the area being improved.* People from outside the area have a different paradigm: they are often able to see things that people who work inside the area are unable to see.

- *Select seven to ten people for the team.* Generally, it is best to avoid a large kaizen team. It is best to limit the scope of the project and select a small team than to have too large a scope and a correspondingly large team.

- *Select at least two operators from the area.* It is important to include two or more people from the area for two reasons:
    - First, they have knowledge that comes from working in the area.
    - Second, it is important to have ownership in the proposed improvements from at least two people in the area. Without ownership in the improvements, it will be difficult to maintain what has been implemented in the event.

- *Consider suppliers for team members.* Suppliers often give a fresh perspective to a problem that insiders simply cannot see.

- *Consider people from your organization with lean expertise* (in addition to the facilitator).

Planning Step 3: Selecting the Team Leader and Facilitator

The team leader will be responsible for organizing the event and providing leadership to the team members. The team leader should be one of the supplier's key people, someone who has lean manufacturing and leadership experience.

The traits of a successful team leader include:

- *Previous success in leadership.* Particularly for the first event, strong leadership skills will be needed to keep the team on track.

- *At least a basic understanding of lean manufacturing and its tools.* The team leader does not need to be a lean "guru," but he or she does need to understand all of the tools.

- *Familiarity with the processes of the event area*

- *High level of comfort with the factory floor.* Kaizen events are hands-on activities; a team leader must be comfortable getting his or her hands dirty.

- *Potential to become a kaizen event facilitator*

The facilitator will be responsible for conducting the training and facilitating implementation during the event. Someone with extensive experience outside the organization should facilitate the first few events. The facilitator may be either an outside consultant or an in-house expert from a customer or supplier, but it is important to choose someone who has facilitated successful kaizen events at other organizations.

Always keep in mind when selecting team members that kaizen events should be used to train future facilitators and team leaders.

Planning Step 4: Preparing the Area

Although it depends on the details of the event itself, supplies needed during a kaizen event typically include:

- Hand tools

- Tape

- Tape measures

- Utility quick-change hookups

- Flip charts, markers, white board

- Stopwatches

- Conference room/Breakout room

- Cleaning supplies

Planning Step 5: Obtaining Necessary Background Information

The team leader is responsible for obtaining all of the following materials, which should be made available to the team members on the first day of the event:

- *Work instructions and/or standardized work charts.* All documentation for each area process should be at the fingertips of the team members. This avoids having to search for information during the event.

- *Customer requirements.* Required for calculating takt time accurately, this is usually in the form of a forecast rather than hard orders.

- *Current facility and area layouts.*

- *Flowcharts/process maps for area processes.* If available, any process maps or flowcharts are very useful to the team. However, the team will still need to validate the information during the event.

• **Product/operation matrix.** This matrix will show all of the products in the area and each process with which they interact. This is often done prior to value-stream mapping to identify value streams. It becomes useful again during kaizen events.

Planning Step 6: Determining the Event Timetable

The event will generally follow the timetable shown in Figure 9-1; however, depending on the experience level of the participants and the subject matter, the timing may change. Many times, kaizen activities are spread out over a longer period of time. This actually makes achieving success more difficult; it requires the discipline to ensure that activities are done in between meetings. Kaizen events are more effective when they are done over a period of consecutive days.

For less complex implementations and with experienced team members who have already been trained, three-day kaizen events can be done instead by eliminating the training and doing most of the current-state analysis prior to the event.

Activity	When
Management Kickoff and Introduction	Day 1
Training in Lean with Emphasis on Relevant Tool(s)	Days 1–2
Teambuilding Exercise	Day 2
Map Current Condition	Day 2
Brainstorming	Day 3
Develop Future Condition	Day 3
Implementation	Days 3–5
Develop Follow-up Action Plan	Day 5
Team Report-out to Management	Day 5

Figure 9-1. Suggested Kaizen Event Timetable

Conducting a Kaizen Event

As mentioned at the beginning of this chapter, ten elements comprise a kaizen event. The next sections describe each of these in detail.

Element 1: Management Kickoff/Introductions

The event should begin with a top manager or executive speaking to the participants. He or she should discuss the importance of the event to the organization, the value of the people involved, and the goals of the event. Each participant should then introduce him or herself and talk about his or her lean and kaizen experience. Alternatively, any "icebreaker" activity can be used to get participants talking and involved.

Element 2: Training

Training should be broken into three parts.

Training in lean basics. First, the team needs to be trained in the basics of lean. Depending on the team members' experience, this can be a refresher course or can be more detailed, but it should cover the following topics:

- 7 wastes
- Takt time calculation
- Process mapping
- Basics of one-piece flow
- Standard work charts
- Basics of value-stream maps
- 5S principles

Training in the particular tool of emphasis. Second, the team needs to be trained in more detail in the tool of emphasis, such as:

- 5S
- One-piece-flow cells
- Quick changeover/SMED
- Kanban
- Poka-yoke
- Visual controls
- Total Productive Maintenance (TPM)

Training in teambuilding. Finally, the team needs to be trained in teambuilding. We have found that even a small amount of teambuilding training results in more productive kaizen events, particularly for a team that has not worked together before. This training should encompass the following activities:

- Train on the subject of teams, including advantages and disadvantages and why teams are useful for lean manufacturing success.
- Break the kaizen team into subgroups and give them a consensus-building exercise or other team exercise. One simple exercise that has been useful to me is to have each person individually rank the top five problems and issues. Then, have the subteams reach consensus on the top five problems. This helps identify the key problems before even moving into the current-state mapping or analysis stage.

Always make the training session interactive: questions and exercises will help the team to begin thinking lean.

Element 3: Documenting the Current Condition

Before actually documenting the current condition, the team should review the goals of the event. This will refresh team members' minds and get them focused on the goal. Then, provide and review the background information collected during the kaizen preparation with the team (see Planning Step 5).

In most cases, the first step in documenting the current condition is to calculate takt time, which is the available working time divided by customer demand. After each person understands the takt time, each process must be mapped in detail. This depends on the type of kaizen event being conducted. The following sections describe some examples of the activities involved in documenting the current condition for different types of kaizen events.

Example: *One-piece-flow cell layout kaizen.* Some steps to be included in current-state mapping are:

1. Break work into work elements.

2. Collect times for each work element.

3. Map process and use a spaghetti diagram to show current work flow.

4. Calculate distance traveled.

Example: *5S kaizen event.* Some steps to be included in current-state mapping are:

1. Map every process done in an area—even if it is a support process within the area (e.g., paperwork procedure, cleaning procedure, etc.). Getting exact times for a 5S activity is not critical.

2. Draw a 5S map showing the process flow for each process.

Note: For 5S, it sometimes works better to go through the "Sort" activity prior to mapping current condition.

Example: *SMED/Quick-changeover kaizen event.* Some steps to be included in current-state mapping are:

1. Videotape the changeover process.

2. Document times for each individual step.

3. Classify each step as internal or external.

Element 4: Other Current Condition Data

The team may also want to collect other current condition data, such as the following:

- Current staffing
- Changeover frequency
- Floor space usage
- Scrap rate
- Support personnel
- Bottlenecks
- Observed WIP inventory

Element 5: Brainstorming

The purpose of brainstorming is to gather as many improvement ideas as possible. Before actually facilitating a brainstorming session, establish some ground rules and review the goals of the event. The most important ground rule to communicate is that ideas should not be evaluated until the brainstorming session is complete: evaluating ideas during brainstorming inevitably prevents some people from giving all of their ideas.

There are several techniques for brainstorming. As mentioned in the discussion of brainstorming for value-stream mapping (in Chapter 3), we have found that the most effective technique for eliciting the most ideas is the "sticky note" method. Each participant is given several sticky notes. There is a set period of time (usually 30 minutes) in which the participants are to write down as many ideas as they can (one per sticky note) to improve the current condition and meet the goals of the event. Participants should place sticky notes on a board in front of the room.

When the session is complete, each idea is given a sequential unique number and is ranked high, medium, or low (indicating level of difficulty in implementation):

- **High (H):** This idea will be difficult to implement. Save the idea for a longer-term project. It will not be part of the follow-up action plan.

- **Medium (M):** The idea can be implemented in a short time with some validation and analysis, but not during the event. It will be part of the follow-up action plan.

- **Low (L):** This idea will be easy to implement. The idea will be implemented during the event.

Some ideas may be alternatives to ideas classified as H, M, and L; such ideas should be noted as such. Of course, there may be other ideas that will be rejected during the evaluation phase; these should not be classified. Each idea to be implemented should have a person or subteam responsible for implementing. Also, each idea should be categorized if appropriate. By the end of the evaluation phase, the ideas should be in the form of an action plan. See Figure 9-2 for a template you can use to create your action plans.

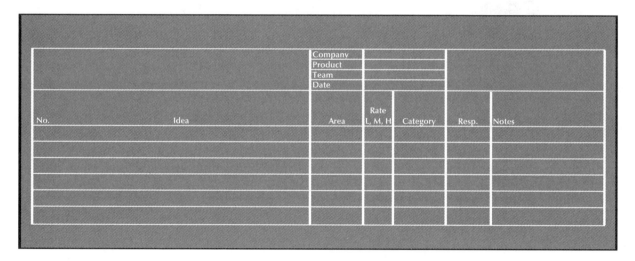

Figure 9-2. Sample Action Plan Template

Element 6: Developing the Future State

The action plan forms the basis of the future state. Additional activities during the development of the future state include:

- *Developing new standard work charts/documentation/checklists.* It is important that standard work charts are developed during the event itself and are updated quickly as changes are made during the first month after the event.

- *Developing new process maps.* New process maps showing the improvement over the old process should be developed during the event. They will aid in implementation.

- *Developing new layouts using "paper doll" layouts.* This simply involves cutting out equipment footprints from a current paper layout (that is, to scale) and moving them to new locations on a paper layout from which the equipment has been removed. This approach remains one of the simplest yet most effective methods for developing a new layout.

- *Identifying/purchasing any additional supplies (if necessary)*. In almost any kaizen event, there will be items that have too long of a lead time to purchase and implement during the event; in such cases, a list of additional supplies to purchase should be generated.

Element 7: Implementation

A kaizen event will not be effective without a strong implementation effort. The goal is to implement as much as possible during the event. Other implementation keys include:

- Providing maintenance with new layout to make moves overnight if possible
- Documenting changes to the future-state plan and standard work charts as they are made
- Training all operators in new processes

Implementation is specific to the kaizen event topic:

- Using the example of a 5S Kaizen event, implementation includes *sort*, *set-in-order*, *shine*, *standardize*, and *sustain*, with many of the "standardize" and "sustain" tasks being implemented after the event.

- For a SMED kaizen, implementation often includes the adoption of standard work charts for the new changeover process, modification of tooling and equipment, and training setup operators.

Element 8: Action Plan

The action plan needs to be updated on day five; the team should identify incomplete tasks, who is responsible for completion, and completion date. After an event is complete, the team should meet at least weekly to ensure that the action plan is being driven to completion. This is a final key to successful implementation. The team needs to understand that its job is not complete until all of the follow-up items have been completed.

Without effective follow-up, a kaizen event cannot truly be viewed as a success. In supplier kaizen events, it is critical that the customer driving the lean implementation supports its supplier in completing the follow-up plan.

Element 9: Report Out and Celebrate

The facilitator then should work with the team to develop the final report-out. This report-out *should not* consist of simply a PowerPoint presentation. The main part of the report-out should be presented on the shopfloor (or area in which the kaizen was conducted). Several (if not all) team members should be presenters. At least one person from top management should be in the audience of the report-out. A question-and-answer session should complete the report-out. After the report-out, the team should have a lunch celebration to celebrate what it has accomplished during the week.

Now that we've walked you through the nine elements of a kaizen event process, let's see how EVS implemented it at one of its suppliers.

Case Study:
How a Kaizen Event Was Implemented at the San Simeon Assembly Plant

Let's walk through an example of kaizen event planning and implementation. One of the improvement activities identified in the San Simeon Assembly future-state value-stream map (done in Chapter 7) is to create a one-piece-flow cell that incorporates all subassembly, final assembly, and test operations previously done in separate areas. EVS Corporation and San Simeon decided that this would be the best kaizen event to implement first; it is the key part of the future-state value-stream map, and it will have a huge impact in terms of lead time and inventory reduction. EVS and San Simeon will work together to plan and conduct a kaizen event to accomplish this major task.

Preparing for the Event

Selecting the team. EVS and San Simeon put together a small team consisting of the following personnel:

- EVS Lean Coordinator (facilitator)
- San Simeon Industrial Engineer (team leader)
- Three Operators: one from subassembly, one from final assembly, and one from test
- San Simeon Test and Assembly Supervisor
- Operator from another manufacturing process
- Maintenance Manager
- EVS Industrial Engineer

Gathering data. The team leader gathered the following data prior to the event's start:
- Work instructions for subassembly, assembly, and test processes
- Current detailed layout of each area
- EVS demand requirements/forecast
- Product/operation matrix showing each product and which processes they go through

Gathering supplies. The team leader also gathered the following supplies prior to the event:
- Three stopwatches, for team members to use for timing work elements
- Colored tape, for taping the floor
- Various tools and cleaning supplies
- Flip charts and markers
- Sticky notes, for brainstorming session

Conducting the Kaizen Event

The event was to begin Monday morning at 8:00 AM. The team leader introduced the President of San Simeon to kick off the meeting. The President welcomed everyone to the event. He then talked briefly about the relationship between EVS Corporation and San Simeon, emphasizing the importance of lean and kaizen. He then explained how important this team was to the success and survival of the organization and the future success of the implementation of lean. Finally, he discussed some of the key goals of the event, specifically the creation of a cell that would eliminate several days of WIP inventory.

EVS Corporation's lean coordinator then began by asking each participant to introduce him or herself and talk about their role in the company and experience with lean. The lean coordinator than introduced herself and began the training session.

Training for Kaizen

The training included the following elements:

1. Introductory lean training (2 hours)
   - Lean overview/Toyota Production System
   - 7 wastes
   - Takt time
   - 5S principles
   - Value-stream mapping
2. Creating one-piece-flow cells
   - One-piece-flow introduction
   - Selecting products/product families for cells
   - Timing and analyzing work elements
   - Line-balancing
   - Cell design
   - Scheduling
   - Material delivery
3. Teambuilding training
   - Strengths and weaknesses of teams
   - Why teams are important for lean manufacturing success

Identifying Problem Areas

After the training portion of the program was complete, the facilitator broke the team up into three subteams. She then asked each individual to rank the top five problems in the area on a piece of paper. After 10 minutes, she asked the subteams to work together to rank the top five problem areas as a team. After 15 minutes, she asked each subteam to present its version of the top five problems and how the team achieved this (democratically, by consensus, etc.). Finally, as a complete team, the group ranked each key problem. This exercise not only gave the teams an opportunity to work together on decision-making, but it gave the team a working list of the top problems in the area; this list would be used later during current-state analysis.

The top five problems identified by the team were:

1. *Inconsistency.* Operations are done differently by different people.
2. *Poor communication.* There is a lack of communication between manufacturing areas (subassembly and assembly) and between production planning and manufacturing areas.
3. *Material delivery issues.* Frequently, operators get their own parts for assembly, resulting in lower productivity.
4. *Expediting.* Too many orders are expedited through the area.
5. *Tools.* Operators often waste time looking for tools.

(Continued on next page)

(Continued from previous page)

Analyzing the Current State

The next step in the process was analysis of the current state. Using the same three sub-teams as in the team exercise, they focused on breaking work into work elements, collecting times for each work element, and drawing spaghetti diagrams for each work flow. The three teams focused on subassembly processes, final assembly processes, and test processes. After the subteams completed this task, each subteam posted the information in the conference room and presented its findings to the entire group. This completed the current-state analysis.

Brainstorming

Next, the facilitator gave each team member several sticky notes and asked everyone to write down one improvement idea per sticky note and place the sticky notes on a board in front of the room. During this 30-minute brainstorming exercise, team members were permitted to visit the plant floor and observe operations, review the current-state data, and look at other ideas posted. Team members were not allowed to critique any ideas until later. At the end of the process, the facilitator read each idea aloud; the team then discussed and evaluated each idea. Each idea was categorized into three categories:

- Cell design
- Material handling
- Fixtures/special equipment/maintenance

Also, each idea that was accepted was rated as High (H), Medium (M), or Low (L) indicating level of difficulty in implementation, as illustrated earlier in the chapter. After each idea was thoroughly discussed, categorized, and ranked, the subteams were then assigned to one of the three categories:

1. The cell-design team's job was to design and implement the cell and create standard work charts.
2. The material-handling team was to design a system for delivering material to the cell and design standard work charts.
3. The fixtures/special equipment/maintenance team's job was to design and/or purchase any necessary fixtures, supplies, or equipment.

Developing the Future State

On Wednesday, each team completed the future-state development task, which produced the following:

- Layout including cells and material delivery points
- Standard work charts for each operator in the cell and for material delivery to the cell
- Fixtures designed and supplies on-hand

Overnight Wednesday, the maintenance group made the equipment moves per the layout. By midday Thursday, the teams were testing their implementation on the factory floor. Each standard work chart was being tested and retimed. The cell was able to run at about 80 percent of plan by day-end Thursday, a significant accomplishment. The team then put together a follow-up plan, which included all activities that needed to be completed over the next 30 to 60 days.

Reporting on the Process and Following Up

The final step was the report-out. On Friday morning, the team put together a 30-minute presentation that included both a factory-floor demonstration as well as a slide show. Each team member had a role in the presentation, and the audience consisted of the President of San Simeon Assembly, EVS Corporation's Vice President of Operations, and various management and front-line personnel from San Simeon Assembly. After the presentation was complete and all questions answered during a brief Q & A Session, the lunch celebration began.

Following the event, the team met twice weekly for eight weeks until all action items were completed from the follow-up list.

Other (Non-Kaizen) Improvement Implementation Techniques

The first half of this chapter described how to conduct kaizen events; in addition, there are some types of improvements that would be better implemented using methods other than a kaizen event. In this section, we will cover two different methods: problem-solving or continuous-improvement team implementation and individual implementation.

Method 1: Problem-Solving/Continuous-Improvement Teams and the DMAIC System

Some improvements that would be identified in a value-stream-mapping activity do not lend themselves well to a kaizen event. Two key examples are (1) process improvements (such as "Six-Sigma" type analysis) aimed at yield improvement and (2) variation/scrap reduction. For example, a value-stream-mapping activity might reveal that a particular process has a first-pass yield of only 85 percent when it would need to be much closer to 100 percent to run in a one-piece-flow environment. If the process must be analyzed using experiments and statistical methods, it would make sense to utilize a team but not a kaizen event. To implement these types of improvements, a team that meets regularly over a period of time works better than a kaizen team meeting for five consecutive days.

Some improvements should be assigned to an individual rather than a team. When should a team be used rather than just an individual? An effective team can accomplish more together than all the individuals can separately; if the project requires significant input from a group and requires buy-in from several people, it might be best to use a team. If one person can do a project effectively (although he or she might need to get input from others), a team is unnecessary and will result in wasted time.

Team make-up would be similar to that of a kaizen team. If the problem is in a particular manufacturing area, include two or more operators from that area. At least 50 percent of the team should consist of people from outside the area. In fact, many times a kaizen team itself will act as a problem-solving team, having shorter weekly meetings spread out over several weeks or months.

The team leader should have the same characteristics as a kaizen team leader; most importantly, he or she should have leadership skills and experience. The team leader's role is to guide team activities, work with team members to resolve conflict and make decisions, and provide technical guidance and training. If the company has a formal Six-Sigma program, the team leader would be a "Black Belt."

Getting any group of people to meet on a consistent basis is one of the biggest challenges for teams. It is important for teams to meet regularly (usually weekly), and it is important that meetings begin on time with all members present. One of the best ways to ensure that people will attend meetings is to include each member's performance on teams in his or her overall performance review. This would involve the team leader's providing input to the individual's manager.

Another way to provide an incentive to team members to attend meetings is to hold *brief* meetings; meetings should not be longer than one hour. In fact, if the team leader is well prepared with an agenda for each meeting and if he or she is a good facilitator, meetings should average only 30 to 45 minutes. The reason meetings often run over their allotted time is because too much time is spent debating one particular issue; in this situation the team leader must show his or her leadership and facilitation skills.

To be successful, a problem-solving team must have a *systematic method* for solving problems. Too many teams simply meet and talk without a systematic approach; this lack of structure often results in projects that go one far too long, many times without ever reaching or implementing a solution.

One of the most effective systems problem-solving teams can use is the DMAIC (Define, Measure, Analyze, Improve, Control) system of Six Sigma. If the team uses an approach like this, it will be much more likely to succeed. It is not necessary for a certified "Black Belt" to lead a team with this approach; the DMAIC method can be used by anyone with strong technical and leadership skills.

The next sections examine the DMAIC method in greater detail.

Phase 1: *Define.* In this step, the problem is defined by identifying the "critical-to-quality" characteristics (CTQs), defined by the customer and identifying the key factors affecting the CTQs.

Phase 2: *Measure.* The measure phase consists of two major steps:

Step 1: Identifying the internal processes that influence the CTQ measurements

Step 2: Conducting a measurement systems analysis, which includes gauge studies and a thorough process-capability study

Phase 3: *Analyze.* In the analysis phase, the project team determines which inputs affect the outputs. This is done using the following three steps:

Step 1: Develop and state a hypothesis about the cause or causes

Step 2: Test the hypothesis through data analysis

Step 3: If your hypothesis is correct, add your cause to a list of significant causes affecting the process

Phase 4: *Improve.* This phase involves quantifying the effects of the key variables on the process and developing an improvement plan that modifies the key factors to achieve the desired process improvement.

Phase 5: *Control.* In the control phase, you put in place a system to maintain the changes and improvements you developed in the improve phase. This phase involves documenting and monitoring processes.

Team Process-Improvement Tools

Teams can use several statistical methods as well as qualitative tools for process improvement using DMAIC. The following sections explain some of the key tools in brief. These tools and many others can be used within a problem-solving or continuous-improvement team. Any comprehensive statistics textbook will describe all of the tools in much more detail. Brainstorming techniques (described in Chapter 3) can be effectively used by such a team as well.

Process mapping/Flowcharting. One of the first steps to process improvement is to map out the process that needs to be improved; this will help give the team a common understanding of the details of the baseline process. Process mapping (or flowcharting) is one simple way to accomplish this. It involves creating a diagram in which each box represents a process step; process boxes typically include such data as:

- Time to complete the process

- Inputs and outputs of a process

- Function(s) of the person(s) involved in the process

- Department

- Any other relevant data

Other icons used in a process map are decision points and an end point. Several standard software programs such as Microsoft Visio™ have templates for mapping. Process mapping works equally well for manufacturing and administrative processes.

Basic statistics. Basic statistics tell the analyst the central tendency and the dispersion of a set of data. For any given set of process data, the following are basic statistics:

- *Mean:* Sometimes called the average or arithmetic mean, the mean is the sum of a series of values divided by the number of values.

- *Median:* The midpoint in a series of data points.

- *Mode:* The value that occurs most often in a set of values.

- *Range:* The range measures a spread of data points. It is equal to the largest value in a set of data minus the smallest value.

- *Variance:* The variance is the average squared deviation of each number in a data set from the mean.

- *Standard deviation:* The most common measure of spread, the standard deviation is the average distance from the mean. It is equal to the square root of the variance.

- *Correlation:* The correlation is the degree to which two variables are related, measured in terms of correlation coefficient.

Basic graphical analysis. This includes the following types of graph:

- *Histogram:* The histogram is a vertical bar graph representing the distribution of a given data set. It is also known as a frequency distribution bar graph. It graphically depicts the central tendency and the variation.

- *Scatter plot:* The scatter plot is a graph in which individual data points are plotted in two dimensions. Scatter plots graphically show correlation.

Cause-and-effect diagram (fishbone diagram). The cause-and-effect diagram or fishbone diagram is a graphic tool for identifying the relationship between a problem and its potential causes. One of the most effective ways of constructing such a diagram is to brainstorm potential causes in a team environment. For example, a cause-and-effect diagram might be used to determine possible causes of a recurring defect in a manufacturing process.

XY matrix. The X-Y matrix is used to link customer requirements to process inputs. It is simply a group of rows and columns, with one set of increments marked along the X-axis and another set of increments marked along the Y-axis. Typically, along the Y-axis, customer requirements would be listed. Along the X-axis, design or process inputs would be listed. Inside the matrix, marks indicating the relationship between the two as strong, medium, small, or nonexistent would be inserted. The X-Y matrix is sometimes called the "House of Quality."

Gauge R&R (repeatability and reproducibility). A gauge R&R ensures that you're measuring what you think you're measuring. It looks at the units of measure and number of variables, calibrates the measurement gauge, and then randomly selects samples to measure against different operators. Gauge R&R should be used to ensure that measuring methods in place are actually working effectively.

Pareto chart. A pareto chart is one of the most commonly used tools for identifying the key factors in a process that have the greatest effect. It graphically depicts the relative importance of causes, defects, and other aspects of a process. For example, a pareto chart may be used for:

- Identifying the defects that recur most often

- Identifying the top causes of a particular recurring defect

- Identifying the biggest contributing factors to the cost of a product

Pareto charts are often used early in the problem-solving process to enable a team to find and focus on the biggest contributing factors.

Hypothesis testing. To determine probable causes of a particular problem or defect, use hypothesis testing. This testing involves the following four steps:

Step 1: Define the problem.

Step 2: Test data assumptions.

Step 3: Select statistically significant samples.

Step 4: Determine whether or not the probability of a defect is caused by random chance or has a specific cause hidden in the process.

For example, hypothesis testing might be used to determine whether or not a particular operator is a statistically significant cause of a defect.

Multivariate analysis. Use multivariate analysis to reduce possible causes of variation in a process to a family of related causes. Multivariate charts present an analysis of three main sources of variation:

- Intra-piece (i.e., within a single piece or batch)

- Inter-piece (i.e., piece-to-piece or batch-to-batch)

- Temporal (i.e., time related)

Failure mode and effects analysis (FMEA). FMEA is a disciplined methodology that identifies potential failures, their effects, and the probabilities of occurrence. Then, the system implements a plan to prevent them from occurring. Two types of FMEAs can be performed: product or design FMEA (DFMEA) and process FMEA (PFMEA).

DFMEA, performed during product development, addresses potential product failures; PFMEA addresses process failures. For example, DFMEA might be used to determine the possible failures and risks of a braking system on an automobile as the system is designed. The DFMEA might drive changes in design or a control plan to prevent the failures from occurring.

Design of experiments (DOE). This powerful tool systematically identifies and quantifies the effects of two or more factors on the outcome of a process by experimenting with many factors and variables simultaneously. For example, DOE might be used in a situation where testing complex systems results in failure, and many possible factors may contribute to the test failures. Using DOE in this situation would reduce the number of tests that would otherwise need to be performed to consider the factors separately.

Control chart. The control chart is the fundamental tool of Statistical Process Control (SPC). It determines whether a process is operating consistently (i.e., in control) or if a special cause has occurred to change the process mean or variance. Control charts are typically used on repetitive manufacturing processes to determine if the process is consistent. For example, a Computer Numerical Control (CNC) machining center might be machining a particular component repeatedly. Particular dimensions of the component might be measured and plotted as time passes to determine if the process is in control. If the process becomes out of control, it will be stopped, and action will be immediately taken to find and correct the problem.

Method 2: Individual Projects

Some companies use teams for almost every project. Although this may be a popular approach, it is often wasteful. Many problems given to teams are ones that an individual can solve equally as well and in much less time. Teams should only be given problems that would benefit from a team approach: for example, complex problems that require a lot of creativity and cross-functional know-how to solve are ideal. If a problem simply needs input from more than one individual, that does not automatically qualify it as a team project. Experienced team leaders can be used to determine whether or not a problem should be solved using a team or individual. An approach that may work well is to have the team leader of a problem-solving team make the decision on a case-by-case basis. The decision may also be made by a value-stream-mapping team as they put together a future-state implementation plan.

If a project is deemed to be appropriate for an individual to handle, the individual needs to have the technical skills and problem-solving skills necessary to handle projects of this level. That does not necessarily mean that he or she needs to be an engineer; in the lean environment, people at all levels of the organization should be able to solve problems. In fact, in a truly lean organization, many problems discovered on the shopfloor should be solved by shopfloor personnel. Nevertheless, some problems require a higher level of problem-solving skills. Let's look at a case study that demonstrates how EVS used a problem-solving team to improve yield at one of its suppliers.

Case Study:
EVS Corporation's Problem-Solving Team

One of the projects from San Simeon's value-stream-mapping activity (see Chapter 7) was to put a problem-solving team together to improve first-pass yield on the test equipment. This project, because it will likely require experimentation and statistical tools, will be completed using a problem-solving team. Because EVS Corporation has experience with problem-solving teams, it has decided to send one of its experienced industrial engineers to San Simeon Assembly to help put together a problem-solving team and to help facilitate the process temporarily.

Selecting the Team Members

The team is made up as follows:
- San Simeon Industrial Engineer (team leader)
- Two Operators: both experienced in assembly and test operations
- San Simeon Test and Assembly Supervisor
- Operator from another manufacturing process
- EVS Industrial Engineer

Charting the Problem

The team's first step was to create a pareto diagram to identify the key reasons for failure on the test equipment. The diagram in Figure 9-3 shows four key reasons for failure in the test process: two are defective circuit boards (part numbers 10999 and 11999), and two of them are incorrectly assembled items (part numbers 33333 and 33334).

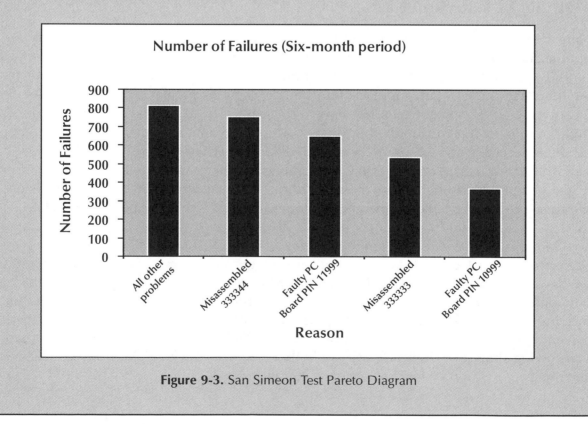

Figure 9-3. San Simeon Test Pareto Diagram

Establishing the Scope of the Project

Based on the pareto analysis, the team has decided to split the problem into two projects. The defective circuit boards are supplied by Electronics, Inc. San Simeon will assign this project to one of its manufacturing engineers who will work with Electronics, Inc., to resolve both circuit board issues. Electronics, Inc., may have to form its own problem-solving team to determine why the circuit boards are failing; however, determining the reason for circuit board failure is beyond the scope and ability of the San Simeon team. The second project, determining the reasons for incorrect assembly of part numbers 333333 and 333344, will be handled by this team.

The team next decided that it needed to dig deeper into the assembly process and determine why these items were being assembled incorrectly. The team created a cause-and-effect diagram ("fishbone" diagram) to identify possible causes for incorrectly assembled parts (see Figure 9-4).

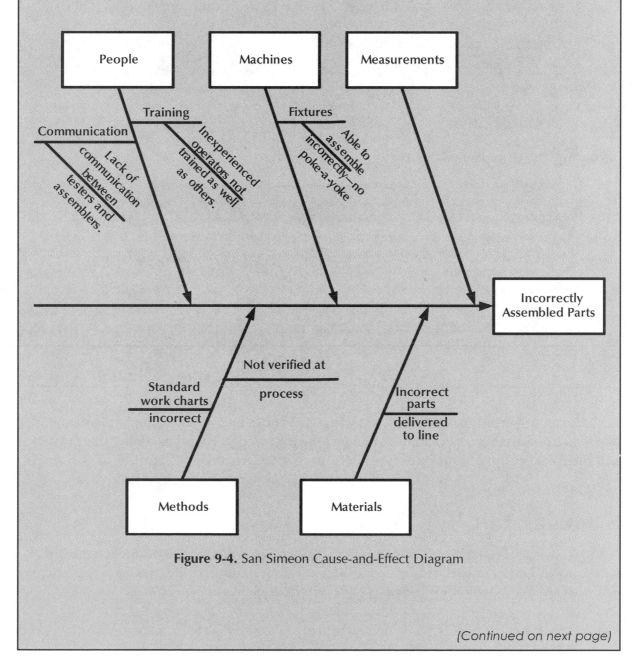

Figure 9-4. San Simeon Cause-and-Effect Diagram

(Continued on next page)

(Continued from previous page)

Investigating and Testing the Process

Using Figure 9-4, the team first investigated the process to determine if there was a problem with the following items:

- **Standard work charts for assembly.** To determine if they are correct and accurate.
- **Standard work charts for material delivery to cell.** To determine if they are correct and accurate.
- **Training levels.** Need to determine level of training of each operator. (Also, part of an experiment will be to determine if there is a correlation between operator inexperience and incorrectly assembled parts.)

The team then set up a test to be done as soon as each of these items was assembled. The test would determine if the item was assembled correctly. The team would track the following over the next 30 days:

- **Operator.** To measure correlation between experience and errors.
- **Specific failure.** To determine what was assembled incorrectly.

Then, after analyzing the results of the above testing, the team determined that two key errors were being made and that there was a positive correlation between operator inexperience and errors.

Solving the Problem

Consequently, the team developed a two-fold solution:

1. The team modified the assembly fixture so it could be used to eliminate the possibility of each of the top errors. The fixture would detect if the assembly was assembled incorrectly and light up a warning light to indicate that the assembly was incorrect. To implement this system, the team developed a standard work chart that identified how to react to each type of failure.

2. The team changed the standard work charts for assembly to clarify the work elements that were causing problems.

After implementation for three months, incorrect assemblies of part number 333333 and 333344 were down to less than 0.5 percent. The team had successfully improved this process.

Once an organization has made improvements at its supplier sites, the implementation of a lean extended value stream is complete. The next step, then, is sustaining this success and focusing on continuous improvement, and for that, we turn to Part III.

Summing Up: Key Points

A kaizen event is a 3- to 5-day breakthrough event that includes a cross-functional team working with an in-house or outside facilitator. Within a short period, the team sets and achieves a specific goal employing the tools of process kaizen.

How to Conduct a Kaizen Event

Events usually include the following activities:
- Management kickoff and introduction
- Training in lean with emphasis on relevant tool(s)
- Teambuilding exercise
- Mapping current condition
- Brainstorming
- Development of future condition
- Implementation
- Development of follow-up action plan
- Team report-out to management

Some tools, such as the tools of Six Sigma, do not lend themselves to rapid improvement events. Instead, alternative methods such as problem-solving teams, which meet regularly over a period of time, or individual projects, are more appropriate.

Applying This Information to Your Organization: Questions to Help You Get Started

1. How would your organization handle the facilitation of kaizen events for suppliers? Does your organization have the skilled resources necessary to assist your suppliers with kaizen events?

2. What experience does your organization (or your suppliers) have with the tools of Six Sigma? Do you envision a need for such tools for supplier process improvement?

Part III

Sustaining and Continuously Improving the Lean Extended Value Stream

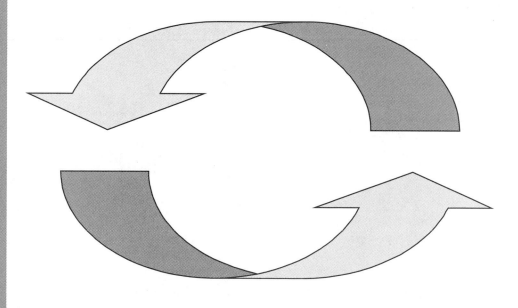

Chapter 10

Techniques for Sustaining Success

Don't Regress: Keep Improving!

Part II covered how to implement a lean extended value stream; however, just because implementation is complete doesn't mean an organization is "done" with this process. In lean or any other culture-changing program, a company either moves forward or regresses; companies that implement lean tools often revert back to the old way of doing things. Sustaining success and moving forward on a lean journey is critical to success. Sustaining success in internal lean operations is a huge challenge to most lean organizations.

Not surprisingly, sustaining lean success in an entire supply chain across several organizations is an even bigger challenge. Fortunately, there are several proven techniques for sustaining lean. Wrapping each of these techniques into a supplier network or association is the best way to sustain a lean system across the entire supply chain.

The Techniques and Functions of a Supplier Association

The concept of a supplier network or supplier association is not completely foreign to most manufacturing companies; many large companies have large annual (or even more frequent) meetings of key suppliers to improve the supply chain. However, most of these companies still do not partner with suppliers as suggested in Chapter 6; most suppliers are still kept at arm's length. A lean organization that intends to spread lean beyond its four walls must partner with its suppliers in such a way that both companies win. A supplier association is critical to ensuring that suppliers not only implement and maintain lean manufacturing but also continuously improve; this is important to maintain the competitive advantage that comes from having a lean supply chain.

A supplier association is a network for sharing information and expertise among a group of suppliers to an organization. After an organization assists its key suppliers with a lean implementation as described in this book, it needs to continue to provide information and assistance to its suppliers. The association should be thought of as a large organization itself, like a supply chain. Imagine if information and assistance were not provided between departments within an organization. (Unfortunately, for many organizations this is the case.) Without this exchange, an enormous amount of time would be wasted searching for information and duplicating efforts. If this is not desirable within an organization, why would it be desirable between organizations in a single supply chain?

An effective supplier association is critical to ensuring long-term that information is shared and assistance is provided as needed. The goal of the supplier association is for the entire network (and entire supply chain) to become better and leaner. An effective supplier association has five key functions:

1. Top management group meetings

2. Committee meetings

3. Quality audits and quality awards

4. Consulting/advisory assistance

5. Training workshops

The first three functions are more familiar to most readers; many supplier development programs have top management meetings, committee meetings, and quality audits and awards. The final two functions, the consulting and training pieces of the association, are much less familiar but critically important. The first half of this chapter describes each function in detail.

Function 1: Top Management Group Meetings

The first function of a supplier association is for top management of the organizations to have meetings for the purpose of information exchange and planning. Many organizations that do not have formal supplier associations have annual supplier meetings (sometimes called "summits" or "symposiums") which serve this function. Supplier association meetings are generally held on a quarterly or monthly basis.

The purpose of these meetings is to share the types of information described in the following sections.

Discuss short-term production plans. Communicating short-term production plans can prevent many of the surprises that suppliers often face; frequently, the spikes in demand that suppliers face could have been communicated earlier. This is one way of sharing all information. Recall from Chapters 2 and 3 that lack of communication and good information is a major waste of the extended value stream/supply chain.

Share long-range forecasts. Having suppliers understand long-range production plans allows them to plan for future capacity and improvement goals. This is information that suppliers rarely see, which forces them to go into crisis mode much more often than they should.

Communicate policy changes. Meetings should also be used to communicate policy changes; this gives the suppliers an opportunity to ask questions and is often more efficient than individually communicating such policy changes to each supplier.

Describe quarterly and/or annual training objectives. Although top management meetings are not used for training, they should be used for communicating training objectives. Specifically, the host organization tells its suppliers what types of training it intends to complete. This aids the suppliers in planning the types of training they need to undergo in order to keep up. (The host organization, as we will see later in this chapter, can help provide and/or develop training resources.)

Function 2: Committee Meetings

Supplier associations can also have committees dedicated to particular topics such as quality, lean manufacturing, design, and safety. Such committees can meet to exchange information and knowledge on their topic or topics. For example, a quality committee member may present project briefings that can serve as assistance to other quality committee members who may be facing a similar problem. A committee or subset of a committee can also serve as a problem-solving or continuous improvement team for an entire supply chain.

Examples of possible committees follow.

Lean manufacturing committee. A committee dedicated to lean manufacturing would lead seminars and information exchange sessions on topics that fall under the lean umbrella such as value-stream mapping, 5S, kanban systems, kaizen event facilitation, Total Productive Maintenance (TPM), and cellular manufacturing.

Equipment maintenance committee. An equipment maintenance committee would be dedicated to exchanging information on the best practices of equipment maintenance. Because very high equipment uptime is critical to achieving one-piece flow, having an equipment maintenance or TPM committee is valuable to the overall financial health of the supply chain.

Quality/Six Sigma committee. A quality committee dedicated to overall quality throughout a supply chain is a requirement for a successful supplier association. Lack of communication often delays the problem-solving process, particularly in a buyer–supplier relationship. Thus, a quality committee would provide an open information exchange and accelerate the problem-solving process. Quality committees can also be used for providing assistance in utilizing the tools of Six Sigma effectively.

Information technology committee. Despite the disdain that some lean purists appear to have for advanced technology, well-designed systems can have a positive impact on a supply chain. For example, good bar-coding systems could aid in setting up supplier kanbans. An e-commerce system could eliminate delays in the transmission of customer orders. There are many similar examples. An information technology committee would provide all the association's members with the latest developments in the field as they relate to a lean supply chain.

Product design committee. As you will discover in Chapter 11, product design has the largest influence on product cost. A product design committee would provide all the value-stream participants with information on best practices in product design.

Safety committee. Workplace injuries drive the cost of worker's compensation insurance up significantly. For example, in California, many companies have moved out of state or outsourced all manufacturing primarily as the result of high insurance costs. A well-run safety program can have a significant impact on the bottom line. Almost every manufacturing company has an in-house safety committee; a safety committee that functions within a supplier organization would provide insight into the most up-to-date safety practices.

Human resources committee. Employee involvement is one of the keys to any successful lean producer. A human resources committee would provide seminars and information exchange on the topic of recruiting and retaining good employees. Such topics as effective reward systems, compensation practices, and recruiting methods would be covered.

Function 3: Quality Audits and Quality Awards

Just as internal audits are effective for sustaining lean operations internally, supplier audits help to sustain the extended lean supply chain. Thus, quality auditing is one of the most important functions of a supplier association. The key to understanding quality auditing in the context of a supplier association is to consider audits to be a help to suppliers within the association rather than a hindrance or "policing" activity. The quality auditing function can be a function of the quality committee.

Audits within a lean supply chain differ from the typical annual quality audit. Many "mass production" organizations audit their key suppliers annually; after an audit, they usually send the supplier a laundry list of items to correct. After the supplier corrects these items and they are verified to be correct, the supplier does not hear from the quality organization until the next audit (or until the next occurrence of a quality issue).

The problem with this type of auditing system is that the organization plays an adversarial role as auditor; it's looking for problems to have a supplier correct rather than finding ways to improve the supplier's operations. In a lean supply chain, the purpose of audits is to *continuously improve quality* throughout the supply chain.

The auditing function of a supplier association is to ensure that suppliers are performing thorough and regular internal audits that cover all key criteria and to assist suppliers in properly performing audits. The supplier association should communicate audit criteria regularly to member suppliers; this communication should be a function of the quality committee. The supplier association should conduct audits on an annual basis and should include the following key elements in the audit:

1. *Review of supplier's internal audits and auditing processes.* Internal audits are critical to sustaining all of the key quality-enhancing elements of a lean system, such as standardized work, 5S, and TPM procedures. Specifically, each of the elements helps to build quality into each process. High process quality results in very few defects. If the internal system is not effective for a given supplier, the supplier association should help the supplier improve the system.

2. *Review of the supplier's corrective action and problem-solving system.* Properly determining the root causes of defects and implementing corrective actions are critical steps to quality improvement. The supplier association should provide assistance to suppliers who have an ineffective system.

3. *Random sample audit of operations.* This audit should be based on the supplier's internal audits; a team from the buyer organization should perform several of the audits that the supplier regularly performs. This has a twofold purpose:

   • It validates that internal audits are actually being done (as opposed to "rubber stamping").

   • It allows the auditing team to make suggestions for improving internal audit procedures.

Quality rewards for suppliers are also effective for sustaining successful lean supply chains. Although suppliers within a successful lean supply chain will be working together as partners, they should be rewarded *individually* for their successes. Based on the results of audits and key metrics, the supplier association should present annual awards to suppliers that have done exceptionally well. For example, if a supplier exceeded quality targets for the year by a significant margin, the supplier should receive a quality reward. Such rewards not only demonstrate an organization's appreciation for good suppliers but will also help the suppliers grow their businesses. (Displaying a quality award from a successful lean customer is an effective marketing tool.) As shown in Chapter 5, it is advantageous to a supply chain to have financially successful suppliers.

Function 4: Consulting and Advisory Assistance

Most U.S. companies would not consider consulting services a necessary function of supplier development. In fact, as discussed in Chapter 6, outsourcing relationships fail because the buyer organization ends up giving more technical support than it originally thought it would. The type of consulting and advisory assistance that would be a function of a supplier organization is generally limited to lean manufacturing and quality-related topics. It certainly would not make sense for a supplier to need to consult with a buyer organization about manufacturing processes. (This should be the supplier's expertise.) However, it is beneficial to have the buyer provide advisory assistance in implementing lean manufacturing. This function goes hand-in-hand with the next function, training.

The extent to which such services can be provided depends on the size of the buyer organization. Of course, a large organization with in-house expertise can find a way to provide consulting resources to its suppliers. It cannot afford not to do so, for investing in suppliers in this way will result in better overall supply chain productivity, lead time, and quality. In particular, consulting services are important for suppliers that are attempting to implement lean manufacturing. Implementing lean without assistance from a person or organization with extensive implementation experience is difficult; organizations that have attempted to do so have usually ended up implementing a few tools with little bottom-line impact.

For situations in which the buyer organization does not have enough resources to provide consulting services, a third party can be used. Many times, this can be the consulting firm that the buyer organization used for lean implementation assistance. In any case, the buyer needs to take an active role in providing consulting services to its key suppliers.

Function 5: Training Workshops

The final but perhaps most important function is to provide training; this function is closely related to the previous function as advisory and training functions are always closely related. Training is important to any lean organization because it is an investment in a truly appreciating asset: people. Suppliers and their people are also appreciating assets to a buyer organization. Yielding similar results to providing advisory assistance, offering training to suppliers will result in a lower-cost, higher-profit supply chain.

Supplier associations should include training workshops on at least an annual basis; the workshops can be held as part of supplier association "summits" or events. This would allow many suppliers to take part in workshops together, thus avoiding the duplication of teaching efforts on the part of the buyer organization.

The workshops should cover the subjects described in the following paragraphs.

Kaizen events workshop. For the supplier just starting on its lean journey, kaizen event support should include training and facilitation of events. As discussed in Chapter 9, kaizen events are powerful methods for improvement. However, because conducting kaizen events requires experience, the buyer organization needs to assist (as outlined in Chapter 9). This is a vital part of supplier development for the lean organization.

Manufacturing technology workshop. Manufacturing technology workshops are necessary for suppliers to share knowledge. These workshops can be done on an annual basis; they would generally be conducted by suppliers for other suppliers. They may also be conducted by outside experts (such as equipment manufacturers) for suppliers.

Lean accounting workshop. One of the biggest hurdles for any company in the process of implementing lean is changing its management accounting system. For lean to work, a lean accounting system must be in place; metrics must drive managers and everyone else to act in accordance with lean. Standard cost accounting systems generally encourage *mass* production rather than *lean* production techniques. Therefore, lean accounting is a relevant topic for suppliers to learn.

Lean/kaizen tools workshop. The tools of lean and kaizen, many of which were covered in Chapter 9, represent the majority of training workshops. These workshops would be conducted annually as well as throughout the year. This type of training would be combined with consulting as described in Function 4.

Problem-solving tools/statistical methods workshop. Problem-solving tools and statistical methods such as the Six-Sigma toolbox should also be part of the training program of a supplier association. As pointed out in Chapter 8, these tools are critical to creating the process stability necessary for one-piece flow.

Teambuilding workshop. Effective teams are another critical factor for a successful lean program. Thus, providing teambuilding training to suppliers will facilitate the successful implementation of lean.

Using Supplier Associations Effectively

Leadership and Team Selection

A purchasing executive, operations executive, quality executive, or even a lean champion can lead the process of setting up a supplier association. The title of the person leading such an effort is not nearly as important as his or her leadership skills. Much time and energy will go into such an effort; it is not for the faint of heart. As with starting any major change initiative, starting a supplier association usually meets with resistance.

Some of the reasons for resistance are as follows:

- *Fear that information will leak to the competition.* This is the fear that information shared with suppliers will be leaked to competitors who purchase from the suppliers. Although it certainly is possible that information will be leaked, it is unlikely that competitors will catch up through the leaking of information. Consider Toyota's situation. It is well known that Toyota not only shares information with suppliers but has shared many of the secrets of its Toyota Production System with the public for years; however, because of Toyota's continual quest to improve, no one has been able to catch up with the company in terms of quality or productivity. Toyota always remains several steps ahead of its competition.

- *Lack of resources.* Before performing any quantitative analysis, it is always assumed that there is a lack of resources and/or time. This is true of both individuals and organizations. Ironically, lean manufacturing itself allows organizations to do more with fewer resources, yet many organizations claim that they do not have the resources to implement lean! It is true that implementing and maintaining a supplier association requires resources; however, the benefits far outweigh the expenditure in resources.

- *Difficulty of quantifying benefits.* It is true that the benefits of implementing a supplier association are hard to quantify exactly. They can be estimated based on the expected improvement planned each year. They can also be demonstrated by examining other organizations that have successfully implemented supplier associations. Toyota, arguably the most successful manufacturer in the world, continues to expand its supplier associations throughout the world and continues to improve productivity and quality. This demonstrates qualitatively that supplier associations are beneficial.

- *Fear that suppliers will become too dependent.* If a supplier association functions properly, suppliers will become less dependent. This is because the workshops and consulting offered by the supplier association teaches suppliers how to continually improve on their own. If suppliers become too dependent, then the supplier association is failing and has not been set up correctly.

Just as implementing lean manufacturing requires strong leadership to overcome resistance to change, implementing a supplier association requires good leadership. The top operations executive or CEO should select a leader. After the leader is selected, his or her first job is to assemble a capable implementation team. The team should be small: no more than five individuals are usually necessary. This team's job is to create a small operating plan for the supplier association and to begin discussions with key suppliers. The team should be less cross-functional than the kaizen or problem-solving teams discussed in Chapter 9. Instead, the team should be made up of key purchasing and quality personnel. The organization's lean champion, if he or she is not the team leader, should also be on the team.

Implementing a Supplier Association: Developing an Operating Plan

The first step in the process is to develop a vision and mission for the supplier association. The mission statement must not be too complicated; it must simply state the purpose of the supplier association's existence. An effective mission statement will provide the supplier association's members with direction. It can be used as a basis for setting specific goals and strategies for the supplier association. The mission statement should be brief: it should not exceed one paragraph.

Next, the plan should describe the key goals and objectives for the supplier association. The goals should be based on financial and operational metrics: cost savings, inventory reductions, productivity improvement, quality improvement, etc. The goals should follow the S.M.A.R.T. acronym: that is, they should be Specific, Measurable, Achievable, Realistic, and Time-bound.

Then, the operating plan should outline the key functions of the supplier association for achieving the goals and objectives and the key people involved with each function. The goals and objectives should be immediately related to the functions. As described earlier in the chapter, the typical functions are:

- Top management group meetings
- Committee meetings

- Quality audits and quality awards
- Consulting and advisory assistance
- Training workshops

Each of these functions should contribute to one or more of the goals and objectives. Clearly identifying which goals and objectives are to be accomplished by which function or functions clarifies the purpose of each function and improves the likelihood that the goals and objectives will be achieved.

Expanding the Supplier Association

Just as there are several approaches to expanding lean throughout an organization, there are several ways to expand a supplier association. Most of these approaches fall into the following four categories:

- *Tier-by-tier expansion approach.* A supplier association may begin with tier-one suppliers only and expand to additional tiers. This is the approach that Toyota used primarily. It began with tier-one suppliers only and then branched out to include other tiers, as well as capital equipment and tooling suppliers. This approach will work best when many of an organization's value streams are similar and can share the supply base.

- *Value-stream or product-line expansion approach.* A supplier association may begin with several tiers of a single product line or value stream and then expand to other product lines or value streams. This approach might work well for organizations that have very different value streams with a unique supply base.

- *Function-by-function expansion approach.* A supplier association may begin with a small number of key functions and expand to several functions (as described at the beginning of this chapter). For example, an organization might begin a supplier association with the purpose of implementing lean only. Thus, the only functions it might employ are top management group meetings and lean training and consulting services. After it meets some key objectives, the association might be expanded to include other functions such as committee meetings, quality audits and awards, and additional training workshops.

- *Hybrid expansion approach.* A hybrid of the above approaches may also be taken instead. For example, an organization might begin with a single tier for a single value stream with only a few functions and then expand tier-by-tier and then add additional value streams and functions.

The approach to expanding a supplier association depends on several key factors:

- *Organization size.* If an organization is relatively small and has few value streams, it may choose to begin a multitier supplier association with one value stream and expand to other value streams relatively quickly. Perhaps over a two-year period or less, such an organization can have a multitier, multiple-value-stream supplier association in place. A small organization may begin with only a few functions and may expand to only those functions it deems critical to its success.

- *Similarity of value streams and supply chains.* If an organization's value streams are very similar and have similar supply chains, the best approach might be to create a supplier association that includes several value streams and expands by tier.

• *Supply-chain length or number of tiers.* If a supply chain has many levels, then it may be easier for an organization to expand tier by tier. For example, in industries with complex assemblies (such as the automotive industry), the supply chain is often multi-tiered. This may explain why organizations in this industry, such as Toyota, have expanded using the tier-by-tier approach.

Now that we've walked you through the steps, functions, and factors involved in establishing an effective supplier association, let's look at a case study and see how EVS did it.

Case Study:
How EVS Corporation Implemented Its
Supplier Association: EVSSA

After having gone through the process of extended value-stream mapping and assisting key suppliers with their internal value-stream maps and process kaizen implementation, EVS Corporation began to put together a supplier association to sustain and improve on the supply chain improvement it had initiated thus far. Because EVS is not a huge worldwide company like the leading automotive companies that have pioneered supplier associations, it needed to customize the guidelines and functions to its particular situation.

Selecting a Leader and Implementation Team

The first step for the association was to select a leader and an implementation team. The leader selected was EVS Corporation's Director of Operations; the leadership would remain in place for the first year and then be changed to an individual whose focus would be 100 percent supplier relations. The reason that the Director of Operations was chosen was because EVS wanted to have its top operations person in charge. The Director of Operations had led the charge in lean implementation, and EVS felt that it would be best to have this individual lead the implementation effort of the supplier association for the first year.

The team consisted of the following individuals:

• EVS Director of Operations (team leader)
• EVS Sr. Industrial Engineer
• EVS Sr. Buyer (responsible for 4400 product line)
• EVS Purchasing Manager
• EVS Quality Manager

Developing a Mission Statement and Goals for the Supplier Association

The mission statement. The team began by developing a mission statement and some key goals and objectives, both short-term and long-term. The mission statement the team developed was as follows:

> *EVSSA is committed to achieving a world-class supply chain for each of its product lines by providing lean manufacturing advisory and training resources and forums for the sharing of information among association members.*

Short-term goals. The team's short-term goal was an 8 percent improvement in overall supply chain productivity in one year for the 4400 product line.

(Continued on next page)

(Continued from previous page)

Its one-year objectives were as follows:

- To include all key suppliers in the 4400 value stream in the association and to begin top management level meetings within four weeks of founding the association.
- To provide lean manufacturing training for implementation teams at each key supplier in the association.
- To conduct four kaizen events at each key supplier in the association within the first year.
- To hold annual quality audits for all suppliers in the association.
- To create an expansion plan for including additional suppliers from other value streams in the association.

Long-term goals. The team's long-term goal was to achieve an average annual productivity improvement of 10 percent per year over the next ten years and a 5 percent average quality improvement for the next ten years. Its long-term objectives were:

- To include representation from all value streams (but not all tiers) in the association by the end of the second year of its existence.
- To provide twice-annual lean training programs for suppliers onsite (at EVS) beginning in the second year.
- To have all members of the association in the first year capable of conducting kaizen events on their own by the end of their second year of membership in the association. (This will require the association to incorporate train-the-trainer kaizen training into their lean training programs offered).
- To include lean accounting workshops in the association by the end of the second year.
- To include product design workshops in the association by the end of the second year.
- To include committees focused on quality, technology, and lean by the end of the second year.
- To include technology workshops in the association by the end of the third year.
- To begin co-locating supplier processes onsite by the end of the third year. (Part of Chapter 11 is dedicated to this topic.)
- To have tier-one suppliers taking the lead in product design for certain subsystems by the end of the third year.
- To include all tiers and value streams in the association by the end of the fourth year of its existence.

Implementing the Expansion Plan

The expansion plan would be a hybrid of approaches. EVSSA began with one single value stream and multiple tiers and expanded by value stream and tiers per its long-term objectives. Although the association would initially focus on lean, it would expand to include other related functions over its existence.

EVSSA began with the following key suppliers as members:

- San Simeon Assembly (Tier one)
- Tau Metalworking (Tier two)

> - Omega Manufacturing (Tier two)
> - Electronics, Inc. (Tier two)
>
> The association began with a top management meeting to outline all its key short-term and long-term goals and objectives. In the minds of EVS Corporation's implementation team, getting the above four organizations on board with the program would prove to be relatively easy, because they had experienced lean improvement from their relationships with EVS already. The team needed to develop a plan to get other suppliers from other value streams on board. Thus, the team decided to invite executives from other key suppliers to the initial top management meeting to familiarize them with the program of which they would eventually become a part.
>
> ### Establishing a Training Program
>
> EVS Corporation developed a train-the-trainer program that would be administered to a small implementation team from each key member organization in the supplier association. The training program was to be given at EVS Corporation's site. This program would be the basis for a program that EVS would offer future association members twice annually as outlined in the association's long-term objectives.
>
> EVS would then proceed to accomplish its short-term objectives throughout the coming year, including conducting kaizen events and quality audits and developing a detailed plan for expansion of the supplier association.

Establishing a supplier association is not the only way to continuously improve; Chapter 11 describes how some companies involve their suppliers in product design and/or co-locate their suppliers near them, to further eliminate waste and achieve a lean extended value stream.

Summing Up: Key Points

A supplier association is a network for sharing information and expertise among a group of suppliers to an organization.

Key Functions of a Supplier Association

An effective supplier association includes the following five key functions:

1. *Top management group meetings.* The first function of a supplier association is for top management of the organizations to have information exchange and planning meetings.
2. *Committee meetings.* Committees would be dedicated to particular topics, such as quality, lean manufacturing, design, and safety.
3. *Quality audits and quality awards.* Supplier audits and awards would be given to suppliers to help sustain the extended lean supply chain.
4. *Consulting and advisory assistance.* Consulting and advisory assistance would usually include lean manufacturing and quality-related topics but not manufacturing know-how (which should be the suppliers' expertise).

5. *Training workshops.* Hand-in-hand with consulting assistance, training workshops should cover such topics as:

   - Kaizen events
   - New manufacturing technology (usually supplier-to-supplier training)
   - Lean accounting
   - Lean/kaizen tools
   - Problem-solving tools and statistical methods
   - Teambuilding

Choosing a Leader and Team to Start the Supplier Association

As with any major change initiative, starting a supplier association usually meets with resistance. Thus, a strong leader needs to be selected to head up the effort. A purchasing executive, operations executive, quality executive, or a lean champion can lead the process of setting up a supplier association. The leader needs to select a small implementation team, which should develop an operating plan that addresses the following functions:

- Setting the vision and mission for the supplier association.
- Identifying the key short- and long-term goals and objectives for the supplier association.
- Implementing the key functions of the supplier association to achieve the goals and objectives and assigning the key people involved with each function.

Expanding the Supplier Association

After a supplier association is formed, there are several ways to expand it. Most fall into the following four categories:

- Tier-by-tier expansion approach
- Value-stream or product-line expansion approach
- Function-by-function expansion approach
- Hybrid expansion approach

Selecting the appropriate approach depends on the organization's size, similarity of value streams and supply chains, and supply chain length and number of tiers.

Applying This Information to Your Organization: Questions to Help You Get Started

1. If your organization were to begin a supplier association, which functions and committees should be included in the initial implementation? Why?

2. Who in your organization would be best suited to lead the implementation of a supplier association?

3. Which approach to expanding a supplier association would you choose for your organization? Why?

Chapter 11

Continuous Improvement of the Extended Value Stream

Moving Beyond Supplier Associations

Chapter 10 described how supplier associations can help an organization sustain and expand its success. This final chapter provides, in addition, several techniques for further improvement. As mentioned several times throughout the book, involving suppliers in product design is one key to extended value-stream improvement; thus, the first part of this chapter will explain the reasoning behind involving suppliers in product design and the methods for involving them.

Another waste-reducing trend in manufacturing is the development of supplier parks, in which key suppliers are co-located with the customer. We will explore this issue in the second part of this chapter, and we will include concepts relevant to small and medium-size organizations that may not be able to create a major supplier park but may be able to gain some of the benefits through alternatives.

Involving Suppliers in Product Design

The Need for Lean Product Design: To Eliminate the 7 Wastes of Product Design

Product design is an often overlooked aspect of lean. If it is examined, product design is often examined only from the standpoint of streamlining the product design process itself. Although this is valuable, it is more value creating to an organization to improve designs themselves in terms of their manufacturability. This discipline, called design-for-manufacturability, is a key part of lean manufacturing. Just as manufacturing and administrative processes should be lean, designs themselves should be lean. The single reason that design of products should be improved is the well-established fact that 70 to 80 percent of a product's cost is predetermined by its design. Just as there is *muda* or waste in manufacturing, there are various types of waste associated with product designs. Let's consider what I call "the seven wastes of product design," described in the following paragraphs.

Waste 1: *Overspecification and over-tolerancing.* New designs are frequently based on previous designs. This often causes designs to have tight specifications and tolerances, even when such specifications are not necessary for the new product being designed.

Also, often engineers will simply over-tolerance "just-in-case." This is much like overproducing and holding inventory just in case it is needed. Although over-tolerancing on CAD software costs no more than properly tolerancing, over-tolerancing can add significant manufacturing cost to the product. In industries such as the medical device industry, loosening tolerances later is a costly endeavor. It is much less expensive to design properly up front.

Waste 2: *Underutilization of components.* This is the waste of having components whose full capacity is not utilized. To eliminate this waste, either the full capacity of the components should be used or lower-cost components with less capacity should be used. A common example is the designing of electronic components that have far more capacity than necessary.

Waste 3: *Unnecessary materials.* Often, more expensive materials than necessary are used in design. Of course, if the materials add value in the eyes of the customer, then they are not unnecessary; often however, unnecessary materials are used because they have been used in previous designs or because the designer is more familiar with the materials. The manufacturability of materials needs to be considered during design. For example, manufacturing folks know that certain types of material are easier to machine than others; in most cases, design engineers are unaware of or do not consider this. Specifying the wrong material results in increased manufacturing cost.

Waste 4: *Excess components.* Almost all assemblies contain more components than actually needed. This results in long assembly times. By eliminating components and combining multiple features and functions into one component, you can reduce assembly times and costs considerably. Whenever more than one component is being specified, the designer needs to consider the reason for using more than one. In most cases, any two attached components that do not need to move and do not need to be made of different material can be combined.

Waste 5: *Excess fasteners.* Many designs use multiple fasteners, which result in long assembly times. Instead, combining fastened components or using alternatives to fasteners will reduce assembly times and cost.

Waste 6: *Use of components that require special equipment.* In this case, the designer creates a component that requires special equipment or tooling to manufacture or handle it. Sometimes it is necessary to design components that require special equipment or tooling; however, doing it unnecessarily is pure waste.

One of the key considerations is expected product volume; it makes sense to avoid specialized tooling or equipment if volume is expected to be low. This may result in a higher per-unit cost, but the total cost may end up being lower.

Waste 7: *Non-value-creating features.* Designs often incorporate features that are not value creating for the customer. Through talking to customers themselves, it should be determined whether or not features are actually needed. Many well-intentioned designs do not sell as products because they have too many "bells and whistles" for which the customer is not willing to pay.

Conclusion

Eliminating the above wastes of product design and using lean principles in product design will result in lower-cost, more competitive products. Involving suppliers in design, as you will see in the next section, will eliminate a significant amount of design waste.

Determining the Role of Suppliers in Product Design

Suppliers who manufacture components and assemblies usually know better than anyone inside the organization how to identify and eliminate waste from designs. They see the results of design waste in the manufacturing process: manufacturing waste. Involving suppliers in product design is one practical method of leveraging the knowledge suppliers have. Having suppliers lead design efforts for particular components, assemblies, or subsystems is effective as well.

Although it is almost always appropriate to involve suppliers in product design, it does not always make sense to have them take the lead in design efforts. The determining factors in the role that suppliers will play are the design expertise and resources of the supplier and the level of in-house expertise:

- If a *supplier* has product design resources and experience, it may be considered for playing a leadership role in design.

- If an *organization* has in-house experience designing and manufacturing a component or assembly, then the organization rather than its supplier should lead the design. The supplier, of course, should be involved in the design. This is usually the case in situations in which a component or assembly has been recently outsourced.

Involving suppliers in design can be at several levels (from least participation to greatest):

- Suppliers may sit in on design reviews and be asked for input. Design reviews may occur on a monthly or quarterly basis during the product development process. In such reviews, suppliers would be able to provide input from a manufacturing standpoint.

- Suppliers may participate in design kaizen events. As with kaizen events whose aim is to eliminate manufacturing waste, kaizen events aimed at eliminating design waste are an effective way for suppliers to provide input. Input and ideas provided during kaizen events are usually greater in quantity and quality than at design reviews.

- Suppliers may have a representative on a product development team. A supplier can send a representative to regular (usually weekly) product development team meetings.

- Suppliers may play a leadership role on a product development team.

- Suppliers may design the entire component, assembly, or product with input from the buyer.

These levels of supplier participation in the design process are described in more detail in the next sections.

Design Kaizen Events

When people think of kaizen events, they usually think of shopfloor improvement, the focus of Chapter 9. Rarely, if ever, do people associate product design with kaizen. This is unfortunate, however, because one area for which kaizen blitz events can be quite powerful is product design; changing the design itself will often result in significant reduction of design and manufacturing waste. Sometimes called Design for Manufacturability (DFM) Workshops, these kaizen events typically result in 20 percent or greater reductions in product cost. DFM kaizen events result in less complexity: fewer parts and fewer operations. Fewer parts to order, plan, fabricate, and assemble result in significant cost savings. Such kaizen events are an effective way to involve suppliers in the design process.

In DFM kaizen events, design engineers, manufacturing engineers, buyers, quality engineers, suppliers, and other interested parties meet for several days and follow a process for reducing the complexity of a design and eliminating waste from a design. Such events involve seven major steps, analogous to the steps of a kaizen event aimed at manufacturing improvement:

Step 1: *Educate.* The team is trained in the concepts of design for manufacturability and eliminating the seven design wastes. Interactive exercises are done to begin the process of helping the team to think differently.

Step 2: *Set goals.* When working with a new product, the goal might begin with the "target cost" for the product. The target cost of a product should be based on the expected selling price and profit margin. If the event is aimed at reducing the cost of an existing product, the goal might be a percentage reduction in cost, reduction in the number of operations to produce the product, and/or reduction in the number of the product's components.

Step 3: *Map out the current condition.* The team maps out the current state (or baseline) design by mapping the steps required to produce the product in great detail. Mapping out the steps to produce a product reveals opportunities for design changes that can improve manufacturability.

Step 4: *Brainstorm ideas.* Based on the training and current-state information, the team brainstorms using the "sticky note" method outlined in Chapter 9. This allows for the greatest number of ideas for improvement.

Step 5: *Select ideas and formulate the future state.* The team then selects ideas and creates several future-state designs, based on the probability of successful implementation.

Step 6: *Develop a plan to implement the future state.* The team develops an implementation plan that details tasks, dates, and people responsible for implementing the design. Steps included often involve investigation of new materials, functional testing, prototyping, 3-D modeling, and working with suppliers.

Step 7: *Report out and celebrate.* As with a shopfloor kaizen event, the team reports the results of the event and has a lunch or dinner celebration.

After the event, the team should meet periodically to update the status of the plan and drive the implementation phase to completion. Unlike the 30- or 60-day action plan that typically comes out of a shopfloor kaizen event, the implementation plan that results from a design kaizen is typically a longer-range plan, usually three to six months. In six months, the product cost savings should begin to be realized on a design change to an existing product.

Organizations can use DFM kaizen events to achieve their goal of lower cost without sacrificing value to their customers; in fact, additional value can often be created in the process. This underutilized tool can be applied across all industries and typically results in 20 to 30 percent reductions in cost. Instead of going with their initial inclinations to squeeze suppliers and reduce value to decrease cost, management teams should champion DFM efforts in their organizations to reduce cost and add significantly to the bottom line. Finally, conducting DFM kaizen events is an effective way of leveraging supplier design-for-manufacturability know-how.

Having Suppliers Lead Product Development Efforts

For suppliers without design resources, participating in design kaizen events or on a product development team may be the most involvement they can have in product design. However, suppliers having the design resources and expertise can go much further: they may take a lead role in design efforts in many cases.

How does an organization go about transitioning from internal design to outsourced design? This transition should probably be done in stages, as shown in Table 11-1.

Table 11-1. Stages of Supplier Involvement

Stage	Buyer's Role	Supplier's Role
1	Designs, Manufactures	Nothing
2	Designs	Manufactures
3	Leads design	Has input to design, Manufactures
4	Has input to design	Leads design, Manufactures

Frequently, an organization begins at either Stage 1 or 2. The organization is designing or manufacturing components, assemblies, or products or is at least designing them and having a supplier manufacture them. In Stages 1 and 2, a supplier has no involvement in the design.

In Stage 3, the supplier is asked for input to designs. The several levels of involvement in this stage range from having suppliers involved in periodic design reviews to participating in design-for-manufacturability workshops to participating on a product development team.

In Stage 4, the supplier leads the design effort with input from the buyer. In almost every case, either Stage 3 or 4 is desirable. Stage 4 is not always desirable; there are several cases in which Stage 3 would be preferred to Stage 4:

1. The internal design expertise of the buyer organization may be a core competency and only design input may be required from suppliers from a manufacturability standpoint. This is true in cases of highly complex technologies.

2. A key supplier may not have or desire to have the design expertise necessary to support Stage 4.

3. In the case of an end product, particularly if it is a complex product, Stage 4 is not usually desired. Most organizations prefer to control the design of complex end products, even if they are to be completely manufactured by suppliers. (Some end products, however, are perfectly suitable for outsourcing product design; for example, if an organization decides to develop a new product in an area for which it does not have expertise, utilizing a supplier with both design and manufacturing expertise would make perfect sense.)

How does the transition from stage to stage work?

- The transition from Stage 1 to 2 is addressed in Chapter 5; it is the process of selecting and contracting with suppliers to manufacture products internally designed.

- The transition from Stage 2 to Stage 3 is not difficult. One of the best ways to begin this is to invite suppliers to design reviews or have the design team meet with suppliers to gather their input on designs. Next, suppliers should be involved in design kaizen events. Then, suppliers might play an active role on a product development team.

- After a year or more of Stage 3 involvement, a supplier might be ready for Stage 4. Of course, this depends on the supplier's design resources. A supplier without design resources must decide whether or not it would be advantageous to obtain the resources and move on to Stage 4 or remain at Stage 3.

Design—A Core Competency?

Outsourcing manufacturing has been an accepted practice for decades; however, many organizations think their design function is a core competency. In the past, most organizations both designed and manufactured products. Over time, organizations outsourced more and more of their manufacturing while keeping design processes internal. However, manufacturing and design are linked. If a design engineer designs a product with intimate knowledge of the manufacturing process (and immediate access to it), he or she will be much more likely to design a manufacturable, lower-cost product. As the manufacturing know-how is lost internally, designs become more difficult to transition into manufacturing.

Thus, the next logical step is to outsource the design process to the supplier who is manufacturing the component, assembly, or product. Before taking this leap, an organization must weigh the pros and cons listed in Table 11-2.

Table 11-2. Pros and Cons of Outsourcing Design

Pros	Cons
Ability to "test" the manufacturability of designs more quickly	Loss of control over design
More manufacturable design	Less ability to control time and resources
Decreased likelihood of many design iterations	Design moved one more step upstream from the customer
Faster transition from design to manufacturing (and thus faster time to market)	

Ultimately, it is a case-by-case decision. In some cases, the pros may outweigh the cons. This depends on the expertise of the supplier(s) involved, the complexity of the product, and internal design skills. Organizations must make an honest assessment of their individual situations and decide whether or not outsourcing design makes financial and strategic sense.

Outsourcing Design to a Third Party

The key benefit of outsourcing design is a faster transition to market. Most organizations that outsource design may have lower product development costs at the forefront of their thought process. This may lead them to outsource design offshore thousands of miles removed from the manufacturing process. They may think that they have manufacturing "experts" manufacturing their products and design "experts" designing their products.

However, such thinking is flawed: outsourcing a design to a third party with no link to manufacturing decreases the benefits that would be had by outsourcing to a manufacturer and actually increases the time to market. In fact, even though the hourly rate of an offshore designer may be low, *the total design process may actually cost more* if there are many iterations of design.

If a design process is closely linked to the manufacturing process, it is much more likely that a design will emerge as a manufacturable design with a lower per-unit cost to manufacture. A fast product release and a lower cost to manufacture rather than the one-time cost of design are what should matter most. The benefits of lower cost are obvious. A faster product release gives an organization several key advantages as well:

- First-to-market advantage over the competition

- Freed-up resources to work on the next new product

- More revenue

For example, Toyota has some of its suppliers designing components and assemblies for its automobiles. It is not coincidental that Toyota also has the fastest product development process in the world. Whereas the competition takes two to three years to design a new automobile, Toyota takes only 12 months.[1]

Compensation for Design Involvement

If a supplier is involved in the design process, how should it be compensated for its efforts? Here are some guidelines:

- In the case of a supplier who is asked for design input (e.g., a supplier is asked to review a design), no compensation is necessary. This, of course, assumes that the supplier already has assurance that it will be the manufacturer of the product.

- In the case of a supplier who is asked to participate in a design kaizen event, again no compensation is necessary. The learning that the supplier will gain from the event should clearly outweigh the cost of participation. The buyer should reimburse any expenses incurred (such as travel).

- A supplier that is a team member on a product development effort should be compensated for its time. This can be a fixed cost or hourly cost written into the contract with the supplier.

Fully outsourced design efforts, however, are to be treated differently. If a supplier is contracted to both design and manufacture a component or assembly, a fixed cost to design the component should be built into the contract. If the supplier designs a component or assembly below the target cost, the financial gain experienced from this should be shared with the supplier.

The buyer should give the supplier incentives to design the product in a timely manner. If the supplier meets or beats the deadline, it should be given a financial incentive. If it fails to meet the deadline, it should be penalized financially. A fixed cost with gainsharing and timing incentives is better than an hourly cost because it benefits both parties. In such a sce-

---

1. *The Toyota Way*. Jeffrey K. Liker. McGraw Hill, 2004, p. 5.

nario, the supplier has incentive to design a low-cost product in a timely manner and no incentive to "pad the bill."

Now that we've walked through various levels of supplier involvement in the design process, let's look at a case study and see how EVS involved its suppliers.

Case Study:
How EVS Introduced Supplier Involvement Into Its Design Process

Part of EVS Corporation's strategy to improve its extended value stream was to involve its tier-one suppliers in the design process. EVS Corporation plans on maintaining control over the overall design of its products; however, there are several assemblies and components whose designs EVS believed could be outsourced. For example, on the existing 4400 product line, the manufacturing of most assemblies that went into the product was outsourced, primarily to San Simeon Assembly. EVS believed that the design of these assemblies and their components should ultimately be outsourced to San Simeon Assembly.

The first step in the process was to involve San Simeon Assembly in the design of EVS's next major product model in the 4400 line. EVS did this by including a San Simeon Assembly engineer on its product development team. EVS Corporation, as part of its development process, had a kaizen event focused on manufacturability of the next 4400 model. On this team, EVS included two San Simeon Assembly representatives. After the entire design process was complete, EVS Corporation would make a decision as to which designs should be outsourced to San Simeon Assembly for the next model.

The next step for EVS Corporation would be to work with San Simeon Assembly on its internal design process. EVS would allow San Simeon Assembly to propose a redesign to some existing assemblies that it was currently manufacturing. This would give San Simeon the opportunity to prove its ability to design manufacturable and lower-cost components and assemblies. Rather than paying San Simeon directly for its time to do this, EVS decided to allow San Simeon to keep the savings gained from its efforts.

After San Simeon proved its ability to design low-cost assemblies, EVS would allow San Simeon to take ownership of several designs on its next product development program. EVS planned on setting up an agreement with San Simeon as follows:

- EVS will agree to a fixed cost for San Simeon to design a set of components and assemblies.

- If San Simeon is able to design a component or assembly below target cost, it will share the savings with EVS Corporation 50/50.

- If San Simeon meets deadlines set for design, it will receive additional compensation outlined in the contract. If it does not meet a deadline, it will pay a penalty. The penalty is greater than the additional compensation San Simeon would receive for meeting the deadline.

The last step in the transition to outsourcing design was to expand the outsourcing to other tier-one suppliers. To accomplish this more effectively, EVS decided to include lean product design training and consulting through its supplier association. This would allow the principles of eliminating design waste to be applied consistently by several suppliers.

In addition to involving suppliers in product design, there are other ways to continuously improve the lean extended value stream. Let's take a look.

Establishing Supplier Parks

Ironically, outsourcing—whose purpose is to *eliminate waste* in the supply chain by hiring companies with the best resources to manage a part of the value stream—actually *causes the waste of transportation*. Recall from Chapter 1 that transportation is a major waste of the extended value stream; a significant portion of the total lead time of a product is time the product is being shipped from facility to facility. This movement does not create value. Proper selection of supplier location is critical to a lean value stream; having mostly local suppliers reduces overall lead time. In some cases, it is not possible to choose a local supplier, and even if a relatively local supplier has been chosen, there is still room for improvement.

Ideally, transportation should be eliminated throughout the supply chain. To get much closer to achieving this ideal situation, the concept of the *supplier park* was born.

The supplier park marries the benefits of outsourcing with the benefits of vertical integration. A supplier park is a campus on which several dedicated supplier manufacturing facilities are located next to the buyer/customer. The purpose is to provide just-in-time delivery of parts directly to customer manufacturing lines in the proper sequence.

The benefits of the supplier park system include:

- *Elimination of transportation waste.* Time wasted shipping products from a supplier is eliminated.

- *Elimination of multiple packing/unpacking operations.* Because of the proximity of the value-stream participants, there is no need to package products for shipment, and then unpack products, place them in appropriate containers, and then deliver them to the manufacturing line. Instead, products can be placed into their proper containers for use and delivered in exactly the quantity needed.

- *Inventory reduction.* Less inventory is needed at the supplier and customer sites. Variation in delivery times, which increases with distance, is no longer a factor. Suppliers will be able to avoid the enormous costs associated with obsolete parts inventory.

- *Improved response time.* Because the facilities are dedicated to the customer and are co-located with the customer, the ability to respond to changes in demand is dramatically improved.

- *Improved time-to-market.* Having suppliers "on campus" facilitates supplier involvement in design. Gathering input from onsite suppliers is much easier than gathering input from suppliers that are a drive or airplane flight away.

- *Improved communication.* Even though we live in a world of so-called global communication where distances are not supposed to matter, anyone who has been involved in long-distance supplier relationships knows that lack of communication is a major problem. Co-locating suppliers onsite with the customer can eliminate many of the communication issues.

- *Shared services.* Sharing of information technology services as well as logistical services benefits suppliers and the customer.

Setting Up a Supplier Park

Automotive giants such as Toyota and Ford have set up supplier parks in various places around the world to improve their value streams. What are the nuts and bolts of such supplier parks? In general, most supplier parks have the following characteristics:

- The buyer/customer (e.g., Toyota) is the owner of the property. Suppliers lease facilities from their customers.

- Key suppliers are invited by the customer to participate in the supplier park. In the United States, the largest number of suppliers in an automotive supplier park is 18; these will be located in San Antonio, Texas, as the site of Toyota's sixth North American automotive plant. Toyota suppliers will employ 1,500 and make a capital investment of $150 million in facilities and equipment.

- The buyer/customer may give its suppliers incentives to participate, such as low-cost leasing and free training.

- The customer usually runs the supplier park. That is, the customer provides the logistics and material handling for the park.

- The park benefits both the suppliers and the buyer/customer.

Supplier parks are still unique to the automotive industry as of the writing of this book; however, there is no reason why the benefits of the supplier park cannot be had by companies in different industries, even smaller companies.

Practical Applications of the Supplier Park Concept

I have made several presentations on this topic and have found that although most people see the *benefits* to a supplier park, they usually do not see *possible applications* for their own organizations. Yet, the supplier park concept is applicable for organizations that are not multi-billion-dollar automotive giants.

To see the possibilities, let's examine how the service industry works. Consider service organizations that provide information technology support, janitorial services, maintenance services, or other such services. Even relatively small organizations utilize such services, and such services must be performed onsite even though they are usually provided by an outside vendor. I have often asked the question, "How can this business model be applied to the manufacturing supplier–buyer relationship?"

Consider a mid-size organization that has several key suppliers for a typical value stream. The suppliers have been selected using the process described in Chapter 5; that is, they have more expertise in particular processes than the buyer organization does. Ideally, the process that the supplier performs should be next to the downstream process being performed by the buyer organization. Even if the mid-size organization does not have the need, resources, or financial justification to build a separate building on campus to house the supplier's process, is there a reason that the process cannot be co-located with the mid-size organization's downstream process and staffed by the supplier? Such an arrangement would work as follows:

- The buyer (customer) would provide space within its own facility to house the upstream process of its key supplier(s). Suppliers would lease floor space from their customers.

- Key suppliers are invited by the customer to locate the supporting process within the customer facility. One key factor is whether or not the demand that the customer places on the supplier is such that a dedicated piece of equipment or manufacturing cell can be created inside the customer's facility.

- Just as in the case of the supplier park, the customer may give its suppliers participation incentives, such as low-cost leasing and free training. The customer may also offer to pay the expenses of moving equipment from its suppliers' facilities to its own facility.

In our case study example, it wasn't practical for EVS to develop a supplier park, but let's see how EVS did work with its suppliers to "co-locate" some of their process.

Case Study: How EVS Implemented Supplier Process "Co-location"

EVS Corporation is an example of a company for which it would be impractical to create a supplier park; it simply does not have the resources for one, nor would its product volume support a supplier park. Co-location of processes; however, is a practical alternative that it will explore in the future.

Let's consider how EVS could improve upon the future-state value-stream map it has created. Figure 11-1 shows the future-state map created in Chapter 3. The "new supplier" process box could now be replaced with the two new suppliers selected in Chapter 4: Omega Manufacturing and Tau Metalworking.

How EVS Worked with Its Suppliers

If EVS Corporation were to collaborate with its suppliers, what would be a practical way to co-locate processes? To answer this question, we need to have more information about the internal processes at each of the four key supplier locations that support EVS Corporation's 4400A–Q line.

Supplier #1: *San Simeon.* San Simeon Assembly operations supporting the EVS 4400A–Q product line include:

- Several manufacturing cells, working two shifts per day, dedicated to the EVS 4400A–Q product line. The cells include assembly and testing operations.

- A shipping function, which does a final visual inspection of product prior to shipment. This is not dedicated to any product line.

- A buyer/planner who is dedicated to EVS Corporation products including but not limited to the 4400A–Q product line.

- A material handler dedicated to EVS 4400 line cells.

- A maintenance function, which services all equipment at San Simeon Assembly.

- A manufacturing engineer dedicated to the 4400 line.

Supplier #2: *Tau Metalworking.* Tau Metalworking operations supporting the EVS 4400A–Q product line include:

- A machining center, which is about 45 percent dedicated to the EVS 4400A–Q product line and other customers.

- An operator who runs the above machining center plus one other machine.

- An inspection department that inspects all product on a sample basis including EVS.

- A buyer who purchases raw materials for the entire plant.

- A planner, who schedules several machines including the machining center that services EVS Corporation.

- A material handler, who services many customers and many machines.

- A maintenance function, which services all machines.

- A shipping function, not dedicated to any customer or product line.

(Continued on next page)

(Continued from previous page)

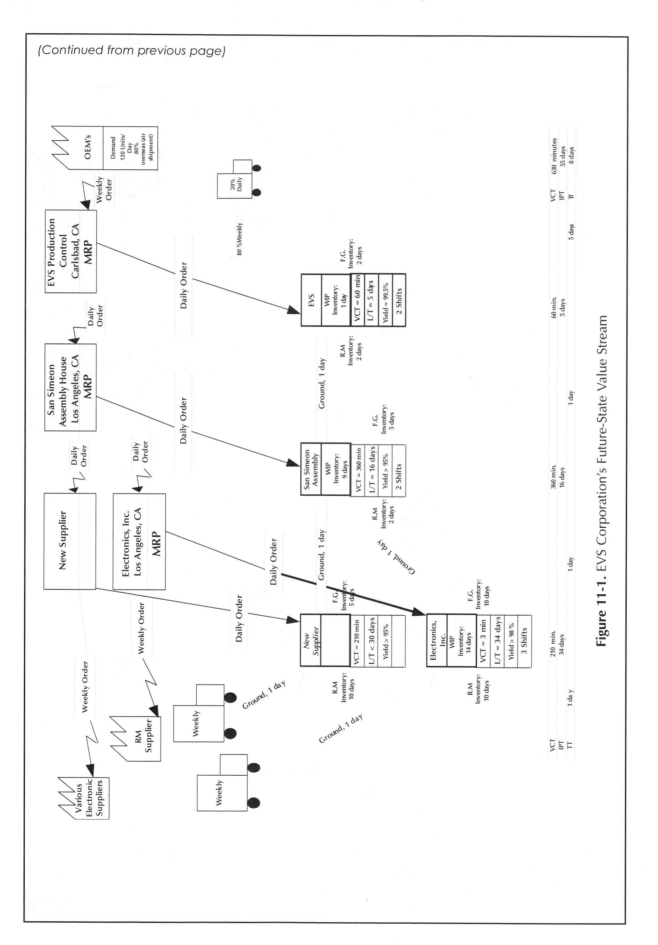

Figure 11-1. EVS Corporation's Future-State Value Stream

Supplier #3: *Omega Manufacturing.* Omega Manufacturing operations supporting the EVS 4400A–Q product line include:

- A machining center, which is about 90 percent dedicated to the EVS 4400A–Q product line and 10 percent for emergency work for other customers.
- An operator who runs the above machine plus one other machine and inspects parts from the machine. (No other inspection is done.)
- A buyer who purchases raw material for the entire plant.
- A planner who schedules 50 percent of EVS Corporation products plus other customers.
- A material handler who services many customers and many machines.
- A maintenance function, which services all machines.
- A shipping function, not dedicated to any customer or product line.

Supplier #4: *Electronics, Inc.* Electronics, Inc., operations include the following:

- Various manufacturing cells that manufacture and test a set of high-mix products including EVS product lines. No cell alone manufactures more than 40 percent EVS Corporation products.
- A buyer who purchases components for several customers including EVS.
- Planners who plan several manufacturing cells each.
- A shipping function, not dedicated to any customer or product line.
- A material handler who services many customers and many manufacturing cells.
- A maintenance function, which services all machines.

Table 11-3 is a summary of the extended value-stream resource analysis for EVS Corporation's 4400 product line.

Table 11-3. Value-Stream Resource Analysis

Supplier	Value-Stream Dedicated Resources	Customer-Dedicated Resources	Non-Dedicated Resources
San Simeon Assembly	Manufacturing cells, Operators, Material handling function	Buyer/Planner	Shipping function, Maintenance function
Tau Metalworking	None	None	Shipping function, Inspection dept., Buyer, Planner, Maintenance function, Material handling function
Omega Manufacturing	90% dedicated equipment	50% dedicated planner	Shipping function, Machine operators, Buyer, Maintenance function, Material handling function
Electronics, Inc.	None	None	Manufacturing equipment, Operators, Buyer, Planners, Shipping function, Maintenance function, Material handling function

(Continued on next page)

(Continued from previous page)

How EVS Decided to Co-Locate Some Supplier Operations

The Top Management Committee of EVS Corporation's Supplier association used Table 11-3 and the supporting information to make the following decisions regarding co-locating supplier operations within the EVS plant:

1. San Simeon Assembly's manufacturing cells can be located within EVS Corporation's facility. The operators and material handler can also be relocated. The EVS dedicated buyer/planner can be moved to EVS Corporation's site.

2. Omega Manufacturing's machining center that is 90 percent dedicated to EVS Corporation can be 100 percent dedicated. Raw material ordering can be set up using a kanban system to the raw material supplier with vendor management so that material can be delivered directly to the machine. Emergency raw material orders can be delivered from Omega's main plant.

3. Tau Metalworking, because it does not have dedicated equipment, will not be considered for the program at this time. It will continue to manufacture onsite. As the 4400A–Q product line grows and its equipment becomes consumed with EVS product, Tau can relocate equipment and functions.

4. Electronics, Inc., will not relocate any equipment or personnel at this time. Its system of high-mix manufacturing cells that include several customers is not conducive to supplier co-location. In the future, if it does make sense to set up a customer-dedicated cell, it will be considered for relocation.

Cost Savings from Co-Locating EVS's Suppliers

Before making a decision to move suppliers, EVS Corporation and its suppliers must do a cost-benefit analysis to determine if this is the right decision.

Cost savings at San Simeon. By co-locating San Simeon Assembly's manufacturing cells and performing just-in-time delivery of the assemblies to EVS Corporation's manufacturing cells, inventory could be reduced from 12 days of San Simeon finished goods (10 days at San Simeon plus 2 days at EVS) *to less than one day.*

The following costs are reduced as a result:

* **Annual shipping costs:** Daily shipping costs of $300, resulting in annual shipping costs of $75,000

* **Annual inventory holding cost:** 20% × $10,000/unit × 120 units/day × 11 days = $2,640,000

It will cost $2,250,000 of capital for facility expansion and $75,000 for moving expenses to relocate the cells to the EVS plant. The San Simeon material handler will be able to move material from the San Simeon assembly cells to the EVS assembly cells at no additional cost.

The cash flow analysis is shown in Table 11-4.

Table 11-4. Cash Flow Analysis of EVS's Investment in Co-Locating San Simeon

Investment	$2,325,000
Annual Cash Savings	$2,715,000

Without performing any further analysis, it is clear that this would be a wise investment that would pay back in less than one year. Performing a net-present-value analysis with a 15 percent required rate of return confirms that the net present value of the discounted cash flows over only a three-year time horizon would be $3,368,657.

Cost savings at Omega Manufacturing. By co-locating Omega Manufacturing's machining center and performing just-in-time delivery of the assemblies to San Simeon Assembly's cells onsite at EVS, inventory of machined components could be reduced *from 12 days to about 6 days*. This is because Omega Manufacturing would do more than half of production for the 4400. The following costs would be reduced as a result:

- *Annual shipping costs:* Daily shipping costs of $150, resulting in annual shipping costs of $37,500
- *Annual inventory holding cost:* 20% × $4,000/unit × 120 units/day × 6 days = $576,000 (cost of machined components is approximately $4,000 per finished good product)

It will cost an additional $100,000 for facility modification and $25,000 for moving expenses to relocate the machining center to the EVS plant. The machining center would be co-located with the San Simeon assembly cells; thus, the San Simeon material handler would be able to move material from the machining center to the San Simeon assembly cells at no additional cost.

Cash-flow analysis is shown in Table 11-5.

Table 11-5. Cash Flow Analysis of EVS's Investment in Co-Locating Omega Manufacturing

Investment	$125,000
Annual Cash Savings	$613,500

Without performing any further analysis, it is clear that this would also be a wise investment that pays back in less than three months. Performing a net-present-value analysis with a 15 percent required rate of return confirms that the net present value of the discounted cash flows over only a three-year time horizon is $1,109,355.

Total cost savings. Co-locating Omega Manufacturing's machining center and San Simeon Assembly's assembly cells with EVS Corporation's final assembly processes will result in a total value-stream savings of $3,328,500 and a total net present value of $4,478,012. The majority of the inventory reduced is owned either by San Simeon Assembly or Omega Manufacturing; thus, they would receive the lion's share of the benefits of this move. The suppliers, of course, will lease the floor space that they occupy. This will not outweigh the benefits that they would receive.

Implementation of EVS's Supplier Process Co-location

EVS Corporation's supplier co-location program would have the following characteristics for implementation:

- EVS will provide space within its own facility to house the upstream process of its key supplier(s); EVS will pay to expand its existing facility to accommodate the suppliers. Modifications will cost $2.35M to accommodate San Simeon Assembly and Omega Manufacturing.
- EVS will pay the expenses of moving equipment from its suppliers' facilities to the EVS facility.
- San Simeon Assembly and Omega Manufacturing will lease floor space from EVS Corporation; EVS will give them a favorable rental rate.
- San Simeon Assembly and Omega Manufacturing will provide their personnel to run their leased areas.

(Continued on next page)

Sustaining and Continuously Improving the Lean Extended Value Stream

---

(Continued from previous page)

EVS Corporation will begin to incorporate supplier co-location three years from its original future-state-mapping activity. The implementation team for this initial implementation will consist of the following individuals:

- EVS Director of Operations
- EVS Facilities Manager
- San Simeon Plant Manager
- Omega Manufacturing Plant Manager
- EVS Industrial Engineer
- San Simeon Manufacturing Engineer

These six individuals would be responsible for setting up San Simeon's assembly cells and Omega Manufacturing's machining center onsite at EVS Corporation. After the completion of this project, EVS Corporation will expand this program.

Expansion of EVS's Supplier Process Co-location

Ultimately, EVS Corporation would like to expand its supplier co-location program to additional suppliers and additional value streams beyond the 4400A-Q value stream to its two other value streams, the 4400XYZ and the 7700. To accomplish this, EVS will utilize its supplier association. EVS plans to utilize a new committee, called the Logistics and Facilities Planning Committee, to plan supplier co-location activities over the coming years. These activities will include the following:

- Monitoring, evaluating, and measuring success of the co-location program
- Expanding the 4400A-Q program to other suppliers
- Creating a program for the 4400XYZ value stream
- Creating a program for the 7700 value stream
- Planning facility expansions
- Exploring the alternative of supplier co-location at supplier sites

---

Customer Process Re-location

The goal of co-locating processes (as we've seen in the first part of this chapter and in the detailed case study of EVS) is to create an ideal lean extended value stream with less inventory and much shorter lead time. However, there are cases where organizations have outsourced almost 100 percent of their manufacturing and assembly processes. Using the logic of supplier co-location, a huge amount of factory square footage would need to be built at the customer site to support the supplier manufacturing functions. For such firms, it would probably not make sense to build a facility to house supplier processes. Is there an alternative to co-locating supplier processes onsite at the customer facility?

As unorthodox as it may sound, co-locating customer processes at a supplier site may be a viable alternative to co-locating supplier processes onsite at the customer facility. For example, consider the case of a company whose only manufacturing function is a final assembly and test process, which takes up only a small amount of square footage, whereas its tier-one supplier is occupying considerably more square footage performing the vast majority of the manufacturing and assembly processes. Because the company believes it needs to control the final assembly and test processes, it may choose to locate those functions onsite. However, we must challenge the physical location of these processes. Relocating processes does not imply that they are no longer owned. The same logic that we applied earlier in relocating processes from a supplier site to a customer site can be applied here as well.

How would this process work? In the case of relocating a supplier process to the customer, the customer would provide the space for the supplier to occupy. If expansion were necessary to do this, the customer would pay to expand the facility. However, in the case of relocating a customer process to a supplier, a supplier would not be willing to pay for facility expansion in order to accommodate the customer's process. If the supplier has the floor space available, then it would simply lease the floor space to the customer. If, on the other hand, additional facility space were needed, then the customer would have to invest in the expansion for the supplier. Because this case assumes that the floor space occupied by the customer process is small, facility expansion would probably be unnecessary in the vast majority of cases.

Other Relocation Concepts

Let's revisit the previous scenario with some additional information. Let's assume that the organization has several global distribution centers that ship the finished product to the end customer. An alternative to moving operations to the supplier would be moving operations to the distribution centers. In this case, the suppliers would ship unfinished product to the distribution centers, where the final assembly and test would be done prior to shipment. Although this solution may cost more in floor space requirements because every distribution center would require space for final assembly and test, it would reduce transportation, lead time, and potentially inventory.

The best reason to implement this type of solution would be that inventory could be reduced using the concept of postponement or delayed customization. For example, if we were to apply this concept to ink jet printer manufacturing, we would have distribution warehouses that hold the printer, various instruction packages depending on the language, and various power supplies depending on the country to which it will be shipped. By postponing the packaging of printers with a specific instruction package and power supply, the manufacturer can reduce printer inventory. It is easier to predict aggregate demand than demand for individual finished-good part numbers. In other words, it is easier to predict approximately how many ink jet printers will be sold in December than it would be to predict how many of each variation will be sold. Thus, fewer printers will need to be in inventory because they can be customized just prior to shipment.

Similarly, in the example in which final assembly and test process could be done at the distribution centers, the final assembly and test process could be thought of as the customizing process. In other words, the assembled product sent from the supplier can be made into a number of finished-good part numbers; thus, less inventory can be held at the distribution centers because they have the power to customize the product just prior to shipment. This would translate into significant financial savings.

Think Waste Elimination

Whatever the scenario, there is always the potential to improve any supply chain. The goal is to identify and eliminate non-value-creating activities and situations. To accomplish this, an organization must never be content with what it has accomplished. Contentment and arrogance based on what has been achieved inevitably leads to decline. Truly world-class organizations recognize that they have much room to improve; consequently, they are always able to find better ways to do things. Toyota has been perfecting the automobile supply chain for more than five decades, and it certainly recognizes that it has room to improve.

The concepts in this chapter are meant to inspire creative thinking about how to further improve a supply chain, whether it be through improving product designs, the design process, or the location of processes. If an organization is not continually progressing toward a waste-free supply chain, it will begin regressing. It is critical to keep moving forward in eliminating waste from the entire supply chain; this is what allows world-class companies to continue to stay ahead of their competition.

Summing Up: Key Points

Although supplier associations will help an organization sustain and expand its successes, involving suppliers in product design and implementing supplier parks are two methods for further improving the lean supply chain.

Product designs often have multiple iterations due to manufacturability issues. Furthermore, it is a well-established fact that 70 to 80 percent of a product's cost is predetermined by its design. Thus, lean manufacturers need to improve the design of products to reduce cost and decrease the development time to market. Because suppliers have manufacturing process knowledge, involving suppliers in product design is a necessity.

The 7 Wastes of Product Design

Most product designs contain the following seven wastes, which contribute to increased manufacturing cost and longer development time to market:

Waste #1: Over-specification and over-tolerancing

Waste #2: Underutilization of components

Waste #3: Unnecessary materials

Waste #4: Excess components

Waste #5: Excess fasteners

Waste #6: Use of components that require special equipment

Waste #7: Non-value-creating features

Suppliers who are manufacturing components and assemblies usually know better than anyone inside their customers' organizations how to identify and eliminate waste from designs.

Involving Suppliers in Product Design at Various Levels of Participation

Involving suppliers in design may be at several levels, varying from least participation to greatest:

- Suppliers may sit in on design reviews and be asked for input.
- Suppliers may participate in design kaizen events.
- Suppliers may have a representative on a product development team.
- Suppliers may play a leadership role on a product development team.
- Suppliers may design the entire component, assembly, or product with input from the buyer.

In most cases, suppliers will transition from little participation to much participation. Some suppliers may be qualified to play a leadership role in the development of a product, whereas others may provide only input to product design. In any case, it is important to involve suppliers in the product design process in some capacity.

The Benefits of Establishing Supplier Parks

The supplier park, another supply chain improvement concept, marries the benefits of outsourcing with the benefits of vertical integration. A supplier park is a campus on which several dedicated supplier manufacturing facilities are located next to the buyer/customer. The suppliers lease manufacturing facilities from their customers, usually at a favorable rental rate. This concept is currently being implemented by the large automotive manufacturers.

Benefits of a supplier park include:

- Elimination of transportation waste
- Elimination of multiple packing/unpacking operations
- Inventory reduction
- Improved response time
- Improved time to market
- Improved communication
- Shared services, such as information technology and logistical services

An Alternative to Supplier Parks: Co-Locating Supplier Processes

As an alternative to actual supplier parks, organizations may choose to have supplier processes co-located with their downstream processes within their own facilities. This allows mid-size organizations to take advantage of the supplier park concept. In such cases, suppliers would lease manufacturing floor space from their customers and provide their own equipment and staff.

In cases where organizations have outsourced almost 100 percent of their manufacturing and assembly processes, it would not be cost-effective to co-locate supplier processes at their facilities. For such firms, co-locating their own processes at a supplier site may be a viable alternative to co-locating supplier processes onsite at the customer facility.

Applying this Information to Your Organization: Questions to Help You Get Started

1. What is your organization's average product development time? What level of involvement do suppliers currently have?

2. What level of involvement do you envision your suppliers having in product development? Which suppliers do you believe will be able to contribute the most?

3. Think of an example of how the supplier park concept can be applied to one of your organization's value streams. What lead-time savings would be realized through implementation?

Recommended Readings

Lean Manufacturing

Lean Thinking. James P. Womack and Daniel T. Jones. Simon & Schuster, 1996.

The Machine That Changed the World: The Story of Lean Production. James P. Womack, Daniel T. Jones, Daniel Roos. Harper Perennial, 1991.

The Toyota Way. Jeffrey K. Liker. McGraw Hill, 2004.

Kaizen and Six Sigma Tools

5 Pillars of the Visual Workplace: The Sourcebook for 5S Implementation. Hiroyuki Hirano. Productivity Press, 1995.

A Revolution in Manufacturing: The SMED System. Shigeo Shingo. Productivity Press, 1985.

Autonomous Maintenance in Seven Steps. Masaji Tajiri, Fumio Gotoh. Productivity Press, 1999.

Creating Continuous Flow: An Action Guide for Managers, Engineers and Production Associates. Mike Rother and Rick Harris. Lean Enterprise Institute, 2001.

Creating Level Pull: A Lean Production-System Improvement Guide for Production-Control, Operations, and Engineering Professionals. Art Smalley. Lean Enterprise Institute, 2004.

Kanban Made Simple: Demystifying and Applying Toyota's Legendary Manufacturing Process. John M. Gross, Kenneth R. McInnis. American Management Association, 2003.

Lean Assembly: The Nuts and Bolts of Making Assembly Operations Flow. Michel Baudin. Productivity Press, 2002.

Lean Logistics: The Nuts and Bolts of Delivering Materials and Goods. Michel Baudin. Productivity Press, 2005.

Making Materials Flow: A Lean Material-Handling Guide for Operations, Production-Control, and Engineering Professionals. Rick Harris, Chris Harris, Earl Wilson. Lean Enterprise Institute, 2003.

The Six Sigma Handbook: The Complete Guide for Greenbelts, Blackbelts, and Managers at All Levels. Thomas Pyzdek. McGraw Hill, 2003.

Zero Quality Control. Shigeo Shingo. Productivity Press, 1986.

Outsourcing

The Outsourcing Revolution. Michael F. Corbett. Dearborn Trade Publishing, 2004.

Product Design for Manufacturability

Design for Manufacturability Handbook. James G. Bralla. McGraw-Hill Professional, 1998.

Design for Manufacturability: Optimizing Cost, Quality, and Time-To-Market. David M. Anderson. CIM Press, 1990.

Value-Stream Mapping

Creating Mixed Model Value Streams: Practical Lean Techniques for Building to Demand. Kevin J. Duggan. Productivity Press, 2002.

Learning to See Version 1.3. Mike Rother, John Shook, Jim Womack, Dan Jones. Lean Enterprise Institute, 2003.

Seeing the Whole: Mapping the Extended Value Stream. Jim Womack, Dan Jones. Lean Enterprise Institute, 2002.

Index

About the Author

Darren Dolcemascolo is co-founder of EMS Consulting Group, Inc., a management consulting firm focused on lean manufacturing strategies. He has worked with clients in a wide variety of industries including medical device, pharmaceutical, aerospace, capital equipment, consumer goods, and industrial goods. He has focused his implementation efforts on the complete supply chain, including the operations within client organizations and their extended value streams.

In addition to working directly with clients, Darren also trains individuals in a variety of public workshops and seminars. He has been published in several manufacturing and trade publications and has spoken at such venues as the Lean Management Conference, Outsourcing World Summit, Biophex, APICS, and ASQ. His articles are also featured in the monthly *Learning to Lean* newsletter published by his firm. Darren has a Bachelor of Science in Industrial Engineering from Columbia University and a Master's in Business Administration with Graduate Honors from San Diego State University.

www.emsstrategies.com